DALLAS BUDDHIST ASSOCIATION
515 APOLLO RD.
RICHARDSON, TX 75081
TEL: (214) 234-4401
FAX: (214) 234-8342

Buddhism of
Wisdom & Faith

Other Books in the Pure Land series*

Pure Land Buddhism
Dialogues with Ancient Masters
(3rd ed.: 1992)

Pure-Land Zen
Zen Pure-Land
Letters from Patriarch Yin Kuang
(2nd ed.: 1993)

Pure Land of the Patriarchs
Zen Master Han-Shan on Pure Land Buddhism
(1st ed.: 1993)

*Available from the following sources:

Sutra Translation Committee of the
United States and Canada
2611 Davidson Avenue
Bronx, NY 10468 (USA)
Tel. (718) 584-0621

International Buddhist Monastic Institute
9250 Columbus Avenue
Sepulveda, CA 91343 (USA)
Tel. (818) 893-5317

Corporate Body of the Buddha
Educational Foundation
11th Floor, 55 Hang Chow S. Road Sec. 1
Taipei, Taiwan R.O.C.
Tel. (02)3951198
Fax (02)3913415

BUDDHISM OF WISDOM & FAITH

Pure Land
Principles and Practice

Dharma Master Thích Thiền Tâm

Translated and edited by the Van Hien Study Group

SUTRA TRANSLATION COMMITTEE OF
THE UNITED STATES AND CANADA
New York - San Francisco - Toronto

5th edition: Vesak 1994
4th edition: Tet ... 1994
3rd edition: 1993
2nd edition: Vesak 1991
1st edition: Tet ... 1991

First published in the United States of America
by the International Buddhist Monastic Institute

*The supreme and endless blessings
of Samantabhadra's deeds,
I now universally transfer.
May every living being, drowning
and adrift,
Soon return to the Land of Limitless
Light!*

The Vows of Samantabhadra

About the Author

The late Dharma Master Thích Thiền Tâm specialized in both the Pure Land and Esoteric traditions. Shunning the limelight and practicing in seclusion for most of his adult life, he translated a number of Mahayana sutras and wrote several well-known commentaries -- all of which have gone through many editions and printings. This treatise, his best known work, is the outgrowth of a multi-year retreat devoted to the study of the Tripitaka, with emphasis on Pure Land related texts.

The translators and editors are members and friends of the Van Hien Buddhist Study Group.

Diệu Phụng
Minh Thành
P. D. Leigh

Contents

Acknowledgements

We acknowledge our debt to numerous good spiritual advisors, who through their comments, corrections, encouragement and sometimes gentle prodding, have made this translation possible. Special thanks go to Dharma Master Lok To of the Sutra Translation Committee for his generous sponsorship of the fourth revised edition and his continuous moral support; Dharma Master Thích Đức Niệm for his incisive observations and clarification of crucial points of doctrine; Dharma Master Thích Phước Bổn for his patient and thorough explanation of many difficult passages; Dr. C.T. Shen for kindly reviewing the manuscript of the first edition in 1990, during the busy Christmas/New Year season, in between two major retreats; and Mr. Lee Tsu-ku, without whose crucial initiative and timely follow-up this book could never have achieved the worldwide dissemination it now enjoys.
   We would also like to thank the following Dharma friends, in the order of our association with them on this project: Mr. D. Bakhroushin (for his prodigious comments and late night exchange of ideas); Ms. Tomoe Arai (for spotting a Dharma friend and providing materials on Jodo Shinshu); Mr. Nguyễn Đức Hoàng (now Rev. Thích Minh Hạnh of Chicago); Mr. Dương Đình Hỷ (our consulting sinologist-cum-Zen expert, who cheerfully went over the fine print of all our translations); Rev. Mitsuye Kamada; Mr. Vinh Nguyen (a most prolific and enthusiastic writer of Dharma books); Mr. Thomas Leung; Dr. Thiện Huệ; Ms. Jean Kames; Mrs. Nguyễn Thành Diêu (whose assistance with the "Micro-Dictionary of the Avatamsaka Sutra" made this translation possible); Mr. Lê Quang Thông (for his extensive and discerning comments at extremely short notice); Ms. Minh-Tâm Lê and Ms. Lien Smith (ever generous in their support of the Dharma).

   Last but not least, we wholeheartedly acknowledge our great debt to Prof. A.J. Prince for his incisive observations and pertinent comments on the early chapters; Prof. J.C. Cleary, whose thoughtful ideas and pointed suggestions concerning aspects of the Dharma were deeply appreciated; and Prof. Forrest G. Smith -- his incisive comments and observations could fill a book in themselves!
   As this book was being readied for printing, we learned of the passing of Dr. Trần Vỹ as well as the grave illness of Mrs. Y. Tashiro. May they always dwell, together will all sentient beings, in the Pure Land of their own mind.

Foreword

This Pure Land treatise is, to our knowledge, the first and only compendium of Pure Land teaching and thought currently available in a Western language. In the tradition of the *Avatamsaka Sutra* (which D.T. Suzuki described as the epitome of Buddhist thought, sentiment and experience), the author sometimes shifts from one plane of meaning to another, at times down-to-earth, at times metaphysical, so as to reach readers at every level and to *sever attachment to his very words*. It is in this light that certain paradoxes already familiar to students of Zen (illusory but not non-existent, recitation with no thought of recitation, etc.) should be viewed and understood.

While the primary focus of this treatise is Pure Land theory and practice, more than half of the book is devoted to questions of concern to all Buddhist schools. Therefore, we suggest the following approach to reading the text, according to the background of the reader:

> *Zen School*: Chap. VII to IX first.
> *Tantrism*:   Chap. VI to X first.
> *Pure Land*: Chap. I-V first.

> *The bereaved*: Chap. X.
> *All others*:   Note on Pure Land and
>   Epilogue.

The reader might also familiarize himself with a number

of key concepts explained in the Glossary (Amitabha, Awakening vs. Enlightenment, Buddha Recitation, Merit and Virtue, Noumenon/phenomena,[1] Pure Land, etc.).

Whatever his approach, he will be forever enriched. *Once reborn in the Pure Land*, like the proverbial seeker of the Way, he will not only discover the treasure trove (*Great Awakening*), but also, in time, partake at will of its priceless gems (*attain Enlightenment*) -- for the common benefit of all sentient beings. *(Van Hien Study Group / New York, Vesak '94)*

Note on Pure Land

Of the various forms of Buddhism that developed after the demise of the historical Buddha in 480 B.C., Mahayana (the "Great Vehicle") became the dominant tradition in East and parts of Southeast Asia. This broad area encompasses China, Korea, Vietnam and Japan, among other countries.

In time, a number of schools arose within Mahayana Buddhism in accordance with the capacities and circumstances of the people, the main ones being the Zen, Pure Land and Esoteric schools. Among these schools, Pure Land has the greatest number of adherents, although its teachings and methodology are not widely known in the West.

Given its popular appeal, [Pure Land] quickly became the object of the most dominant form of Buddhist devotion in East Asia. (M. Eliade, ed., *Encyclopedia of Religions*, Vol. 12.)

The present book, part of a series published by the Sutra Translation Committee of the US and Canada, is a modest attempt to enlarge the understanding of East Asian Buddhism, which (with the possible exception of some segments of Japanese Buddhism) is essentially eclectic in approach and outlook.

What is Pure Land?

[Pure Land comprises the schools] of East Asia which emphasize aspects of Mahayana Buddhism stressing faith in Amida, meditation on and recitation of his name, and the religious goal of being reborn in his "Pure Land," or "Western Paradise." (Keith Crim, general editor, *Perennial Dictionary of World Religions*, p.586).

In practice, the most common technique of the Pure Land school is the recitation of Amitabha Buddha's name.

Along with this popular form of Pure Land, there is also a higher aspect, in which Amitabha, the Buddha of Infinite Light and Life, is equated with our Buddha Nature, infinitely bright and everlasting *(Self-Nature Amitabha, Mind-Only Pure Land)*.[2]

Pure Land: a Compassionate Tradition

Several main elements define Pure Land:

i) Its teachings are based on *compassion*, on faith in the compassionate Vows of Amitabha Buddha to welcome and guide all sentient beings who so desire to His Pure Land;

ii) It is an *easy method*, in terms of both goal (rebirth in the Western Pure Land as a stepping-stone toward Buddhahood) and form of cultivation (can be practiced anywhere, any time with no special liturgy, accoutrements or guidance);

iii) It is a *panacea* for the diseases of the mind, unlike other methods or meditations which are directed to specific illnesses (for instance, meditation on the corpse is designed to sever lust, while counting the breath is for the purpose of reining in the wandering mind);

iv) It is a *democratic* method that empowers its adherents, freeing them from arcane metaphysics as well as dependence on teachers, gurus, roshis and other mediating authority figures. [3]

For these reasons, since the thirteenth century, Pure Land has been the dominant tradition in East Asia, playing a crucial role in the democratization of Buddhism and the rise of the lay movement. Honen Shonin(1133-1212), the Patriarch of the Jodo (Pure Land) school in Japan, expressed the very essence of Pure Land teaching when he wrote:

There shall be no distinction, no regard to male or female, good or bad, exalted or lowly; none shall fail to be in his Land of Purity after having called, with complete faith, on Amida.[4]   (Quoted by Elizabeth ten Grotenhuis in Joji Okazaki, *Pure Land Buddhist Painting*, p. 14.)

Van Hien Study Group
Rye Brook, NY: Feb. 1994

It is like a great regal tree growing in the rocks and sand of barren wilderness. When the roots get water, the branches, leaves, flowers, and fruits will all flourish. The regal bodhi-tree growing in the wilderness of Birth and Death is the same. All living beings are its roots; all Buddhas and Bodhisattvas are its flowers and fruits. By benefitting all beings with the water of Great Compassion, one can realize the flowers and fruits of the Buddhas' and Bodhisattvas' wisdom.

The Vows of Samantabhadra

1

Birth and Death

Pure Land, a Buddhist Approach for Today
1) Mahayana Buddhism and the Pure Land School

Traditionally, in Mahayana temples and pagodas, monks and nuns recite the *Amitabha Sutra* in their evening prayer session, followed by the sacred names of the three Pure Land Sages: Amitabha Buddha and the Bodhisattvas Avalokitesvara (Kuan Yin/Kannon) and Mahasthamaprapta (Shih Chih/Seishi). Moreover, Buddhist followers, whether clergy or laymen, usually greet fellow cultivators with palms joined and the words "Amitabha Buddha."

***

Pure Land teaching effectively suits today's times and the Buddhas' intentions and has quietly penetrated the psyche of Buddhists. Wherever Buddhism is practiced, the majority of followers always have the sacred words "Amitabha Buddha" in mind. Japanese Buddhism has the following saying: "the Esoteric School and the T'ien T'ai School are reserved for the nobility. Zen practice is the domain of the samurai, and Pure

Land is for ordinary people." And, ordinary people always form the majority.

It follows, therefore, that in Mahayana countries, those who practice Buddha Recitation (i.e., recite Amitabha Buddha's name) represent the majority.

2) Predictions concerning the Pure Land

In the *Longer Amitabha Sutra*, Buddha Sakyamuni made the following prediction:

> In the days to come, the paths of the sutras will come to extinction. I, with compassion and mercy, will purposely make this sutra survive for a hundred years. Anybody who encounters this sutra will, according to his wish, surely attain Enlightenment. (tr. in *Shozomatsu Wasan: Shinran's Hymns on the Last Age*, Ryukoku University Press, p. xv.)

In the *Great Heap Sutra*, Buddha Sakyamuni predicted:

> In the Dharma-Ending Age, among the multitude of practitioners, very few will attain the Way. The most they can expect is to rely on the Pure Land method to escape Birth and Death.

Elder Zen Master T'ien Ju also admonished:

> In the Dharma-Ending Age, all sutras will disappear, and only the words "Amitabha Buddha" will remain to bring liberation to sentient beings.

This is because [in the distant future] deep in the Degenerate Age, when all sutras have disappeared and people's capacities are at a low level, they will not be aware of any method other than Buddha Recitation. If they do not believe in and practice Pure Land, they will certainly remain mired in the cycle of Birth and Death. Within that cycle, good actions are difficult to perform while bad deeds are easy to commit. Thus, sooner or later they are bound to sink into the hellish realms.

The Patriarch Yin Kuang, a Chinese Pure Land Master of recent times, also said:

In the current Dharma-Ending Age, sentient beings bear heavy karma and their minds are deluded. If they practice other methods rather than Buddha Recitation, they can expect to sow the seeds of merit, virtue and wisdom but not to escape the cycle of Birth and Death in their present lifetimes. Although there are a few instances of great monks exhibiting extraordinary achievement, they are in reality transformation Bodhisattvas. In accordance with their vows, they act as examples for sentient beings in the Dharma-Ending Age, as is taught in the *Surangama Sutra* [a key Zen text]. Even then, these Bodhisattvas, adapting themselves to people's capacities, can only take the expedient appearance of having awakened to the Way, but not of having attained Enlightenment.[5] In the specific case of Pure Land, very few sentient beings can achieve the Buddha Recitation Samadhi these days, compared to earlier times. However, through Buddha Recitation, they can "take their residual karma along with them" to the Pure Land -- by relying on their own vows and those of Amitabha Buddha. Once there, they have escaped Birth and Death, achieved non-retrogression, and can progress in cultivation until they reach the stage of Non-Birth.

These predictions show clearly that the Pure Land method is well adapted to the causes and conditions of the current period and the capacities of today's people. For this reason, Buddha Sakyamuni made the compassionate vow to preserve and disseminate the *Longer Amitabha Sutra*, to teach Buddha Recitation to sentient beings. This is also true of the Bodhisattvas and Patriarchs, who, through their compassionate vows and in accord with the current times, also teach the Pure Land method.

It is due to the power of these vows that the Pure Land method has become popular among the majority of Buddhists.

3) The Shift from Zen to Pure Land

From ancient times, Zen has been especially popular in China, Korea and Japan. In Vietnam, as well, with its people rich in intuition and influenced by Chinese thought, Buddhism and Zen used to be synonymous. From the seventh to the thirteenth centuries, during the Ly and Tran dynasties, Buddhist monks and nuns formed a significant percentage of the population, and almost all followed the Zen School. In those days Buddhism was at its apogee in Vietnam [with three monarchs abdicating to become Zen monks]. Numerous monasteries were known to house a great many monks and nuns, to the point where it was said that "the monks quarters [in a certain temple] numbered up to three thousand, and each morning some seventy persons were required to clean and sweep them."

However, from the thirteenth century onwards, the influence of Zen began to wane in both China and Vietnam. On the other hand, Pure Land began to predominate, ultimately taking the lead, until it became the most popular school throughout East Asia.[6]

Some readers may ask, "Who says that our capacities are not the same as those of the ancients? It seems so only because we lack self-confidence and do not exert enough effort."

Answer: Effort and self-reliance should always be encouraged. However, the statement is not really valid. If the majority of today's people were not mediocre, why would Sakyamuni Buddha have taught about the three periods: the Perfect Age of the Dharma, the Dharma Semblance Age, and the Dharma-Ending Age? Moreover, Buddhist sutras mention the five periods of consolidation, from the True Dharma Time to the Dharma Fighting Time [during which monks and laity alike would engage in endless rivalry instead of cultivation]. Furthermore, with sutras and commentaries much more available than in earlier times, why is it that practitioners who attain the Way are now so rare? Is it not because the capacities of people today are in general lower and weaker than in earlier times?

As the Patriarch Yin Kuang said:

Cultivation is no different from wearing cotton garments in the summer and heavy padded clothing in winter; we cannot go against the times, capacities and conditions of sentient beings. Even if the Patriarch Bodhidharma himself were to be reborn today, and wished to preach in accordance with the current times and conditions and swiftly emancipate sentient beings, there would be no better method than Pure Land.

Thus, if what we teach is not in accord with the times and the capacities of sentient beings, the latter will surely drown in the sea of suffering. I sincerely call upon you all, even though you may practice a different method, to make the Pure Land your goal. However, if you have reached the stage where a white plum blossom is no different from a yellow chrysanthemum, this writer will gladly rejoice in your attainment!

Pure Land and the Issue of Birth and Death

4) Recitation according to the Buddhas' Intentions

As was said earlier, in those countries which follow Mahayana Buddhism, Pure Land practitioners are in the majority. Not only do many monks and laymen practice Buddha Recitation, even followers of various cults invoke the name of the Lord of the Western Paradise. Nevertheless, though many recite the Buddha's name, very few truly understand the goal of recitation. Thus, their recitation is not in accordance with the true intention of the Buddhas.

There are those who, visiting Buddhist temples and monasteries and seeing people engaged in Buddha Recitation, also join in, without a specific goal. This action, while garnering merits and virtues for the future, is not in accordance with the Buddhas' true intention.

There are those who practice Buddha Recitation seeking escape from danger and calamities as well as health, happiness and tranquillity for their families and ever-growing success in their careers and business dealings. Such goals, although worthy, are not consonant with the Buddhas' true intention.

There are those who, faced with hardships and the frustration of their wishes, become despondent. They recite Amitabha Buddha's name, praying that they will be spared such adversity in their present and future lives, that they will be endowed with beauty and honor, and that everything will turn to their advantage and accord with their wishes. Such goals are of course worthy, but they are not consonant with the Buddhas' true intention.

There are those who realize that life on earth does not bring any lasting happiness; even the noble, rich, powerful and influential are beset by worry and suffering. They hope that through the merits and virtues of Buddha Recitation, they will be reborn in the celestial realms, endowed with longevity and leisure, joy and freedom. Such a goal, although worthy, is not consonant with the Buddhas' true intention.

There are those who, having committed many transgressions, think that they cannot easily be saved in this life. They therefore recite the Buddha's name, praying that in their next life they will be reborn as a male, leave home to be a high-ranking monk, and become awakened to the Way. Such a goal, while exemplary, is still lacking in wisdom and faith, and is not consonant with the Buddhas' true intention.

***

What, then, is the true intention of the Buddhas?

Buddha Sakyamuni clearly recognized that all conditioned dharmas are impermanent, and that all sentient beings have always possessed in full the virtues and wisdom of the Tathagatas (Buddhas). However, because of delusion about their Original Nature, they create evil karma and afflictions and revolve forever in the cycle of Birth and Death. Even if they were to be reborn in the Heavens, once their merits were exhausted, they would descend into the lower realms. For this reason, the real intention of Sakyamuni Buddha is that through the Pure Land method, sentient beings may realize an early escape from the sufferings of Birth and Death.

Throughout countless eons, all Buddhas have accumulated merits and wisdom. Anyone who recites their names will engender immeasurable virtues. Moreover, Buddha Amitabha has made this Vow: Any sentient being who singlemindedly recites His name and seeks rebirth in His Land will, at the final moment, be welcomed and guided to the Pure Land, and attain non-retrogression.[7] To exchange the immeasurable virtues accumulated through Buddha Recitation for the small merits and blessings of the realm of gods and men -- forfeiting liberation and rebirth in the Pure Land -- would be no different from an innocent child bartering an invaluable diamond for a piece of candy. That would be a great waste indeed!

Moreover, the power of Amitabha Buddha's Vows is so immense that no matter how heavy our karma may be, by reciting His name in all earnestness, we can, in this very lifetime, achieve rebirth in the Pure Land. To seek rebirth, for instance, as an enlightened, high-ranking monk is to lack wisdom and faith. It cannot ensure rebirth in the Pure Land in this very life or attainment of Bodhisattvahood at the stage of non-retrogression. Therefore, the real intention of the Buddhas is for sentient beings to practice Pure Land so that they can be liberated from Birth and Death -- and this liberation is to be achieved in one lifetime.

***

But why do we need to escape the cycle of Birth and Death? It is because, in the wasteland of Birth and Death, we truly undergo immense pain and suffering. If students of Buddhism do not sincerely meditate on this truth of suffering, they cannot achieve results despite all their scholarship, as they do not experience fear and seek liberation. The sutras say:

> If the fearful mind does not come easily, the sincere mind cannot spring forth easily.

This is the reason why Sakyamuni Buddha, when preaching the Four Noble Truths to the five monks led by Kaundinya, taught them first the Truth of Suffering. According to this truth, if we meditate on the suffering of the human condition, we will have a clearer idea as to why we must swiftly escape the cycle of Birth and Death.

5) The Eight Major Sufferings

Sakyamuni Buddha explained the eight causes of suffering in his Truth on Suffering. The human condition has always entailed countless sufferings, as exemplified by the eight types enumerated below:

a) Suffering of birth

While still in the womb, human beings already have feelings and consciousness. Because of this they move and experience pleasure and pain. When the mother eats cold food, the embryo feels as though it were packed in ice; when hot food is ingested, it feels as though it were burning. The embryo, living as it is in a small, dark and dirty place, immediately lets out a scream upon birth. From then on, all it can do is cry when it feels cold, hot, hungry, thirsty, or suffers insect bites. Buddha Sakyamuni in his wisdom saw all this clearly and in detail and therefore describes birth as suffering. The ancient sages had a saying in this regard:

> As soon as sentient beings escape one womb,
> they enter another,
> Seeing this, sages and saints are deeply moved to such
> compassion!
> The illusory body is really full of filth,
> Swiftly escaping from it, we return to our Original
> Nature.

b) Suffering of old age

As they approach old age, human beings have diminished faculties; their eyes cannot see clearly, their ears have lost their acuity, their backs tire easily, their legs tremble, eating is not as pleasurable as before, their sleep is not sound, their memories fail, their skin dries out and wrinkles, their teeth ache, decay and fall out. Even those who were most handsome and beautiful in their youth can only feel sorrow and regret when they grow old.

In old age, many persons become confused and mixed up when eating or dressing or they become incontinent. Their children and other family members, however close to them, soon grow tired and fed up. The human condition is like that of a flower, ruled by the law of impermanence, which, if it can bring beauty and fragrance, also carries death and decay in its wake. In truth, old age is nothing but suffering and the human body has nothing worth cherishing. For this reason, Buddha Sakyamuni said: old age is suffering!

c) Suffering of disease

To have a body is to be open to disease, from those small ailments which have an external source to those dreadful diseases coming from the inside. Some people are afflicted with incurable diseases such as cancer or debilitating ailments, such as osteoporosis, etc. In such condition, they not only experience physical pain, they also have to spend large sums of money for treatment. Should they lack the required funds, not only do they suffer, they create additional suffering for their families. This is suffering on top of suffering. The suffering of disease is self-evident and requires no further elaboration.

d) Suffering of death

All sentient beings desire an easy birth and a peaceful death. However, these conditions are very difficult to fulfill, particularly at the time of death, when the physical body is generally stricken by disease and in great pain. With the body in this state, the mind is panic-stricken, bemoaning the loss of wealth and property, and saddened by the impending separation from loved ones as well as a multitude of similar thoughts. This is suffering indeed. Very few of us want even to hear about death, let alone "like" it.

e) Suffering due to separation from loved ones

This truth is particularly easy to discern in time of war. In this situation, how many families have to endure separation, with some members in the "North," others in the "South?" How many young men have lost their lives on the battlefields, the survivors stricken by their losses, the departed suffering tragic deaths? This is the suffering of separation. How many still in their prime have lost their loved ones to the demon of death, leaving them alone, helpless and forsaken? Should we also mention those whose parents, brothers, sisters and children have been killed by bombs and bullets? How many children, having lost their families, lacking all means of support and guidance, must lead precarious lives in orphanages? This is suffering due to death.

Thus, in times like these, the sea of remembrance and the river of love are deep and long, but the mountain of hate and the sky of grief are also high and wide! Separation from loved ones, whether in life or through death, is suffering indeed!

f) Suffering due to meeting with the uncongenial

This is suffering due to encountering enemies. To endure those to whom we are opposed, whom we hate, who always shadow and slander us and look for ways to harm us -- which is hard to tolerate, as we are always worried and ill at ease -- this is true suffering. There are many families in which fathers and mothers, brothers and sisters, husbands and wives are not of the same mind, and which are constantly beset with disputes, anger and acrimony. This is no different from encountering enemies. Where is happiness then?

g) Suffering due to unfulfilled wishes

We all have many desires and hopes in our lives. For example, the poor hope to become rich, the ugly wish for beauty, the childless pray for a son or daughter. Those who have children wish them to be successful, intelligent and filial. Such wishes and hopes are legion, and cannot all be fulfilled. Thus, they are a source of suffering.

h) Suffering due to the raging skandas (aggregates)

This is the suffering of those whose faculties are too sharp and full. The five skandas (or aggregates) are form, feeling, perception, volition and consciousness. The skanda of form relates to the physical body, while the remaining four concern the mind. To put it simply, this is the suffering of the body and the mind.

The suffering of the skandas encompasses the seven kinds of suffering mentioned above. Our physical bodies are subject to birth, old age, disease, death, hunger, thirst, heat, cold and weariness. Our minds, on the other hand, are afflicted by sadness, anger, worry, love,[8] hate and hundreds of other vexations. It once happened that Prince Siddhartha (the young Buddha Sakyamuni), having strolled through the four gates of the city, witnessed the misfortunes of old age, disease and death. Endowed with profound wisdom, he was touched by the suffering of the human condition and left the royal palace to find the way of liberation. Those with limited understanding and shallow thinking, on the other hand, do not ponder the truth of suffering and often mistake suffering for happiness.[9]

***

There are those who, upon being told that birth is suffering, will answer: When I was born I was too young to know anything, so I do not know of any suffering! If told that old age is suffering, they answer: I am not old yet! When told that disease is suffering, they answer: Since infancy, I have always been in good health, seldom experiencing any disease. Even when I was sick, it was only a minor discomfort; therefore, I do not see any suffering! When told that death is suffering, they say: Death has not come. Who knows that it is not a peaceful sleep? Upon being told that separation from loved ones is suffering, they say: The members of my family have always lived happily together, without experiencing any separation! If told that the company of the uncongenial is suffering, they answer: I haven't done anything to deserve anyone's wrath. There is no reason for anyone to plot against me! If we say that not getting what we want is suffering, they answer: I have everything I desire and need from life; I do not want anything else!

Can we say, however, that these people have no suffering? No. Precisely because they are well-endowed in body and mind, they are undergoing the suffering of the five raging skandas. Why is it that a well-endowed mind and body constitute suffering? Let us remember the trials for murder, robbery, rape and other violent crimes in our society. These occurrences derive in part from persons with too much time on their hands. With mind and body over-satisfied, they are subject to mental and biological stimulations. They are not at peace either sitting or standing and create problems where there are none, which leads to violent events. As an example, nowadays many people throughout the world lead self-indulgent lives, prone to hard liquor, drugs, illicit sex and every kind of indulgence -- fond of danger and cruelty. They are not physically and mentally at peace with themselves and, like a raging fire, engage in wrongful acts leading to inevitable suffering. This is the "suffering of the five raging skandas."

The eight conditions described above are known as the Eight Sufferings. They are described here in a general way and can be subdivided into many other types of suffering. If we examine ourselves and others, are we not to a greater or lesser extent under the sway of the eight sufferings? If those who study the Dharma continuously ponder the Eight Great Sufferings of mankind, they can be said to be close to the Way.

Liberation from Suffering

6) Contemplating the Suffering of Birth and Death

Sentient beings revolve in the cycle of Birth and Death, along the Six Paths, life after life. These are the paths (realms) of celestials, human beings, asuras (titanic demons), animals, hungry ghosts and hell-dwellers. The Eight Sufferings, while common to all sentient beings, concern humans in particular.

Although the celestial path is blessed with more happiness than our world, it is still marked by the Five Signs of Decay and the "things that go against our wishes." The path of the asuras is filled with quarrelling and acrimonious competition. The path of animals, such as buffaloes, cattle, donkeys and horses, is subject to heavy toil. Other domestic animals, such as goats, pigs, chicken and ducks, are subject to violent, untimely death. Still other animals suffer from stupidity, living in filth, and killing one another for food. On the path of hungry ghosts, sentient beings have ugly, smelly bodies, with bellies as big as drums and throats as small as needles, while flames shoot out of their mouths. They are subject to hunger and thirst for incalculable eons. As to the hellish paths -- the sufferings there are so great no words can describe them.

These last four paths (realms) are referred to in the sutras as the "Four Paths of Misery." The degree of suffering, from the path of the asuras downward, is multiplied manyfold for each path. Within these realms, sentient beings revolve in Birth and Death through one realm after another, like a spinning wheel, with neither beginning nor end.

In general, rebirth on the celestial or human paths is difficult and rare, while descent onto the four lower paths is easy and common. For this reason, the ancients lamented:

Born and reborn endlessly along the Six Paths,
When impermanence strikes, we must let go of everything.

Once while he was still alive, Buddha Sakyamuni scratched a tiny bit of soil with his finger and asked his disciple Ananda, "Where is there more dirt, on my fingertip or in the whole wide world?" Ananda replied, "Great Master, of course there is infinitely more soil in the big, wide world than on your fingertip; it is beyond all possible comparison." The Buddha then said, "Likewise, Ananda, the sentient beings who are reborn on the celestial and human paths are like the dirt on my fingertip, while those who descend onto the lower paths are like the soil in the whole wide world." This example should ring like a bell in the morning calm, waking up cultivators.

In short, as stated in the *Lotus Sutra:*

The Triple Realm is impermanent and conditioned dharmas bring no happiness.

Those who recite the Buddha's name should seek rebirth in the Western Pure Land to escape the cycle of Birth and Death and gradually attain Buddhahood. They should not seek the false blessings of this earth. Only in this way is Buddha Recitation consonant with the goal of liberation and with the compassionate Mind of Sakyamuni Buddha.

To achieve this aim, the practitioner should constantly meditate on the Eight Sufferings of the human condition, including the untold sufferings of the Six Paths. Otherwise, the determination to escape Birth and Death will not easily arise and the vow to be reborn in the Western Pure Land will not be in earnest. How, then, can he step upon the "other shore" [of liberation] in the future, and, with his wisdom, save all sentient beings?

Buddha Sakyamuni once sighed:

In the Dharma-Ending Age, my disciples will always chase after worldly blessings; very few will pay attention to the major question of Birth and Death.

This is so because they lack wisdom and do not meditate realistically on the suffering in the world. They are not only ungrateful to the Buddhas, they are also ungrateful to themselves. Is it not a great pity?

7) To escape suffering, follow the Pure Land method

Some Buddhist followers, preferring mysterious and transcendental doctrines, at times misunderstand the Pure Land method. Little do they realize that Pure Land is the wonderful gateway to the depth of our Buddha Nature, that it is the "guaranteed boat" to escape Birth and Death. Even persons of the highest capacity sometimes do not understand Pure Land and therefore, continually tread the path of delusion. On the other hand, there are instances of ordinary people with merely average capacities who, through the Pure Land method, have begun to step swiftly towards emancipation. I will cite a few examples here for your consideration.

***

In T'ang Dynasty China, in a temple called Fragrant Mountain in the district of Loyang, there was a Buddhist monk named Mirror of Emptiness.

He came from a destitute family, and, though diligent in his studies, was a mediocre student in his youth. As an adult, he used to compose poems, few of which are quoted or remembered. He would travel throughout central China seeking support from local leaders, without much result. As soon as he would accumulate some savings he would fall ill, exhausting all his funds by the time he recovered.

Once, he travelled to a neighboring district, which at that time was struck by famine. He was thinking of reaching the Temple of the Western Land to eat and regain strength, but on the way, felt too hungry to go further. He decided to rest by a snow-covered spring, reciting verses of self-pity and despondency.

Suddenly, an Indian monk appeared and sat down beside him. Smiling, he asked, "Elder Master, have you already exhausted the sweet dew of distant travel?" He answered, "I have indeed exhausted the nectar of travel; however, my name is ... and I have never been a high-ranking Buddhist master." The Indian monk replied, "Have you forgotten the time you were preaching the *Lotus Sutra* at the Temple of ... ?" -- *Answer*: "For the last forty-five years, since I was born, I have always been in this vicinity. I have never set foot in the capital and therefore cannot have preached at the temple you mentioned." The Indian monk answered, "Perhaps you are starving and have forgotten all about the past." Thereupon, he took an apple as big as a fist from his bag and gave it to the famished poet, saying, "This apple comes from my country. Those of high capacities who eat it can see the past and future clearly. Those of limited capacities can also remember events of their past lifetimes."

The poet gratefully accepted the apple, ate it, and proceeded to drink the spring water. Feeling suddenly drowsy, he rested his head on the rocks and began to doze off. In an instant, he awakened and remembered his past life as a high-ranking Buddhist monk, preaching the Dharma along with fellow monks, as clearly as though everything had happened the previous day.

He wept and asked, "Where is the Great Abbot Chan these days?" The Indian monk replied, "He did not cultivate deeply enough. He has been reborn a monk in Western Szechuan." The starving poet asked further, "What has become of the great masters Shen and Wu?" "Master Shen is still alive. Master Wu once joked in front of the rock monument at the Fragrant Mountain Temple, 'If I cannot attain Enlightenment in this life, may I be reborn as a high-ranking official in the next one.' As a result, he has now become a top general. Of the five monks who were close in the past, only I have managed to escape Birth and Death. The three others are as described ... and you, the fourth and last one, are still plagued by hunger in this place."

The starving poet shed a tear of self-pity and said: "In my previous life, for forty long years I took only one meal a day and wore only one robe, determined to rid myself of all mundane preoccupations. Why is it that I have fallen so low as to go hungry today?"

The Indian monk replied: "In the past, when you occupied the Dharma seat, you used to preach many superstitions, causing the audience to doubt the Dharma. In addition, you were not entirely faultless in keeping the precepts, resulting in today's retribution."

Having finished, the Indian monk took a mirror from his bowl, with flawless reflection on both sides, and said "I cannot undo what happened in the past. However, If you want to know your future destiny, whether you will be rich or poor, have a long or short life, even the future ups and downs of the Dharma, just have a look in the mirror and all will be clear." The poet took the mirror and gazed into it for a long time. Returning it, he said, "Thanks to your compassionate help, I now know causes and retribution, honor and disgrace."

The Indian monk put the mirror back in his bowl, took the poet by the hand, and started to walk away. After about ten steps, he disappeared.

That same night, the poet entered the Order at the Temple of the Divine Seal, and was given the Dharma name "Mirror of Emptiness." After receiving the complete precepts of a Bhikshu, he travelled throughout the country practicing the Way, his high conduct and ascetic practices being praised by all.

Later on, Zen Master Mirror of Emptiness once

met with a certain layman from the Temple of the Western Land. Telling the latter about his past, he said: "I am now 77 years old, my Dharma age is 32. I have only nine more years to live. After my death, who knows if the Dharma will still exist as it is now?" The layman, puzzled, tried to inquire further. The Master did not reply. He just requested a pen and began scribbling some lines on the north wall of the tower which housed the Tripitaka (Buddhist canon)...The words represented the prophecy of Zen Master Mirror of Emptiness, the gist of which is as follows:

> The Dharma will experience a decline. There will be ruthless persecution of Buddhism, the period of persecution beginning in the 840's. However, the Dharma will survive; the light of the Dharma will not be extinguished.

This prophecy is consonant with the destruction of Buddhism under the Chinese Emperor T'ang Wu Tsung, who ordered the razing of some 47,000 temples and forcibly returned hundreds of thousands of monks and nuns to the laity.

***

Around the year 1330, there was a long period of famine in China. In the town of Hangchou, the bodies of those who had died of starvation could be found everywhere, cluttering the streets. Every morning, corpses were dumped in a mountain cave behind the Pagoda of Great Harmony.

Among the dead was the body of an old woman, which did not decompose for ten days. Each day, her body would somehow rise above the others and lie on top of them all. Surprised at the sight, the people lowered a rope and dragged her body up. They found a small pocket on her robe containing three sheets of paper, decorated with a picture of Amitabha Buddha, and recording the number of her daily recitations. This became known to the local magistrate, who ordered that her body be placed in a coffin and cremated. As flames engulfed the coffin, people reported seeing images of Buddhas and Bodhisattvas emitting brilliant rays. Thanks to this event, many people began to take up Buddha Recitation.

***

Through the first story, we can deduce that the monk Mirror of Emptiness, had been, in his previous life, a high-ranking master lecturing on the Dharma; he had reached a certain level of achievement and had expended a fair amount of effort in his practice. However, because he had not *attained* the Way[10] and still had some minor flaws, he was reborn as a hungry, destitute scholar. Of the five Buddhist monks, only the Indian monk had managed to escape the cycle of Birth and Death.

In addition to Zen Master Mirror of Emptiness, we may also read a) the life story of a great Elder Master whose rebirth as a buffalo was due to his greed for money and his stinginess with the Dharma, b) the story of a Master of high repute who, because he improperly accepted offerings, was reborn as a daughter in the household of his disciple, c) the story of a monk who led an illustrious life but, because of the reappearance of evil karma accumulated from time immemorial, had to undergo rebirth as a person lacking intelligence and resentful of cultivators, d) the story of a well-known Master who, having seen the Way through meditation, was reborn as a monk praised and respected by all, but then, swayed by his blessings, forgot all about the path of liberation, e) the story of the disciple of a great master who became enlightened to the source of the Mind, but who, because he had not yet attained the Way, was reborn as a brilliant monk. He could not, however, control thoughts of power and arrogance, and from then on, there was no evil karma he did not commit.

There is also the story of a nun who had recited the *Lotus Sutra* for thirty years, but because she had not rid herself of attachment to form and sound, was reborn as a beautiful courtesan with a most alluring voice and lotus fragrance emanating from her mouth.

We can read of many such instances in books and commentaries. The lesson we can derive is that if we rely only on our own strength (self-power) to cultivate without having extinguished evil karma and severed greed anger and delusion, we are bound to be deluded upon rebirth. Out of ten cultivators, as many as eight or nine will fail. On the other hand, take the case of the old woman mentioned earlier, who merely practiced Buddha Recitation, ignorant though she was on questions of doctrine and knowing nothing about this school or that teaching. Because she earnestly recited Amitabha's name, many extraordinary events occurred after her death, pointing to her rebirth in the Pure Land.

***

Thus, the Dharma doors of Zen, Sutra Recitation and other methods are all praiseworthy schools to be encouraged. However, in this Dharma-Ending Age, we should practice Buddha Recitation in addition, dedicating all merits to rebirth in the Pure Land, to ensure escape from the cycle of Birth and Death. If we do not take the Pure Land as our goal, the virtues gained from practicing other methods can only provide good roots, merits and blessings, and serve as the causes and conditions of liberation in the future.

This being the case, we should fear the prospect of being deluded during rebirth, and mired for a long time in the wasteland of Birth and Death. How many of us have as much intelligence as the Great Master Wu Ta? He was a high-ranking Zen monk for ten lifetimes; in his last lifetime, before attaining Enlightenment, he was able to lecture in depth on the *Great Nirvana Sutra* when barely fourteen. However, because of one delusive thought of pride [over the sandalwood throne offered to him by the Emperor as a symbol of loftiness], his past karma reappeared as a sore, in the form of a human face, on his lap. He was finally saved and reborn in the Pure Land through Buddha Recitation. Those who would rely solely on their own wisdom, discoursing on lofty and profound principles, respecting only self-power and belittling Buddha Recitation, should pay heed to this example and reflect upon it.

2

The Bodhi Mind

Essay on the Bodhi Mind

8) Meaning of the Bodhi Mind (Bodhicitta)

Exchanging the virtues of Buddha Recitation for the petty merits and blessings of this world is certainly not consonant with the intentions of the Buddhas.[11] Therefore, practitioners should recite the name of Amitabha Buddha for the purpose of escaping the cycle of Birth and Death. However, if we were to practice Buddha Recitation for the sake of our own salvation alone, we would only fulfill a small part of the Buddhas' intentions.

What, then, is the ultimate intention of the Buddhas? *The ultimate intention of the Buddhas is for all sentient beings to escape the cycle of Birth and Death and to become enlightened, as they are.* Thus, those who recite Amitabha Buddha's name should develop the Bodhi Mind (aspiration for Supreme Enlightenment).[12]

The word "Bodhi" means "enlightened." There are three main stages of Enlightenment: the Enlightenment of the Sravakas (Hearers); the Enlightenment of the

Pratyeka (Self-Awakened) Buddhas; the Enlightenment of the Buddhas. What Pure Land practitioners who develop the Bodhi Mind are seeking is precisely the Enlightenment of the Buddhas. This stage of Buddhahood is the highest, transcending those of the Sravakas and Pratyeka Buddhas, and is therefore called Supreme Enlightenment or Supreme Bodhi. This Supreme Bodhi Mind contains two principal seeds, Compassion and Wisdom, from which emanates the great undertaking of rescuing oneself and all other sentient beings.

To reiterate, the Bodhi Mind I am referring to here is the supreme, perfect Bodhi Mind of the Buddhas, not the Bodhi Mind of the Sravakas or Pratyeka Buddhas.

***

The *Mahavairocana (Dai Nichi) Sutra* says:

The Bodhi Mind is the cause
Great Compassion is the root (foundation)
Skillful means are the ultimate.[13]

For example, if a person is to travel far, he should first determine the goal of the trip, then understand its purpose, and lastly, choose such expedient means of locomotion as automobiles, ships, or planes to set out on his journey. It is the same for the cultivator. He should first take Supreme Enlightenment (Buddhahood) as his ultimate goal, and the compassionate mind which benefits himself and others as the purpose of his cultivation, and then, depending on his preferences and capacities, choose a method, Zen, Pure Land or Esotericism, as an expedient for practice. Expedients, or skillful means, refer, in a broader sense, to flexible wisdom adapted to circumstances -- the application of all actions and practices, whether favorable or unfavorable,[14] to the practice of the Bodhisattva Way. For this reason, the Bodhi Mind is the goal that the cultivator should clearly understand before he sets out to practice.

Thus, while the previous chapter dealt with the importance of the Pure Land method and its immediate purpose of escaping Birth and Death, this chapter goes into the Supreme Bodhi Mind (Buddhahood) as the ultimate goal of the cultivator.

When Buddha Sakyamuni preached the Four Noble Truths, we might expect that he would have explained the "cause" of suffering first. Instead, He began with the Truth of Suffering, precisely because he wanted to expose sentient beings to the concept of universal suffering. Upon realizing this truth, they would become concerned and look for the cause and source of suffering. Likewise, this author, following the intent of the Great Sage, first brought up the Pure Land method of escaping Birth and Death as a most urgent matter, and will proceed next to discuss the Bodhi Mind.

The *Avatamsaka Sutra* states:

> To neglect the Bodhi Mind when practicing good deeds is the action of demons.

This teaching is very true indeed. For example, if someone begins walking without knowing the destination or goal of his journey, isn't his trip bound to be circuitous, tiring and useless? It is the same for the cultivator. If he expends a great deal of effort but forgets the goal of attaining Buddhahood to benefit himself and others, all his efforts will merely bring merits in the human and celestial realms. In the end he will still be deluded and revolve in the cycle of Birth and Death, undergoing immense suffering. If this is not the action of demons, what, then, is it? For this reason, developing the supreme Bodhi Mind to benefit oneself and others should be recognized as a crucial step.

9) The Bodhi Mind and the Pure Land Method

The Dharma, adapting to the times and the capacities of the people, consists of two traditions, the Northern and the Southern. The Southern tradition (Theravada) emphasizes everyday practical realities and swift self-emancipation, leading to the fruits of the Arhats or Pratyeka Buddhas. The Northern tradition (Mahayana, or Great Vehicle) teaches all-encompassing truths and stresses the goal of liberating all sentient beings, leading to the complete Enlightenment of the Tathagatas. Pure Land is a Mahayana teaching and therefore is not only directed toward the goal of self-enlightenment, but stresses the enlightenment of others at the same time.

When Buddhism spread to China [around the first century A.D.], it evolved, through the teachings of the Patriarchs, into ten schools. Among them are two schools which belong to the Southern (Theravada) tradition, the Satysiddhi School and the Abhidharma School. However, the faculties and temperament of the Chinese people did not correspond to the Southern tradition, and, therefore, within a short period of time it faded away. The other eight schools, are all Mahayana: the T'ien T'ai (Tendai) School, the Avatamsaka School, the Madyamika (Three Treatises) School, the Mind-Only (Yogacara) School, the Vinaya (Discipline) School, the Zen School, the Esoteric School and the Pure Land School. The vehicle for popularizing the Pure Land School is the Buddha Recitation method.

Pure Land being a Mahayana teaching, if the practitioner, in addition, develops the *Supreme Bodhi Mind*, mind and method will be perfect. This leads to Buddhahood, which encompasses both "self-benefit" and "other benefit." If he recites the Buddha's name seeking rebirth in the celestial or human realms, Buddha Recitation becomes a celestial or human method. A practitioner who develops such a mind will receive only the blessings of the celestial or human realms. When such blessings are exhausted, he will sink into a lower realm. If the practitioner is interested first and foremost in self-enlightenment, he will receive only the less exalted, incomplete fruits of the Sravakas and Pratyeka Buddhas.

Therefore, when reciting the Buddha's name, we should develop the supreme Bodhi Mind. There is a saying, "if you are off by a thousandth of an inch, you are off by a thousand miles." This being the case, Pure Land practitioners should pay particular attention to developing a proper Bodhi Mind.

The Practices of the Bodhi Mind

10) How to Develop the Bodhi Mind

Awakening the Bodhi Mind, as indicated earlier, can be summarized in the four Bodhisattva vows:

Sentient beings are numberless, I vow to save them all;
Afflictions are inexhaustible, I vow to end them all;
Dharma doors are boundless, I vow to master them all;
Buddhahood is unsurpassable, I vow to attain it.

However, it is not enough simply to say "I have developed the Bodhi Mind," or to recite the above verses every day. To really develop the Bodhi Mind, the practitioner should, in his cultivation, meditate on and act in accordance with the essence of the vows. There are cultivators, clergy and lay people alike, who, each day, after reciting the sutras and the Buddha's name, kneel down to read the transference verses: "I wish to rid myself of the three obstructions and sever afflictions ..." However, their actual behavior is different: today they are greedy, tomorrow they become angry and bear grudges, the day after tomorrow it is delusion and laziness, the day after that it is belittling, criticizing and slandering others. The next day they are involved in arguments and disputes, leading to sadness and resentment on both sides. Under these circumstances, how can they rid themselves of the three obstructions and sever afflictions?

In general, most of us merely engage in external forms of cultivation, while paying lip service to "opening the mind." Thus, the fires of greed, anger and delusion continue to flare up, preventing us from tasting the pure and cool flavor of emancipation as taught by the Buddhas. Therefore, we have to pose the question, "How can we awaken the Bodhi Mind?"

In order to develop a true Bodhi Mind, we should ponder and meditate on the following six critical points:

Point 1: the Enlightened Mind

Sentient beings are used to grasping at this body as "me," at this discriminating mind-consciousness which is subject to sadness and anger, love and happiness, as "me." However, this flesh-and-blood body is illusory; tomorrow, when it dies, it will return to dust. Therefore, this body -- a composite of the four elements (earth, water, fire and air) -- is not "me." The same is true of our mind-consciousness, which is merely the synthesis of our perception of the six "Dusts" (form, sound, fragrance, taste, touch and dharmas).

Take the case of a person who formerly could not read or write, but is now studying English or German. When his studies are completed, he will have knowledge of English or German. Another example is a person who had not known Paris but who later on had the opportunity to visit France and absorb the sights and sounds of that city. Upon his return, if someone were to mention Paris, the sights of that metropolis would appear clearly in his mind. That knowledge formerly did not exist; when the sights and sounds entered his subconscious, they "existed." If these memories were not rekindled from time to time, they would gradually fade away and disappear, returning to the void.

This knowledge of ours, sometimes existing, sometimes not existing, some images disappearing, other images arising, always changing following the outside world, is illusory, not real. Therefore, the mind-consciousness is not "me." The ancients have said:

> The body is like a bubble, the mind is like the wind; they are illusions, without origin or True Nature.

If we truly realize that body and mind are illusory, and do not cling to them, we will gradually enter the realm of "no self" -- escaping the *mark of self*. The self of our self being thus void, the self of "others" is also void, and therefore, there is no *mark of others*. Our self and the selves of others being void, the selves of countless sentient beings are also void, and therefore, there is no *mark of sentient beings*. The self being void, there is no lasting ego; there is really no one who has "attained Enlightenment." This is also true of Nirvana, ever-dwelling, everlasting. Therefore, there is no *mark of lifespan*.[15]

Here we should clearly understand: it is not that the eternally dwelling "True Thusness" has no real nature or true self; it is because the sages have no attachment to that nature that it becomes void.

Sentient beings being void, objects (dharmas) are also void, because objects always change, are born and die away, with no self-nature. We should clearly realize that this is not because objects, upon disintegration, become void and non-existent; but, rather, because, being illusory, their True Nature is empty and void. Sentient beings, too, are like that. Therefore, the ancients have said:

> Why wait until the flowers fall to understand that form is

emptiness?

The practitioner, having clearly understood that beings and dharmas are empty, can proceed to recite the Buddha's name with a pure, clear and bright mind, free from all attachments. Only when he cultivates in such an enlightened frame of mind can he be said to have "developed the Bodhi Mind."

Point 2: the Mind of Equanimity

In the sutras, Buddha Sakyamuni stated:

All sentient beings possess the Buddha Nature; they are our fathers and mothers of the past and the Buddhas of the future.

The Buddhas view sentient beings as Buddhas and therefore attempt, with equanimity and great compassion, to rescue them. Sentient beings view Buddhas as sentient beings, engendering afflictions, discrimination, hatred and scorn.[16] The faculty of vision is the same; the difference lies in whether we are enlightened or not. As disciples of the Buddhas, we should follow their teachings and develop a mind of equanimity and respect towards sentient beings; they are the Buddhas of the future and are all endowed with the same Buddha Nature. When we cultivate with a mind of equanimity and respect, we rid ourselves of the afflictions of discrimination and scorn, and engender virtues. To cultivate with such a mind is called "developing the Bodhi Mind."

Point 3: The Mind of Compassion

We ourselves and all sentient beings already possess the virtues, embellishments and wisdom of the Buddhas. However, because we are deluded as to our True Nature and commit evil deeds, we revolve in Birth and Death, to our immense suffering. Once we have understood this, we should rid ourselves of the mind of love-attachment, hate and discrimination, and develop the mind of repentance and compassion. We should seek expedient means to save ourselves and others, so that all are peaceful, happy and free of suffering. Let us be clear that compassion is different from love-attachment, that is, the mind of affection, attached to forms, which binds us with the ties of passion. Compassion is the mind of benevolence, rescuing and liberating, detached from forms, without discrimination or attachment. This mind manifests itself in every respect, with the result that we are peaceful, happy and liberated, and possess increased merit and wisdom.

If we wish to expand the compassionate mind, we should, taking our own suffering as a starting point, sympathize with the even more unbearable misery of others. A benevolent mind, eager to rescue and liberate, naturally develops; the compassionate thought of the Bodhi Mind arises from there. For instance, in a situation of war and famine, the young, who should be cared for by their parents, grow up orphans, helpless and forsaken. Likewise, the old, ideally, are supported by their children. However, their children having been killed prematurely, they are left to grieve and suffer alone. Witnessing these examples, our hearts are moved and we wish to come to their rescue. The compassionate thought of the Bodhi Mind, which up to that time had not developed, will spontaneously arise.

Other examples: there are young men, endowed with intelligence and full of health, with a bright future, who are suddenly cut down by bullets and bombs. There are also young women in their prime who suddenly lose the parents and family members upon whom they depend for support and therefore go astray, or they become orphans, their future livelihood and survival under a dark cloud. Witnessing these occurrences, our hearts are deeply moved and we wish to come to their rescue. The compassionate thought of the Bodhi Mind, which up to that time had not developed, will spontaneously arise.

There are people who are sick but cannot afford the high cost of treatment and must therefore suffer needlessly for months or years, to the point where some even commit suicide. There are the poor and unemployed, whose wives and children are undernourished and sick, their clothing in rags; they wander aimlessly, pursued by creditors, enduring hunger and cold, day in and day out. They can neither live decently nor die in peace. There are people who face difficult mental problems, without family or friends to turn to for advice and solace. There are those who are deluded and create bad karma, not knowing that in the future they will suffer retribution, unaware of the Dharma and thus ignorant of the way to emancipation. Witnessing these occurrences, our hearts are deeply moved and we wish to come to their rescue. The compassionate thought of the Bodhi Mind, which up to that time had not developed, will spontaneously arise.

In broader terms, as the Bodhisattva Samantabhadra taught in the *Avatamsaka Sutra*:

> Great [Bodhisattvas develop] great compassion by ten kinds of observations of sentient beings: they see sentient beings have nothing to rely on for support; they see sentient beings are unruly; they see sentient beings lack virtues; they see sentient beings are asleep in ignorance; they see sentient beings do bad things; they see sentient beings are bound by desires; they see sentient beings drowning in the sea of Birth and Death; they see sentient beings chronically suffer from illness; they see sentient beings have no desire for goodness; they see sentient beings have lost the way to enlightenment. [Bodhisattvas] always observe sentient beings with these awarenesses.
> (Thomas Cleary, tr. *The Flower Ornament Scripture [Avatamsaka Sutra]*. Vol. II. p. 343.)

Having developed the great compassionate mind,

we should naturally develop the great Bodhi Mind and vow to rescue and liberate. Thus the great compassionate mind and the great Bodhi Mind interpenetrate freely. That is why to develop the compassionate mind is to develop the Bodhi Mind. Only when we cultivate with such great compassion can we be said to have "developed the Bodhi Mind."

Point 4: The Mind of Joy

Having a benevolent mind, we should express it through a mind of joy. This mind is of two kinds: a rejoicing mind and a mind of "forgive and forget." A rejoicing mind means that we are glad to witness meritorious and virtuous acts, however insignificant, performed by anyone, from the Buddhas and saints to all the various sentient beings. Also, whenever we see anyone receiving gain or merit, or prosperous, successful and at peace, we are happy as well, and rejoice with them.

A "forgive and forget" mind means that even if sentient beings commit nefarious deeds, show ingratitude, hold us in contempt and denigrate us, are wicked, causing harm to others or to ourselves, we calmly forbear, gladly forgiving and forgetting their transgressions.

This mind of joy and forbearance, if one dwells deeply on it, does not really exist, because there is in truth no *mark of self*, no *mark of others*, no *mark of annoyance or harm*. As stated in the *Diamond Sutra*:

> The Tathagata teaches likewise that the Perfection of Patience is not the Perfection of Patience; such is merely a name. (A.F. Price, tr., "The Diamond Sutra," p. 44. In *The Diamond Sutra & The Sutra of Hui Neng*.)

The rejoicing mind can destroy the affliction of mean jealousy. The "forgive and forget" mind can put an end to hatred, resentment, and revenge. Because the mind of joy cannot manifest itself in the absence of Enlightenment, it *is* that very Bodhi Mind. Only when we practice with such a mind, can we be said to have "developed the Bodhi Mind."

Point 5: The Mind of Repentance and Vows

In the endless cycle of Birth and Death, all sentient beings are at one time or another related to one another. However, because of delusion and attachment to self, we have, for countless eons, harmed other sentient beings and created an immense amount of evil karma.

The Buddhas and the sages appear in this world out of compassion, to teach and liberate sentient beings, of whom we are a part. Even so, we engender a mind of ingratitude and destructiveness toward the Triple Jewel (Buddha, Dharma, Sangha). Now that we know this, we should feel remorse and repent the three evil karmas. Even the Boddhisattva Maitreya, who has attained non-retrogression, still practices repentance six times a day, in order to achieve Buddhahood swiftly. We should use our bodies to pay respect to the Triple Jewel, our mouths to confess our transgressions and seek expiation, and our minds to repent sincerely and undertake not to repeat them. Once we have repented, we should put a complete stop to our evil mind and conduct, to the point where mind and objects are empty. Only then will there be true repentance ... We should also vow to foster the Triple Jewel, rescue and liberate all sentient beings, atone for our past transgressions, and repay the "four great debts," which are the debt to the Triple Jewel, the debt to our parents and teachers, the debt to our spiritual friends, and finally, the debt we owe to all sentient beings.

Through this repentant mind, our past transgressions will disappear, our virtues will increase with time, leading us to the stage of perfect merit and wisdom. Only when we practice with such a repentant mind can we be said to have "developed the Bodhi Mind."

Point 6: The Mind of no Retreat

Although a practitioner may have repented his past transgressions and vowed to cultivate, his habitual delusions and obstructions are not easy to eliminate, nor is the accumulation of merits and virtues through cultivation of the six paramitas and ten thousand conducts necessarily easy to achieve. Moreover, the path of perfect Enlightenment and Buddhahood is long and arduous, full of hardship and obstructions over the course of untold eons. It is not the work of one or two life spans. For example, the Elder Sariputra [one of the main disciples of Buddha Sakyamuni] had reached the sixth "abode" of Bodhisattvahood in one of his previous incarnations and had developed the Bodhi Mind practicing the Paramita of Charity. However, when an externalist (non-Buddhist) asked him for one of his eyes and then, instead of using it, spat on it and crushed it with his foot, even Sariputra became angry and retreated from the Mahayana mind.

We can see, therefore, that holding fast to our vows is not an easy thing! For this reason, if the practitioner wishes to keep his Bodhi Mind from retrogressing, he should be strong and firm in his vows. He should vow thus: "Although this body of mine may endure immense suffering and hardship, be beaten to death or even reduced to ashes, I shall not, in consequence, commit wicked deeds or retrogress in my cultivation." Practicing with such a non-retrogressing mind is called "developing the Bodhi Mind."

***

The six cardinal points summarized above are *sine*

qua non for those who aspire to develop the Bodhi Mind. Those who do not earnestly practice on this basis will never attain Buddhahood. There are only two roads before us: revolving in Birth and Death, *or* liberation. Although the way to liberation is full of difficulties and hardships, each step leads gradually to the place of light, freedom, peace and happiness. The way of Birth and Death, while temporarily leading to blessings in the celestial and human realms, ultimately ends in the three Evil Paths, subjecting us to untold suffering, with no end in sight.

Therefore, fellow cultivators, you should develop a mind of strong perseverance, marching forward toward the bright path of great Bodhi. The scene of ten thousand flowers vying to bloom in the sky of liberation will be there to greet you!

11) Teachings on the Bodhi Mind

The sutras have expounded at length on the Bodhi Mind, as exemplified in the following excerpts from the *Avatamsaka Sutra*.

> In such people arises the [Bodhi Mind] -- the mind of great compassion, for the salvation of all beings; the mind of great kindness, for unity with all beings; the mind of happiness, to stop the mass misery of all beings; the altruistic mind, to repulse all that is not good; the mind of mercy, to protect from all fears; the unobstructed mind, to get rid of all obstacles; the broad mind, to pervade all universes; the infinite mind, to pervade all spaces; the undefiled mind, to manifest the vision of all buddhas; the purified mind, to penetrate all knowledge of past, present, and future; the mind of knowledge, to remove all obstructive knowledge and enter the ocean of all-knowing knowledge. (Thomas Cleary, tr., *The Flower Ornament Scripture [Avatamsaka Sutra]*, Vol. III, p. 59.)

> Just as someone in water is in no danger from fire, the [Bodhisattva] who is soaked in the virtue of the aspiration

for enlightenment [Bodhi Mind] is in no danger from the fire of knowledge of individual liberation ...

Just as a diamond, even if cracked, relieves poverty, in the same way the diamond of the [Bodhi Mind], even if split, relieves the poverty of the mundane whirl.

Just as a person who takes the elixir of life lives for a long time and does not grow weak, the [Bodhisattva] who uses the elixir of the [Bodhi Mind] goes around in the mundane whirl for countless eons without becoming exhausted and without being stained by the ills of the mundane whirl. (Ibid., p. 362, 364.)

***

We can see that in the *Avatamsaka Sutra*, the Buddhas and Bodhisattvas explained the virtues of the Bodhi Mind at length. The above are merely a few major excerpts. The sutras also state:

The principal door to the Way is development of the Bodhi Mind. The principal criterion of practice is the making of vows.

If we do not develop the broad and lofty Bodhi Mind and do not make firm and strong vows, we will remain as we are now, in the wasteland of Birth and Death for countless eons to come. Even if we were to cultivate during that period, we would find it difficult to persevere and would only waste our efforts.[17] Therefore, we should realize that in following Buddhism, we should definitely develop the Bodhi Mind without delay.

That is why Elder Zen Master Hsing An wrote the essay, "Developing the Bodhi Mind" to encourage the Fourfold Assembly. In it, the Master described eight approaches to developing the Bodhi Mind, depending on sentient beings' vows: "erroneous/correct, true/false, great/small, imperfect/perfect." What follows is a summary of his main points.

1) Some individuals cultivate without meditating on the Self-Nature. They just chase after externals or seek fame and profit, clinging to the fortunate circumstances of the present time, or they seek the fruits of future merits and blessings. Such development of the Bodhi Mind is called "erroneous."

2) Not seeking fame, profit, happiness, merit or blessings, but seeking only Buddhahood, to escape Birth and Death for the benefit of oneself and others -- such development of the Bodhi Mind is called "correct."

3) Aiming with each thought to seek Buddhahood "above" and save sentient beings "below," without fearing the long, arduous Bodhi path or being discouraged by sentient beings who are difficult to save, with a mind as firm as the resolve to ascend a mountain to its peak -- such development of the Bodhi Mind is called "true."

4) Not repenting or renouncing our transgressions, appearing pure on the outside while remaining filthy on the inside, formerly full of vigor but now lazy and lax, having good intentions intermingled with the desire for fame and profit, practicing good deeds tainted by defilements -- such development of the Bodhi Mind is called "false."

5) Only when the realm of sentient beings has ceased to exist, would one's vows come to an end; only when Buddhahood has been realized, would one's vows be achieved. Such development of the Bodhi Mind is called "great."

6) Viewing the Triple World as a prison and Birth and Death as enemies, hoping only for swift self-salvation and being reluctant to help others -- such development of the Bodhi Mind is called "small."

7) Viewing sentient beings and Buddhahood as outside the Self-Nature while vowing to save sentient beings and

achieve Buddhahood; engaging in cultivation while the mind is always discriminating[18] -- such development of the Bodhi Mind is called "imperfect" (biased).

8) Knowing that sentient beings and Buddhahood are the Self-Nature while vowing to save sentient beings and achieve Buddhahood; cultivating virtues without seeing oneself cultivating, saving sentient beings without seeing anyone being saved -- such development of the Bodhi Mind is called "perfect."[19]

Among the eight ways described above, we should not follow the "erroneous," "false," "imperfect," or "small" ways. We should instead follow the "true," "correct," "perfect," and "great" ways. Such cultivation is called developing the Bodhi Mind in a proper way.

In his commentary, Zen Master Hsing An also advised the Great Assembly to remember ten causes and conditions when developing the Bodhi Mind. These are: our debt to the Buddhas, our parents, teachers, benefactors and other sentient beings; concern about the sufferings of Birth and Death; respect for our Self-Nature; repentance and elimination of evil karma; upholding the correct Dharma; and seeking rebirth in the Pure Land.

On the subject of rebirth, he stated, quoting the *Amitabha Sutra*:

> You cannot hope to be reborn in the Pure Land with little merit and virtue and few causes and conditions or good roots.

Therefore, you should have numerous merits and virtues as well as good roots to qualify for rebirth in the Pure Land. However, there is no better way to plant numerous good roots than to develop the Bodhi Mind, while the best way to achieve numerous merits and virtues is to recite the name of Amitabha Buddha. A moment of singleminded recitation surpasses years of practicing charity; truly developing the Bodhi Mind surpasses eons of cultivation.[20] Holding firmly to these two causes and conditions assures rebirth in the Pure Land.

Through these teachings of the Buddhas, Bodhisattvas and Patriarchs, we can see that the Bodhi Mind is essential for the practice of the Way.

Key Conditions with respect to the Bodhi Mind

12) The Path of Birth and Death is Full of Danger

There are many gates to the garden of Enlightenment. As long as the practitioner takes the great Bodhi Mind as his correct starting point, whatever Dharma door he chooses, in accordance with his capacities and preferences, will bring results.

If we consider "capacity," Pure Land embraces persons of all levels. Not only ordinary people but also Bodhisattvas (Manjusri, Samantabhadra) and Patriarchs (Asvaghosha, Nagarjuna) have all vowed to be reborn in the Pure Land. If we take "timing" into consideration, we should realize that in this Dharma-Ending Age when sentient beings in general have scattered minds and heavy obstructions, Buddha Recitation is easy to practice and can help the practitioner achieve rebirth in the Pure Land in just one lifetime. However, if we discuss "individual preferences," the Pure Land method alone cannot satisfy everyone; hence the need for many schools and methods.

In general, cultivators endowed with a sharp mind, seeking a direct, simple and clear approach, prefer Zen. Those who are attracted to supernatural power, the mystical and the mysterious prefer the Esoteric School. Those who like reasoning and require a clear, genuine analysis of everything before they can believe and act, prefer the Mind-Only School... Each school has further subdivisions, so that adherents of the same school may have differing practices.

***

The cultivator who has developed the Bodhi Mind, vowing to save himself and others, may follow any of the schools mentioned earlier. Nevertheless, in this Dharma-Ending Age, he should, at the same time, practice Buddha Recitation seeking rebirth in the Pure Land -- thus ensuring success without retrogression. Why is this so? There are three cardinal points:

In the wasteland of Birth and Death, there are many dangers and obstacles to cultivation. In order to escape the dangerous cycle of Birth and Death and ensure that there is no retreat or loss of the Bodhi Mind, we should seek rebirth in the Pure Land. This is the first cardinal point the practitioner should keep in mind.

The ancients often reminded us:

If we cultivate without striving for liberation, then our cultivation in this life is in fact an enemy during our third rebirth.

This is because in the first lifetime, we endure suffering and bitterness in our practice and therefore, in the next life we enjoy wealth, intelligence and authority. In this second lifetime, it is easy to be deluded by power and wealth, "charming spouses and cute children," and other such worldly pleasures. Having tasted lust and passion, it is easy to become attached, and the deeper the attachments, the closer we are to the dark place of perdition, as we resort to numerous evil deeds to strengthen our power, authority and ambitions. Having generated such causes in our second lifetime, how can we fail to descend upon the three Evil Paths in our third lifetime?

***

Some would ask: "If we have expended efforts to cultivate and sow good seeds in our previous life, how can we lose all our good roots and wisdom in the second lifetime, to the point of descending upon the Evil Paths in the third lifetime?"

Answer: Although good roots exist, the bad karma accumulated for eons past is not necessarily wiped out. Furthermore, on this earth, good actions are as difficult to perform as climbing a high tree, while bad deeds are as easy to commit as sliding down a slope. As the sages of old have said:

> The good deeds performed all of one's life are still not enough; the bad deeds performed in just one day are already too many.

For example, people in positions of power and authority whom we meet today have all, to a greater or lesser extent, practiced charity and cultivated blessings and good karma in their previous lives. However, few among them now lean toward the path of virtue, while those who are mired in fame and profit constitute the majority. Let us ask ourselves, how many persons of high academic achievement, power and fame would agree to leave the secular life, opting for a frugal, austere existence directed toward the goal of lofty and pure liberation? Monks and nuns, too, may patiently cultivate when they have not yet reached high positions. However, with power and fame, and many disciples bowing to and serving them, even they may become easy prey to the trappings of the vain world. Nowadays, how many individuals, clergy or laymen, who were practicing vigorously in the past, have gradually grown lax and lazy, abandoning cultivation or leaving the Order entirely, retreating from the Way -- why even mention the next lifetime?

***

If such is the case in the human realm, how much more difficult it is to cultivate in the celestial realms, where the Five Pleasures are so much more subtle!

We have been talking about those who enjoy blessings. Those lacking in blessings and leading a life of deprivation also find it difficult to cultivate. Even if they are middle class, in this life full of heterodox ways, they may find it difficult to meet true Dharma teachers or to discover the path to liberation. Let us not even mention those treading the three Evil Paths, where cultivation is tens of thousands times more difficult, because they are deluded and suffering both in mind and body.

The cycle of Birth and Death is filled with such dangers and calamities. Thus, if we do not seek rebirth in the Pure Land, it is difficult to ensure non-retrogression of the Bodhi Mind.

13) The Need to Seek Liberation in this Very Life

In this Dharma-Ending Age, if we practice other methods without following Pure Land at the same time, it is difficult to attain emancipation in this very lifetime. If emancipation is not achieved in this lifetime, deluded as we are on the path of Birth and Death, all of our crucial vows will become empty thoughts. This is the second cardinal point which the cultivator should keep in mind.

Those practitioners who follow other schools, stressing only self-help and a firm, never-changing mind, believe that we should just pursue our cultivation life after life. Even if we do not achieve emancipation in this life, we shall certainly do so in a future lifetime. However, there is one thing we should consider: Do we have any firm assurances that in the next lifetime, we will continue cultivating? For, if we have not yet attained Enlightenment, we are bound to be deluded upon rebirth, easily forgetting the vow to cultivate which we made in our previous lifetimes. Moreover, in this world, conditions favoring progress in the Way are few, while the opportunities for retrogression are many. How many monks and nuns have failed to pursue their cultivation upon rebirth, as in the examples summarized in the first chapter?

The sutras state:

Even Bodhisattvas are deluded in the bardo stage,
Even Sravakas are deluded at birth.

Bardo is the intermediate stage between death and rebirth ... In the interval between the end of this current life and the beginning of the next life, even Bodhisattvas are subject to delusion, if they have not yet attained [a high degree of] Enlightenment.

Another passage in the sutras states:

Common mortals are confused and deluded when they enter the womb, reside in the womb, and exit from the womb. Celestial kings, thanks to their merits, are awake upon entering the womb, but are confused and deluded when residing in or exiting from the womb. Sravakas are awake when they enter and reside in the womb; however, they are confused and deluded when they exit from the womb. Only those Bodhisattvas who have attained the Tolerance of Non-Birth are always awake -- entering, residing in, and exiting from the womb.

***

In a few instances, ordinary people, because of special karmic conditions, are able to remember their previous lives, but these are very rare occurrences. Or else, they could be Bodhisattvas who took human form in order to demonstrate the existence of transmigration to sentient beings. Otherwise, all sentient beings are deluded when they pass from one life to another. When they are in such a state, all their knowledge of the Dharma and their great vows from previous lives are hidden by delusion and often forgotten.

   This author recalls the story of a Dharma colleague. In his youth, each time he happened to be dreaming, he would see himself floating freely, high up in the air, travelling everywhere. As he grew older, he could only float lower and lower, until he could no longer float at all. In the commentary *Guide to Buddhism*, there is the story of a layman who, at the age of four or five, could see everything by night as clearly as in the daytime. As the years went by, this faculty diminished. From the age of ten onward, he could no longer see in the dark, except that from time to time, if he happened to wake up in the middle of the night, he might see clearly for a few seconds. After his seventeenth birthday, he could experience this special faculty only once every two or three years; however, his special sight would be merely a flash before dying out. Such persons had cultivated in their previous lives. However, when they were reborn on this earth they became deluded, and then, as their attachments grew deeper, their special faculties diminished.

   There are similar cases of persons who can see everything clearly for a few dozen miles around them. Others can see things underground, through walls, or in people's pockets.   However, if they do not pursue cultivation, their special faculties diminish with time and, in the end, they become just like everyone else. Some persons, having read a book once, can close it and recite every line without a single mistake. Others have a special gift for poetry, so that whatever they say or write turns poetic. However, if they do not pursue cultivation, they sometimes end by rejecting the Dharma.

An eminent Master once commented that such persons had practiced meditation in their previous lives to a rather high level and reached a certain degree of attainment. However, following the Zen tradition, they sought only immediate awakening to the True Nature, severing attachment to the concepts of Buddha and Dharma (i.e., letting the mind be empty, recognizing no Buddha and no Dharma). Therefore, those who failed to attain *Enlightenment* were bound to undergo rebirth in the Triple Realm, whereupon, relying on their mundane intelligence, they sometimes became critical of Buddhism. Even true cultivators in the past were thus; how would today's practitioners fare compared to them?

***

As Buddha Sakyamuni predicted, "In the Dharma-Ending Age, cultivators are numerous, but those who can achieve Supreme Enlightenment are few." And, not having achieved it, even with bad karma as light as a fine silk thread, they are subject to Birth and Death. Although there may be a few cultivators who have awakened to the Way, being awakened is different from attaining Supreme Enlightenment. During rebirth, they are bound to be deluded and unfree. In subsequent lifetimes, there may be few conditions for progress and many opportunities for retrogression, making it difficult to preserve the vow of liberation intact.

Concerning the retrogression of practitioners who have merely experienced Awakening, the ancients have provided three analogies:

1) When we crush prairie grass with a stone block, though the grass cannot grow, its roots are not yet rotten or destroyed. If conditions arise that cause the stone to be overturned, the grass will continue to grow as before.

2) When we pour water into a jar, though the impurities are deposited at the very bottom, they are not yet filtered out. If conditions change and the water is stirred up, the impurities will rise.

3) Take the case of clay which is molded into earthenware but not yet fired in a kiln. If it should rain, the earthenware would certainly disintegrate.

The strong probability that those who have merely experienced an Awakening will retrogress during transmigration is similar to the above examples.

Furthermore, in the Dharma-Ending Age, how many cultivators can claim to be awakened to the Way? Awakening to the Way is not easy. There was once a Zen Master who practiced with all his might for forty years before he succeeded. Another Great Master sat for so long that he wore out more than a dozen meditation cushions before he saw his Original Nature. As far as today's Zen practitioners are concerned (with the exception of a few saints who have taken human form to teach sentient beings), the majority only manage to achieve a temporary calming of the mind and body; at most they may witness a few auspicious realms! Even if they have awakened to the Way, they can still encounter dangerous obstacles during transmigration, as previously described. The path of Birth and Death, filled with fearful dangers for those who have not attained Enlightenment, is the same. Therefore, to claim that we should not fear Birth and Death is a superficial point of view.

Furthermore, over the centuries, the Dharma has met with difficulties in some parts of the world. Wherever materialism has spread, Buddhism has come under criticism. There are places where temples and pagodas have been destroyed, sutras and commentaries burned, monks and nuns forcibly returned to lay life, and common citizens barred from practicing their faith.

Even if Buddhism is revived later on, it will have undergone changes and possibly lost some of its vitality ... For this reason, we should follow the Pure Land School, to ensure non-retrogression of the Bodhi Mind. Even if we follow other schools we should, at the same time, practice Buddha Recitation seeking rebirth in the Land of Ultimate Bliss.

This is the common exhortation of such eminent sages as Masters Lien Ch'ih, Ou I, Chien Mi and Yin Kuang.

14) How to Perfect the Bodhi Mind

Having developed the Bodhi Mind and considering our own capacities and circumstances, what expedients should we adopt to perfect that Mind? If we want both the self-centered and the altruistic aspects of the Bodhi Vow to be complete, there is no better way than to seek rebirth in the Pure Land. This is the third cardinal point that the practitioner should keep in mind.

A high-ranking monk of old, having expressed his determination to cultivate, penned the following verses:

I have pondered this world, and the world beyond,
Whose name would one recite, if not Amitabha's?

Truthfully, after reading these verses, pondering, and comparing Dharma methods, people's capacities and the current environment, this author is convinced that Pure Land is the safest and most complete path.

***

Some may say that having awakened the Bodhi Mind, we should remain in the Saha World, because in this world there are many sentient beings in need of help. Why seek rebirth in the Pure Land?

Let me reverse the question: What are the conditions that would allow us to save sentient beings? They are, of course, merit, virtue, wisdom, eloquence, spiritual power and auspicious features and bearing. (Do we have these qualities to any degree?) Particularly, severing afflictions and delusions and developing wisdom, so that we are not led astray by mundane things, is no easy matter! The ancients have said, "Severing Delusions of Views is as difficult as preventing water from running down a mountain forty miles high." If it is so difficult to rid ourselves of Delusions of Views, how much more difficult it is to sever Delusions of Thought, Delusions of "Dust and Sand," and ignorance.

Delusions of Views, simply put, are the afflictions connected with seeing and grasping at the coarse level. Delusions of Thought are afflictions at the subtle level. For countless eons, the infectious filth of greed, anger and delusion, as well as countless other erroneous views, have been instilled in our mind-consciousness. Can we really manage, in the short span of this life, to do away with them all? Today's cultivators, in general, have few blessings and shallow wisdom. Just reciting the words "Amitabha Buddha" in an accomplished manner is difficult enough. Why even mention such distant goals as saving sentient beings at will?

For this reason, the immediate necessity is to seek rebirth in the Western Pure Land, first rescuing ourselves from the cycle of Birth and Death and then relying upon the auspicious environment of that Land to practice vigorously. We should wait until we have achieved Enlightenment and developed wisdom, eloquence, spiritual powers and auspicious features before returning to the Saha World to rescue sentient beings. Only then will we have some freedom of action.

Nevertheless, considering the responsibility and the compassionate mind of the cultivator, we should not completely reject all attempts to save sentient beings in our current life. In truth, however, our present altruistic attempts can only be within the framework of "according to one's means and conditions." This is not unlike the case of someone who, having fallen into the river of delusion, tries his best to reach the shore, all the while shouting to others, exhorting them to do likewise.

***

To speak more broadly, even if we have attained the stage of Non-Birth and must reside in the evil worlds in order to perfect the "paramitas," in reality we cannot be away from the various pure lands.[21] Why is this so? As stated in the sutras, even Bodhisattvas of the First Stage cannot know the "comings and goings" of Bodhisattvas of the Second Stage, much less the realms of the Buddhas! For this reason, in the *Avatamsaka Sutra* [one of the most grandiose texts of the Mahayana canon], after preaching the Ten Great Vows, the Bodhisattva Samantabhadra immediately admonished the Bodhisattvas at all fifty-two levels (i.e., all Bodhisattvas) to seek rebirth in the Western Pure Land. This is because Amitabha Buddha is always teaching in that Land, and Bodhisattvas wishing to enter the lofty, esoteric realm of the Tathagatas should remain close to and study with Him.

Thus, even the highest level Bodhisattvas should spiritually divide themselves -- on the one hand remaining in the various defiled worlds to accumulate good deeds and on the other, being present in the various pure lands to be close to and cultivate with the Buddhas. Rebirth in the Pure Land of Amitabha Buddha is, therefore, important for sentient beings -- from the lowest beings to the highest level Bodhisattvas.

As seen above, there are many obstacles along the path of Birth and Death. If we have not reached the stage of Non-Birth, it is easy to become deluded during transmigration and descend into evil realms. For this reason, to ensure non-retrogression of the Great Bodhi Mind and fulfillment of the Bodhi Vow, common mortals such as ourselves -- who urgently need to resolve the issue of Birth and Death existing before our very eyes -- should seek rebirth in the Pure Land of Amitabha Buddha.[22]   Even the highest Bodhisattvas cannot remain away from the Pure Land, if they wish to enter the lofty, esoteric realms of the Tathagatas and fulfill the Great Bodhi Vow.

3

Faith

Faith: the Door to Pure Land
15) The Importance of Faith

It is not easy for sentient beings in this Saha World to progress in their cultivation, living as they are in the realm of the Five Turbidities, subject to heavy afflictions and surrounded by violence. Moreover, they usually go astray and become deluded each time they die and are reborn, so that it is very difficult for them to attain Enlightenment. As the ancients often noted:

> Those who enter the clergy are as numerous as hairs on a water buffalo, but those who attain the Way are as scarce as rabbits' horns.

Our Master, Buddha Sakyamuni, experienced the Way to Buddhahood first hand, and knew full well which path was easy to tread and which was difficult. Therefore, with his compassionate, enlightened mind, he purposely taught the special method of Buddha Recitation. Followers of this method, even while not entirely rid of afflictions, may "bring their residual karma along" to the Pure Land. Once reborn there, thanks to the highly favorable conditions of that Land, progress in cultivation and attainment of the Way are as easy as holding an object before one's eyes.

Since Buddha Sakyamuni has such great compassion, one would think that all sentient beings would attain the Way through this method. Nevertheless, relatively few are reborn in the Pure Land. Why is this so? It is because sentient beings have little wisdom and heavy karma, or they doubt the Buddha's words and refuse to cultivate. Or else, they may cultivate but their Faith and Vows are not strong and earnest, or they may recite the Buddha's name but their practice is not in accord with Buddhist teachings. For these reasons, though they may cultivate, their practice will not lead to Enlightenment. The fault lies with the practitioner, not the method.

***

The *Avatamsaka Sutra* teaches:

Faith is the basis of the Path, the mother of virtues
Nourishing and growing all good ways...
Faith can assure arrival at enlightenment.
(T. Cleary, tr. *The Flower Ornament Scripture.* Vol. I, p. 331.)

Therefore, Faith is of great importance to the cultivator. If we lose Faith, not only will our base for progress in the Way crumble, but none of our liberating deeds will succeed. This Faith is not blind faith, but is Faith grounded in wisdom, based entirely on the words of the Buddhas, Bodhisattvas and Patriarchs, as taught in the sutras.

Why is it that after relying on wisdom, we should still put our complete Faith in the teachings of the sages? It is because the Pure Land method, belonging as it does to the Mahayana tradition, is concerned with many transcendental realms beyond human knowledge or wisdom. Therefore, there are many realities that ordinary sentient beings cannot readily understand.

Once, when Buddha Sakyamuni was lecturing on the *Lotus Sutra* at the Vulture Peak Assembly, five thousand great Sravakas (Hearers), many of whom were Arhats, did not believe His words and left the Assembly. Even these venerable Sravakas endowed with transcendental wisdom had doubts about the Dharma preached by Buddha Sakyamuni Himself. We can see, then, that Mahayana teachings are not easy to understand and believe.

For this reason, there are many passages in the Mahayana sutras in which Buddha Sakyamuni requested that such and such a teaching not be preached indiscriminately to those without Faith and with too many view-attachments, lest they develop slanderous thoughts and reap evil karma. When the Mahayana doctrine began to spread widely, the ancient sages, too, admonished Buddhist followers to adopt the following approach to studying Mahayana sutras:

Understand with your mind those passages that you can. As for those passages which you cannot fully comprehend through reflection, just put your Faith entirely in the words of the Buddhas. That is the only way to avoid the offense of vilifying the great Dharma and losing merits and virtues thereby.

In the *Amitabha Sutra*, Buddha Sakyamuni reminded us about Faith several times, as in the following passage:

Sariputra, all of you should believe and accept my words and those of all Buddhas... Sariputra, just as I now praise the inconceivable merits and virtues of all Buddhas, all those Buddhas equally praise my inconceivable merits and virtues with the words "Sakyamuni Buddha can accomplish extremely rare and difficult deeds! In the Saha World, in the evil time of the Five Turbidities... he can attain Buddhahood for the sake of all living beings and preach this Pure Land method, which people the world over are inclined to doubt."

If Sakyamuni Buddha, in his wisdom, has spoken these words, we can see that the Pure Land Dharma door is indeed difficult to grasp, and that Faith is very important! The ancients have likewise stated:

It is very difficult to believe deeply in the Pure Land method. Only sentient beings who have planted the good roots of Buddha Recitation or Bodhisattvas at the Equal Enlightenment stage can truly believe and accept it. Other sentient beings, including even Arhats, Pratyeka Buddhas, and Bodhisattvas at the Expedient Stage, sometimes do not believe in or accept this method.

Reading such remarks, this writer was surprised at first and asked himself why Buddhist disciples did not believe Buddha Sakyamuni's words. The sages of the Two Vehicles (Sravakas and Pratyeka Buddhas) and Bodhisattvas at the Expedient Stage have transcendental wisdom and their attainments are already high; why is it that they do not believe in the Pure Land method? Later on, however, upon observing that there are monks and nuns who can explain the Dharma in a thorough manner but do not believe in the Land of Ultimate Bliss and reject the idea of seeking rebirth there, he conceded that this observation was indeed true. Looking for an explanation, he found it written in the sutras that... the perception of the Arhats, Pratyeka Buddhas and beginning Bodhisattvas is limited; they cannot fully participate in what the Buddhas perceive and understand.

***

The critical elements of the Pure Land method are Faith, Vows and Practice. These three conditions interact like the three legs of an incense burner; if one is lacking or broken, the incense burner cannot stand. Among these conditions, Faith is fundamental. If this critical condition is missing, the mind of Vows and sincere Practice cannot truly develop.

This element of Faith consists, in general, of three factors. *First*, we should believe in the words of the Buddhas, truly acknowledging that the Pure Land, from its inhabitants to the environment itself, does "exist."[23] *Next*, we should believe that the Lord Amitabha Buddha is always true to his Vows, and that however deep the evil karma of sentient beings may be, if they earnestly recite His name, they will be reborn in the Pure Land. *Finally*, we should believe that if we recite Amitabha Buddha's name and vow to be reborn in the Pure Land, we will certainly see the Buddha and be reborn there, as cause and effect cannot diverge. These three factors are, of course, only generalities.

The first factor encompasses faith in the words of the Buddhas and in the noumenal and phenomenal aspects of the Pure Land. The second encompasses faith in the great Vows of Amitabha Buddha and in his "other-power" to rescue us and lead us to rebirth in His Land. The third factor encompasses faith in our own Self-Nature, our own vows, and the cause and effect of the practice of Buddha Recitation. To recognize these three factors fully is to have deep Faith.

Moreover, deep Faith is not a question of words or discriminating thought; it is a profound realization, it is the Pure Mind without a trace of doubt. In this regard, a layman of old once asked a wise monk: "How can we fully ensure rebirth in the Pure Land?" The monk replied, "You need only have a mind of deep and true Faith for rebirth in the Pure Land to be assured." Having been enlightened by this answer, the layman acted accordingly and later on did in fact achieve his aspiration.

Deep Faith is, therefore, of great benefit indeed.

16) Actions that Reduce and Destroy Faith

There are cultivators who teach Buddha Recitation, but do so according to the practices of externalists (non-Buddhists).[24] There are others who vilify Buddha Recitation because they lack deep knowledge or because they have an erroneous understanding of Pure Land. Thus, some clarification of the Pure Land method is required.

***

Let us leave aside, for the moment, those who do not believe in cause and effect or the Dharma and consider only those who are connected, at least on the surface, with Buddhism.[25]

There are some externalists who appear to be monks and nuns, residing in temples and pagodas. However, they neither study nor understand Buddhism and only follow the practices of externalist cults. These people are peddling a hodgepodge of other beliefs under the label of Buddhism. They and their followers secretly transmit their beliefs to one another. Many of them, while claiming to practice meditation, in fact specialize in exercises to balance energy currents, with little knowledge of what meditation is all about. As far as the Pure Land method is concerned, they teach that one should visualize the Buddha's name "shooting" from the navel to the back of the body and up the spinal column, and then returning to the navel. This, they say, is "turning the Dharma wheel." This is the practice of "releasing blockages in the energy system," according to certain non-Buddhist schools.[26] Such teaching is not consonant with Buddhism.

Other persons teach that we should stop breathing

and recite the Buddha's name at one stretch, then rapidly swallow saliva. This, they say, consolidates our "true source." Still others teach that we should figuratively distribute the words "taking refuge in Amitabha Buddha" all around our body. Yet others explain the *Shorter Amitabha Sutra* in a non-Buddhist way, claiming that the seven-jewel lotus pond represents the stomach, the seven rows of precious trees stand for the rib cage, the water of the eight virtues represents blood, marrow and other bodily fluids ... Such persons who purport to practice the Dharma do not represent the correct Faith. How, then, can they be reborn in the Pure Land and escape Birth and Death?

***

Apart from these externalists who hide in the shadow of the Dharma, we should mention true followers of the Buddhas. Among them are some who believe in, understand and accept the teachings of the Buddhas with regard to Pure Land, but do not find Buddha Recitation consonant with their deep preferences. They therefore follow other methods. These are, of course, genuine cultivators of the Dharma. However, there are other persons who do not understand Pure Land in depth, or who, because of their attachment to a particular school, not only do not believe in Buddha Recitation but even criticize it.

For example, we can think of some Zen followers with not much practice who object *a priori* to Buddha Recitation. Little do they realize that many high-ranking Zen Masters of the past,[27] having experienced Awakening and seen their True Nature through meditation, subsequently favored Pure Land. Within the Zen tradition, these Masters were renowned spiritual advisors who taught meditation. In the Pure Land tradition, they were Masters of great repute and virtue who taught Buddha Recitation. This shows that Zen and Pure Land are complementary.

We also have the example of Zen Master Hsu Yun, a high-ranking Chinese monk who passed away not many years ago. He was recognized by all as a transcendentally enlightened Master. However, whenever he was in a Zen hall, he would preach meditation; in a Buddha Recitation hall, he would urge followers to recite the Buddha's name. Not only did he not oppose the Pure Land School, he in fact spoke highly of it.

There are also followers of the Mind-Only school, who, barely having taken up their studies, begin to oppose Buddha Recitation. Little do they realize that the founder and first Patriarch of that school in China, the Great Master Hsuan Tsang, whose teachings they are now following, not only did not oppose Pure Land, but actually propagated it. Indeed, when he brought Indian sutras back to China, he took along a copy of the *Amitabha Sutra* in Sanskrit, which he translated into Chinese. Even the Second Patriarch of the Mind-Only school, the Great Master K'uei Chi, authored two commentaries favorable to Pure Land.

Furthermore, the Great Master T'ai Hsu, a high-ranking Chinese monk of recent times, is recognized by everyone as the foremost Master who revitalized the Mind-Only school; yet, whenever Pure Land followers requested his teaching, he would lecture on and explain Buddha Recitation. He wrote numerous books on the Pure Land method, containing thousands of fascicles, which are still being reprinted. This demonstrates that high-ranking Patriarchs of the Mind-Only school not only did not criticize or reject Pure Land, on the contrary, they spoke highly of it and disseminated its teaching.

***

The first criterion of Pure Land is correct Faith and

understanding. If Faith is lacking, how can we make vows, let alone practice? As indicated earlier, there are generally three types of people who create misunderstanding of the Pure Land teaching. First are those ordinary people who do not believe in cause and effect or the Dharma and therefore belittle the practice of Buddha Recitation. Second are those externalists who hide behind the label and appearance of Buddhism to teach Buddha Recitation in a manner inconsistent with the Buddhas' teachings. Third are those within Buddhism proper who criticize Buddha Recitation because they have only an elementary understanding of it. Pure Land followers should be aware of these persons and their views, realize what is false and what is true, and firmly maintain their Faith in the Way.

Explanation on Points of Doubt

17) Ordinary, everyday doubts about Pure Land

Above we were discussing the views of outsiders looking at the Pure Land school. Below we will take up the reservations of those who truly have the intention of cultivating or who have already started Pure Land practice.

There are some people who truly want to recite the Buddha's name or have already engaged in the practice; however, because their study and understanding of the Dharma are still wanting, they develop doubts as soon as they hear the criticisms of others. There are many such doubts; I shall only mention here three of the most common: 1) Pure Land is really just an expedient teaching; 2) the method is too easy; 3) sentient beings lack conditions and merit and therefore cannot achieve rebirth in the Pure Land. What follows is a summary explanation on these points.

1. Seeing the Pure Land described in overly majestic terms in the sutras, some people suddenly develop the idea that the Pure Land is merely an expedient of the Buddhas.   How can there exist a world in which everything, from the ground to the trees and towers, is made of the seven jewels (gold, silver, lapis lazuli...)? Moreover, the inhabitants radiate health and tranquillity; they spring to life from lotus blossoms, free of old age, disease and death.   Ethereal food and clothing appear before them according to their wishes. All these are far removed from the realities spread before our own eyes; how can we believe in them?

In reply to this I will say: all these doubts derive from the limited sights and sounds perceived by the eyes and ears of common mortals. Those who wish to study the Dharma should not assess the realms of the saints with the limited faculties of sentient beings.

Let us not talk of faraway things. In Asia, in the last century, when a certain high-ranking official returned from Europe, he reported that over there, lamps required no fire to light them, while carriages and barges moved on their own, without horses or men to pull them. He then praised Europeans for their intelligence and skills, which in hundreds of instances rivalled those of God -- only life and death remaining within the purview of the Almighty. His words were met with disbelief from the king on down to his entire court. Even the official's closest friends smiled and thought that returning from far away, he was just exaggerating!

Let us ask ourselves: the king and his entire court were all erudite and worldly. Therefore, they did not believe the official because "their ears had not heard, their eyes had not seen, their imagination could not conceive" of such occurrences. However, can we in fact say that they did not exist? Extrapolating from this small example, we can see that if we measure the realms of the saints with the fixed ideas gathered through our limited senses and imagination, everything is distorted.

Moreover, if there is no such thing as Amitabha Buddha "welcoming and escorting back" to the Pure Land, why is it that numerous people who practice Buddha Recitation know the time of their death in advance, and witness scenes of the Pure Land as well as of Amitabha Buddha and Bodhisattvas welcoming them? If the Pure Land is non-existent, why is it that there are Pure Land followers who in this very life suddenly experience an Awakening and clearly see the adorned Pure Land realm, exactly as explained in the sutras?[28] If we who are the followers of the Buddhas or wish to study Buddhism are not guided by the teaching of the Buddhas, upon whom else can we rely?

Therefore, based on the "teachings of the Buddhas and sages" and on the "attainments of cultivators," we should believe that the adornments of the Pure Land all exist.[29]

***

2. Hearing that the Pure Land method is easy to practice but the results are speedy and lofty, some people develop this doubt: How can there be such an easy method leading to Buddhahood? The usual way of Buddhist cultivation centers around concentration and contemplation. When we start cultivating, we practice first concentration (samatha) then contemplation (vipasyana), or we can begin first with contemplation and follow up with concentration. We then progress to the stage where "in contemplation there is concentration, in concentration there is contemplation." Upon reaching the level of "non-dual concentration and contemplation, still-but-illuminating samadhi and wisdom," we have stepped into the realm of the Self-Nature. From then on, if we vigorously keep up with our cultivation life after life, it will take ten thousand eons before we reach the level of

non-retrogression, according to the sutras and commentaries. How is it that after only a few singleminded utterances of the Buddha's name, we can be reborn in the Pure Land in this very lifetime, at the stage of non-retrogression? Is it not really too easy?

When responding to this doubt, we should realize that most other methods involve complete reliance on "self-power," and are therefore bound to be difficult. The Pure Land method characteristically involves two factors, the power of one's own mind and Amitabha Buddha's power of "welcoming and escorting." Therefore, obtaining results is extremely easy. For example, if someone with weak, hobbled feet wanted to climb a mountain unaided, it would be difficult indeed! However, if he were assisted by a great athlete who took him by the arm and climbed the mountain along with him, head held high, the result would not be that difficult to achieve.

The same is true of Pure Land. As we earnestly recite the Buddha's name, our mind-power keeps developing. When one-pointedness of mind is achieved, the mind-power manifests itself perfectly. At that point the power of our karma is subdued and is no longer a hindrance. If we add to that Amitabha Buddha's power to "welcome and escort," we will achieve rebirth in the Pure Land in spite of the fact that not all of our bad karma is extinguished. Once reborn, our lifespan extends over innumerable eons. Non-retrogression until complete Enlightenment and Buddhahood are attained is therefore an easily understandable occurrence.

***

3. the Land of Ultimate Bliss is so extremely lofty and beautifully adorned that we cannot rely merely on "a few good roots, blessings, virtues, causes and conditions" to achieve rebirth in that Land. Reflecting upon

ourselves, we see that our good roots, merits and virtues are indeed shallow, while our bad karma and obstructions are heavy; how can we expect to attain, in this very life, conditions favorable to rebirth in the Pure Land?

I respectfully beg of you, ten million times, not to have such doubts! For, if you can finger a rosary and recite the Buddha's name, you already have deep roots of merit and virtue. Do think again. How many people are there on this very earth who lack the opportunity to hear the Buddha's name? How many, even after hearing Amitabha Buddha's name, continue to seek fame and profit, chasing after mundane dusts and refusing to recite the Buddha's name? You have now heard the Dharma and recited the Buddha's name in all sincerity. Is this not proof enough that you already have many good roots, merits and virtues?

In the *Longer Amitabha Sutra*, Buddha Sakyamuni said to the Bodhisattva Maitreya:

> If any sentient being hears the name of Amitabha Buddha and is transported with delight even for a moment, you should know that he has received great benefit and has perfected supreme merit and virtue.

This quote should be proof enough: the very fact that a person practices Buddha Recitation shows that he already has many good roots, merits and virtues. The book, *Biographies of Pure Land Sages and Saints*, records the life histories of individuals who committed extremely heavy transgressions, yet achieved rebirth in the Pure Land through singleminded recitation of the Buddha's name at the time of death. Your good roots, merits and virtues far surpass those of the evil beings cited in these biographies. Therefore, why should you have doubts about being reborn in the Pure Land in this very lifetime?

18) Doctrinal Doubts about Pure Land

Apart from the three common doubts discussed above, there are a number of doubts of a doctrinal nature, ranging from the shallow to the deep. I will indicate the important details in question and answer form.

Question I:

The Pure Land method is not for those of high capacities, who should follow the Zen or Mind-Only school. Moreover, people should have strong wills, be independent and rely on their own strength to become emancipated. Is it not a sign of weakness to depend on the other-power of Amitabha Buddha?

Answer:

I will answer this question by referring first to the capacities of sentient beings and then to the issue of self-power vs. other-power.

1. Pure Land embraces people of all capacities -- whether limited, moderate or high. Sentient beings of limited and moderate capacities who recite the Buddha's name can rid themselves of afflictions and karmic obstacles and develop merit, virtue and wisdom, leading in time to the state of samadhi. They will then be reborn within the nine "lotus grades" of the Land of Ultimate Bliss, the exact grade depending on the amount of effort they exert in cultivation.

Those of high capacities, on the other hand, enter deeply into the state of samadhi and wisdom as soon as they begin uttering the Buddha's name. Whether walking, standing, lying down or sitting, they are always in the "Buddha Recitation Samadhi." After death they will be reborn in the highest lotus grade. Some of the sages of old who entered this realm described it in the following terms:

> Holding the rosary, I am rid of worldly thoughts,
> Suddenly, I already became a Buddha a long time ago.

Thus, Pure Land embraces people of all levels. For those of high capacities it is a sublime method; for those of limited capacities it turns into a simple method.

High-ranking masters of the Buddhist canon often commented:

> The Buddha Recitation method encompasses the Zen, Sutra Studies, Discipline (Vinaya) and Esoteric (Tantric) Schools.

Why is it that Buddha Recitation encompasses all four schools? It is because when reciting the Buddha's name, we rid ourselves of all deluded thoughts and attachments, which is *Zen*. The sacred words "Amitabha Buddha" contain innumerable sublime meanings, hidden in and springing forth from those words, which is the *Sutra Studies* School. Reciting the Buddha's name at the deepest level stills and purifies the three karmas (of mind, speech and body), which is the *Discipline* School. The words "Amitabha Buddha" have the same effect as a mantra, eliminating grievances and wrongs, severing evil karma, granting wishes and subduing demons. This is the *Esoteric* School.

For example, during a year of long, severe drought, the Great Master Lien Ch'ih, instead of reciting the "rain mantra," just walked around the countryside hitting his gong while reciting the Buddha's name. It was reported that wherever he went, the rain would begin to fall. There is also the case of the Elder Zen Master Yuan Chao Pen, who, rather than practice meditation, would just recite the sacred words "Amitabha Buddha." In the process, he became enlightened to the Original Nature and attained the Buddha Recitation Samadhi. Extrapolating from the above, the words "Amitabha Buddha" include the Five Periods and the Eight Teachings [i.e., all the teachings of Buddha Sakyamuni] and encompass all the paramitas.

The *Meditation Sutra* further teaches:

A single wholehearted recitation of Buddha Amitabha's name will obliterate all the heavy karma committed in [eight billion eons] of Birth and Death. (J.C. Cleary, *Pure Land, Pure Mind*. Unpub. manuscript.)

If Pure Land followers can concentrate their minds, they are bound to develop wisdom, as with other methods. In addition, since they recite the Buddha's name while in concentration, their evil karma and obstructions will easily be dissolved, and they will attain a high degree of merit and wisdom much sooner. For this reason, Elder Master Lien Ch'ih lauded the Buddha Recitation method as "great samadhi" "great wisdom," "great merit and virtue," and "great emancipation."

According to the *Meditation Sutra*, if anyone who has committed the "Five Grave Offenses" or "Ten Evil Deeds" sees evil omens appear as he is on the verge of death, he need only recite the Buddha's name one to ten times with all his heart, and Buddha Amitabha will descend to welcome and escort him to the Pure Land. For an extremely sinful person to be saved and reach the stage of non-retrogression with just a few recitations of Buddha Amitabha's name is quite an accomplishment. The Patriarch Yin Kuang has these words of praise:

Persons of the highest capacities can attain samadhi if they practice Buddha Recitation with an undisturbed mind. Those of the lowest capacities will still succeed with only ten utterances [as they may be reborn in the Pure Land and ultimately achieve samadhi and Buddhahood]. This is an outstanding feature not found in any other method.

2. As far as the question of "self-power" vs. "other power" is concerned, it is wrong to understand the Pure Land method as exclusive reliance on Buddha Amitabha's power. The Pure Land practitioner should use all his own power to rid himself of afflictions, while reciting to the point where his mind and the Mind of Amitabha Buddha are in unison. At that moment, in this very life, the Buddha will emit rays to silently gather him in and at his death, he will be welcomed and guided back to the Pure Land. The "welcoming and escorting" feature is really the principal manifestation of the "other-power."

As an analogy, for a student to exert his own efforts to the utmost is, of course, a laudable thing. If, in addition, he has the benefit of an excellent teacher who follows his progress and assists him, his level of achievement will be higher, resulting in assured success in his final examinations.

Adding other-power to self-power is similar. Therefore, how can it be considered weak or mistaken to exert all of our own efforts to cultivate and then seek additional help to achieve rapid success?

The great and lofty Pure Land method is lauded by such great Bodhisattvas and Patriarchs as Manjusri, Samantabhadra, Asvaghosha, Nagarjuna as well as eminent Masters of various schools and traditions. To belittle Buddha Recitation is to belittle these very Bodhisattvas, Patriarchs and high-ranking Masters. To claim that Buddha Recitation is low-level, relying only on other-power, is to lack a real understanding of the Pure Land method.

Question II:

In the words of an ancient poem,

Cultivating to the point where the body is as
light as a fairy crane,
We return to the Pure Land in a horizontal line.

Therefore, we should keep practicing meditation until such time as we develop spiritual powers. At that point, we can return to the Land of Ultimate Bliss or go to other pure lands at will.[30] Where then is the need to continuously recite the Buddha's name seeking rebirth in His Land of Ultimate Bliss?

Answer:

The meaning of the above verse is that the realm of the practitioner's Self-Mind accords with the "gathering in" power of Amitabha Buddha. It does not refer to the realm of mystical power. I will discuss these subjects, beginning with mystical powers.

The sutras relate an instance where even the great Arhat Maudgalyayana (foremost in mystical powers among the disciples of Buddha Sakyamuni) had difficulty finding the Pure Land through his own strength. For ordinary people in the Dharma-Ending Age to seek the higher stages of Bodhisattvahood (and thus qualify to enter and reside in the Pure Land on their own merit) is sheer delusion. Therefore, seeking the help of Amitabha Buddha is an essential factor for rebirth in the Pure Land.

What is meant by the realm of the Self-Mind harmonizing with the "gathering in" power of Amitabha Buddha? The sutras state:

Amitabha Buddha constantly emits rays of light, gathering in all sentient beings in the ten directions who practice

Buddha Recitation, without exception.

For this reason, when reciting the Buddha's name, the practitioner is immediately "gathered in," silently, by the Vow-power of Amitabha Buddha. As he singlemindedly recites, his bad karma is "sunk and deposited," his pure mind is revealed, and the light of his mind interacts with the light of Amitabha Buddha. This makes it possible for him to see the Pure Land, or the deities strolling there, before his very eyes.

The power of the cultivator's pure vows directed toward the Pure Land is called "self-power;" the power to emit light and to escort the cultivator back to the Pure Land is called the Buddhas' power or "other-power." Thanks to these two powers, the Pure Land cultivator, although not yet possessing extensive mystical powers, can still be reborn in the Pure Land. At the time of death, depending on his virtues, he will see Amitabha Buddha, the great Bodhisattvas, or members of the Pure Land Assembly reaching out to him, to welcome and escort him. Some cultivators, while not witnessing anything, also achieve rebirth in the Pure Land thanks to the power of their vows and the power of Buddha Amitabha's guiding light. Therein lies the importance of "other-power."

Question III:

When practicing Pure Land, we need to attain the Buddha Recitation Samadhi, or at least reach the stage of one-pointedness of mind, in order to achieve rebirth in the Western Land. Those of limited capacities are not necessarily able to practice at such a level. Therefore, how can these sentient beings be reborn in the Land of Ultimate Bliss? And, if such persons cannot achieve rebirth there, how can Buddha Recitation be said to "gather in" all types of people?

Answer:

   In truth, the capacities of people being what they are these days, even one-pointedness of mind is extremely difficult to achieve, not to mention the state of Buddha Recitation Samadhi! However, according to the *Meditation Sutra*, if anyone who has committed the "Five Grave Offenses" or "Ten Evil Deeds" sees evil omens appear as he is on the verge of death, he need only recite the Buddha's name one to ten times with all his heart and Buddha Amitabha will descend to welcome him and guide him back to the Pure Land. Thus, one-pointedness of mind resulting in rebirth in the Pure Land refers to *the time of death*, not the present time.

   However, in order to achieve such a state of mind at the time of death, the cultivator should practice Buddha Recitation in daily life to the point where it becomes second nature. As he constantly recites the Buddha's name in daily life, even though one-pointedness of mind is not yet achieved, the seeds of Buddha Recitation are accumulated and stored away in great quantities. On his deathbed, the practitioner who begins to recite "activates" those seeds immediately and with great force, resulting in one-pointedness of mind. Those of limited capacities who achieve rebirth in the Pure Land through Buddha Recitation usually fall into this category.

Question IV:

   The purpose of Buddha Recitation is to sever the mind of delusion, put an end to afflictions and reach the state of No-Thought (No Recitation). This being the case, we need only keep the mind pure, and we will progress gradually toward the realm of No-Thought. Where is the need to expend time and effort in Buddha Recitation?

Answer:

The aim of the Pure Land method is the Buddha Recitation Samadhi, achieving, in totality, our Self-Nature Amitabha -- the realm of the "Ever-Silent Illuminating Pure Land." However, the most urgent and immediate aim is rebirth in the Pure Land. This ensures an end to transmigration, and then, through the excellent environment of the Land of Bliss, progress in cultivation and swift attainment of Buddhahood. For this reason, Pure Land cultivators should recite the name of Amitabha Buddha. This is the principal approach of Pure Land; it does not consist of rapidly reaching the realm of No-Thought and becoming enlightened to our Original Nature, as in Zen.

However, while working toward that goal, the practitioner should recite until he reaches the state of one-pointedness of mind. Thus, although he does not seek the realm of "No-Thought," that realm will nevertheless appear naturally. Moreover, it will appear that much sooner, thanks to the virtues accumulated through Buddha Recitation, which help to erase bad karma swiftly. Here we can see a new ray of light, a new vista: to achieve "No-Thought" swiftly, to become enlightened to the Original Nature speedily, we should recite the Buddha's name all the more.

Probing deeper, if we have the roots and the temperament of Mahayana followers, we should understand that the *ultimate* goal of Buddha Recitation is to achieve Buddhahood. If we understand that goal to be merely the elimination of deluded thoughts, we have already strayed into the "Five Meditations to calm the mind" approach of the Theravada tradition.

Why is it that the goal of Buddha Recitation is to become a Buddha? It is because as soon as we begin reciting, the past, present and future have lost their distinctions, marks exist but they have been left behind, form is emptiness, thought is the same as No-Thought, the realm of the Original Nature "apart from thought" of the Tathagata has been penetrated. This state is Buddhahood. What else could it be?

If we were to think that to recite is to remain attached to the "conditioned" (mundane dharmas subject to Birth and Death), then, when Buddha Sakyamuni displayed such concrete marks as eating a meal, donning a robe, conversing, preaching the Dharma, walking, standing, lying down, or sitting up, was He not attached to the conditioned and therefore not a Tathagata?

Moreover, if we were to think that reciting the Buddha's name is not yet No-Thought, then, when high-ranking Zen masters are meditating on a koan, preaching the Dharma, or, at times, reciting sutras, genuflecting, seeking repentance, or circumambulating, (all actions having marks), are they therefore not practicing Zen?

We should know that the essence of the "unconditioned" is to "practice all conditioned dharmas without seeing the mark of practice." The same is true of No-Thought. It does not mean that entirely eliminating all actions and words is the unconditioned, the No-Thought! Because they fail to understand this truth, some persons who are attached to the teaching of Emptiness think: Buddha Recitation is like a moving vehicle carrying an added heavy load, impure gold with traces of lead, rice mixed with sand, not light, pure and unmixed. How wrong can they be!

However, reciting to the point of "not reciting," is the sphere of those of the highest capacities. I merely raise the issue to reply to a point of doubt. As far as most of us are concerned, making the effort to recite the Buddha's name in an accomplished manner is already a very worthwhile thing!

Question V:

The nature of all dharmas is "emptiness," from time immemorial, ever non-arising, equal, serene and still. When the mind is pure, though we may be living in an impure world, the mind is just as pure. On the other hand, if the mind is not pure, even if we are living in a "pure land," it will be full of afflictions and disturbances. If there is "arising," there is "extinction;" where there is birth, there is death. Thus, is it not contrary to the Dharma to leave the Saha World and seek rebirth in the Pure Land?

Answer:

This question can be answered on two levels. I will follow the explanations of the T'ien T'ai Patriarch Chih I in his treatise *Ten Doubts about the Pure Land* and add a few explanatory comments of my own, from the two viewpoints of generality and specificity.

On the level of *generality*, if we consider that seeking rebirth in the Pure Land means "leaving here and going there," which is inconsistent with the principle of Equal True Thusness, then what about remaining in the Saha World and not seeking rebirth in the Pure Land? Is that not also making the mistake of "leaving there and grasping here"? Now, if we say that "I neither seek to go there nor am I attached to here," we are also caught in the error of nihilism. For this reason, the *Diamond Sutra* states:

> Subhuti, do not think that to develop the Bodhi Mind is to annihilate all the marks of the dharmas. Why is this so? It is because developing the Bodhi Mind with respect to phenomena is not the same as nihilism.

On the level of *specificity*, I will now explain the truth of No-Birth and the Pure Mind.

"No-Birth" is precisely the truth of No-Birth No-Death. No-Birth means that dharmas are born of illusory combinations of causes and conditions, with no Self-Nature and thus, no true mark of birth. Because they are illusory, they are not really born nor do they appear from anywhere. Therefore, they are said to have No-Birth.

"No-Death" means that when dharmas disintegrate, there is no Self-Nature remaining. Since they have no true place of return, no place of extinction, they are said to be "undying." The truth of No-Birth, or neither Birth nor Death, cannot exist outside of conditioned dharmas. Thus, No-Birth does not mean not seeking rebirth in the Pure Land, or that being reborn in the Pure Land is to be subject to death and extinction (which is contrary to the truth of No-Birth). This is from the viewpoint of principle or noumenon.

On the level of phenomena, those who are reborn in the Pure Land have reached the stage of non-retrogression, with a life extending over innumerable eons. During that period, they will have ample opportunity to progress toward the fruit of No-Birth. Thus, the issue is moot: there is no arising, no extinction, no Birth and no Death to worry about!

The principle of the Pure Mind is similar. Practicing with a Pure Mind in the Saha World, and "anchoring" the Pure Mind in the Pure Land to progress in cultivation are not contradictory. The *Vimalakirti Sutra* states:

Although he knows that Buddha lands
Are void like living beings
He goes on practicing the Pure Land (Dharma)
To teach and convert men. (Charles Luk, tr., p. 88.)

Therefore, the wise, while diligently reciting the

Buddha's name seeking rebirth in the Pure Land, do not grasp at the mark of Birth, because that mark does not really exist. Although they are clearly aware that dharmas from time immemorial are ever pure, empty and still, they do not hesitate to seek rebirth in the Pure Land. This is because they rely on the supremely auspicious environment there to progress in their cultivation and to teach and enlighten others. This is true No-Birth and also the true meaning of a Pure Mind in accord with a pure environment.

On the other hand, those who lack knowledge and true understanding are caught up in the mark of Birth. Hearing of Birth, they immediately think that it really exists, along with death and extinction. Hearing of No-Birth, they immediately become attached to the notion that there is no rebirth anywhere. Little do they realize that Birth is really No-Birth, No-Birth is not incompatible with Birth. With a Pure Mind, where is the worry about seeking rebirth in the Pure Land? Not understanding this truth, they develop a contentious and discriminatory Mind, belittling those who seek rebirth in the Pure Land. How mistaken and lost can they be?

19) Doubts Based on Misreading the Sutras

Apart from the above, there are numerous students of the Dharma who raise a number of issues based on the teachings in the sutras. I will follow the question and answer formula to reply to them.

Question I:

The *Diamond Sutra* states:

All mundane (conditioned) dharmas are like dreams, illusions, shadows and bubbles.

Therefore, the Saha World being illusory, so is the Land of Ultimate Bliss. Why not enter directly into the

True Original Mind instead of seeking rebirth in an illusory world?

Answer:

In truth, all the pure and impure lands in the ten directions are like dreams and illusions; however, only when we have attained the "Illusion-like Samadhi" can we see them as illusory and false. If we have not yet reached that stage, we still see them as real, we are still subject to their sway, we still know sorrow and happiness, we still feel uncomfortable during the summer heat and are even bothered by such small things as mosquito bites. Thus, how can we speak about things being illusory?

We should realize that the Pure Land method is a wonderful expedient of the Buddhas -- borrowing an illusory realm of happiness to help sentient beings escape from an illusory realm of great suffering, full of obstructing conditions and dangers. Then, in that happy, peaceful, illusory realm, cultivation progresses easily, and the ever-silent realm of the True Mind is swiftly attained.

To take an example, in this Saha World of ours, the scenes of stifling family life and noisy downtown business districts are illusory, and so are the scenes of temples and pagodas or mountain wildernesses. However, why is it that cultivators leave the noisy environment of the cities to seek the quiet, sparsely populated landscapes of temples and pagodas hidden in the mountains? Is it not because family life creates many binding ties and bustling urban intersections are not conducive to concentration, while temples, pagodas and mountain wildernesses facilitate cultivation? For this reason, the circumstances of ordinary people are different from those of the saints. For common mortals to put themselves in the place of the saints is far-fetched and unrealistic. We who are still common mortals should follow the path of ordinary people, and cultivate gradually. We should not look with the eyes of saints and comment too far above our level, to avoid the transgression of false speech.

There was once a Zen Master who thought that the Pure Land was illusory and that reciting the Buddha's name seeking rebirth there was useless. Upon hearing this, Elder Master Ch'e Wu said immediately:

> This is a mistake. Bodhisattvas of the Seventh Stage and below are all cultivating in a dream. Even those Bodhisattvas who have reached the level of Equal Enlightenment are still fast asleep within the great dream of delusion. Only the Buddhas can be honored with the designation Great Enlightened, i.e., those who have completely awakened. When our own body is in a dream, happiness and suffering are to be expected; we still experience happiness and still know suffering. How can we consider ourselves awakened from a dream and our environment dreamlike?
>
> This being the case, how can remaining in the suffering dream of the Saha World compare with returning to the blissful dream of the Pure Land? Moreover, the Saha World dream goes from dream to dream, subject to the laws of karma, eternally revolving in the cycle of Birth and Death. The Pure Land dream on the other hand, is from dream to Enlightenment and gradual awakening to the ultimate stage of Buddhahood. Although the illusory dreams are the same, the conditions of the dreaming state in the two instances are really different. Thus, it is truly necessary to recite the Buddha's name seeking rebirth in the Pure Land!

These explanations have clearly demonstrated the need to seek rebirth in the Pure Land. However, the stanza from the *Diamond Sutra* quoted above is still an expedient explanation to help sentient beings abandon the common mortal's concept of attachment. Going one step further, as stated in the *Great Prajna Paramita Sutra:*

Buddha Sakyamuni explained to those of dull capacities that all dharmas are dreamlike, silent, and still, lest they develop view-attachment. To those of sharp capacities He spoke of the embellishments of the Buddhas, because they are like lotus blossoms, untouched by worldly dusts.

For this reason, Subhuti, who of all the Arhat disciples of Buddha Sakyamuni was foremost in the realization of the Truth of Emptiness (devoid of all names and marks), characteristically received a prediction that he would attain Buddhahood in the future under the title of "Name and Mark Buddha." Thus, the sublime truth of no name or mark is inseparable from name and mark -- all illusory dharmas are the Buddhas' dharmas, true and unchanging.

Going still deeper, to the ultimate and perfect stage, as the Sixth Patriarch has said:

Sentient beings are originally Buddhas, afflictions are Bodhi (Enlightenment), all delusions are the perfect and illuminating state, truly enlightened, of the womb of the Tathagatas.

Question II:

The *Platform Sutra* states:

Recitation with no thought of recitation is true; recitation while [grasping at the thought of] recitation is wrong.[31]

Thus, is not Buddha Recitation deviant and false?

Answer:

The meaning of No-Birth, No-Thought of Recitation has been discussed earlier, but I will give a direct explanation here. "No-Thought of Recitation" does not mean no Buddha or Sutra Recitation, but rather habitual recitation of the Buddha's name and the sutras with a completely empty mind, neither seeing nor grasping at the thought that we are the ones doing the reciting. This is called No-Thought of Recitation. On the other hand, though we may sit still and at peace, our minds completely empty, if we are still aware that we are sitting in meditation, this is still grasping at the thought of recitation.

If we think that No-Thought of Recitation is not to recite the Buddha's name or the sutras, not to lecture on the Dharma and not to reflect or meditate, then we have turned into wood and stone. While avoiding the error of grasping at forms, we have fallen into the error of grasping at emptiness -- thus going against the very meaning of the *Platform Sutra*. For this reason, the Sixth Patriarch continued:

> He who is above "affirmative" and "negative"
> Rides permanently in the white bullock cart
> (the vehicle of Buddha)."
> (Wong Mou-Lam, tr. "The Sutra of Hui Neng," p. 65. In *The Diamond Sutra & The Sutra of Hui Neng*.)

High-ranking monks of old often practiced Buddha Recitation seeking rebirth in the Pure Land, but they were not attached to the mark of Buddha Recitation or seeking rebirth. Therefore, they left behind this stanza:

> To recite is the same as not to recite,
> No-Birth is precisely birth,
> Not bothering to move even half a step,
> The body has reached the city of Great Enlightenment.

However, we have spoken so far of the practice of exeptional individuals. Persons of limited or moderate capacities should strive to repeat the Buddha's name as many times as possible. While they may still have attachments and see themselves as reciting the Buddha's name earnestly seeking rebirth in the Pure Land, it is still a good thing. This is because by so doing, they will assuredly achieve rebirth in the Pure Land at the time of death and ultimately enter the realm of No-Recitation,

No-Birth. Where is the worry? Otherwise, seeking a direct and lofty way without gauging their own limitations and grasping at the teachings of Emptiness while incapable of following the truth of No-Recitation -- yet unwilling to practice at the level of seeking rebirth in the Pure Land through Buddha Recitation -- in the end they achieve nothing. They just remain common mortals in the painful cycle of Birth and Death!

Question III:

In the *Platform Sutra*, the Sixth Patriarch stated:

Those living in the East [i.e., our world] who commit transgressions recite the Buddha's name seeking rebirth in the West [i.e., Pure Land]. Where do those transgressors living in the West seek rebirth when they recite?[32]

Thus, we should only aim at eliminating transgressions. What need is there to recite the Buddha's name seeking rebirth in the Pure Land?

Answer:

The Sixth Patriarch and high-ranking Zen Masters were intent on teaching the doctrine of Mind. Thus, all of their words were based on these tenets, pointing directly to the Self-Nature, with the mind as the center. What the Patriarch really meant was that if the mind is pure, even though we may be in the Saha World, we are emancipated and free. If the mind is impure, even though we may be in the Pure Land, we are still subject to the sufferings of Birth and Death.

In truth, for the Pure Land cultivator who understands the Dharma, the Patriarch's words serve only to urge him on, encouraging him to recite the Buddha's name to the level of purity of mind, devoid of all attachment to forms. The Patriarch certainly did not reject the act of reciting the Buddha's name seeking rebirth in the Pure Land as Buddha Sakyamuni, the Buddhas of the ten directions, the great Bodhisattvas and the Patriarchs all recommended seeking rebirth there. In fact, the two foremost Indian Zen Patriarchs, Asvaghosha and Nagarjuna, both recommended the Pure Land method. Nagarjuna himself, according to the *Lankavatara Sutra*, was enlightened to the preliminary Bodhisattva ground of "extreme Joy," and was reborn in the Pure Land.

If the Sixth Patriarch had truly intended to reject Buddha Recitation, he would have been criticizing and rejecting Buddha Sakyamuni, the Buddhas of the ten directions, the Bodhisattvas and the Patriarchs, including the very precursors who established his own Zen School, the Patriarchs Asvaghosha and Nagarjuna. How could that be? Therefore, if we were to misunderstand the Sixth Patriarch's words and use those very words to deprecate Buddha Recitation, we would be slandering and sowing the seeds of injustice toward him.

Moreover, every method has two aspects, noumenon (principle) and phenomena. The quotation from the Sixth Patriarch is at the level of principle. We must also consider the phenomenal aspect of the path to liberation.

Let us restate the question. "Those who commit transgressions in the secular world seek refuge in temples and pagodas, where they cut their hair, become vegetarians, and keep the precepts, looking for a place of purity and tranquillity in order to cultivate. Where do those living in temples and pagodas who transgress go to cultivate?" If we base ourselves only at the level of noumenon and follow the above reasoning, then can such actions as entering the monastic life, being vegetarian, and keeping the precepts, including Buddha, Sutra and Mantra Recitation as well as meditation, all be mistakes?

The Pure Land method is similar. In truth, people in the East do not recite the Buddha's name seeking rebirth in the West merely because they have committed transgressions; rather, they do so precisely to take advantage of the excellent conditions of that Land to cultivate and swiftly attain the level of No-Birth and liberation. This is also the goal pursued by those who have committed evil deeds but who now repent and recite the Buddha's name.

Moreover, the inhabitants of the Western Pure Land cannot commit transgressions because once reborn there, they are surrounded by Buddha Amitabha, Bodhisattvas and "morally superior beings." Around them are "birds singing the Dharma and music expounding the sutras," while they are free from such daily worries as food, clothing, disease, calamities, hatred and resentment. Thus, they can only progress along the path of cultivation. Where are the causes and conditions for creating bad karma?

In conclusion, we should understand the Sixth Patriarch's words as an explanation and exhortation based exclusively on pure noumenon or essence. We should not misunderstand them and use them to reject phenomena and marks. This being the case, Pure Land cultivators should redouble their efforts and practice to the point of emptiness of mind. Only then will they be in accord with the intent of the Patriarch.

20) The Need to Sever Dualistic Attachments

Many similar doubts remain concerning the Pure Land method. This is because most cultivators are still attached to "duality," and have not reconciled essence and marks,[33] existence and non-existence, noumenon and phenomena. That is why they embrace essence to reject marks, noumenon to reject phenomena, Emptiness to reject Existence, and vice versa -- thus creating disputes, doubts and perplexity.

Little do they suspect that there is mutual identity between noumenon and phenomena -- phenomena are noumenon, noumenon is phenomena. If we divide them and consider them separately, phenomena are not true phenomena, noumenon is not true noumenon. This is true also of essence and marks, existence and non-existence and other dualistic dharmas.

For this reason, the *Vimalakirti Sutra* speaks of the non-dual method to destroy this attachment. Non-dual means reconciling all things, penetrating into their very nature; it does not mean "one." This is the true realm of "Mind-Only." Any other doctrine based on the Dharma Doors of Existence or Emptiness is merely an expedient for teaching purposes.

The sutras state:

To tire of and abandon "conditioned" virtues is the action of demons. Yet, to be greedy and attached to transcendental, unconditioned virtues is also demonic action.

Ancient sages have also said:

Conditioned dharmas, while illusory, cannot be abandoned if we are to attain the Way. Although unconditioned dharmas are true, if we become attached to them, our wisdom-nature will not be comprehensive.

These words clearly show that on the path to Enlightenment, unconditioned and conditioned dharmas, noumenon and phenomena are inseparable.

It is also stated in the *Treatise on the Middle Way:*

Because common sentient beings grasp at external forms, the sutras destroy this attachment with the truth of Emptiness. If as soon as they are free of the disease of attachment to Existence they fall into the error of grasping at Emptiness, there is no medicine that can help them.

As the Prajna Paramita Truth of Emptiness sounds lofty and miraculous, when educated people read this literature, they usually get caught up in the error of "speaking on the level of principle" about everything and look down on those who follow forms and marks in their practice. Thus, they create the karma of arrogance and self-importance. While they expound the Truth of Emptiness, their actions are entirely in the realm of Existence, as exemplified by the following couplet:

Above, their mouths speak about the totally wonderful,
Below, their feet do not part with even a mote of dust.

***

In the past, high-ranking spiritual teachers often used the Truth of Emptiness to cure the disease of attachment to Existence. However, the achievements of these masters were genuine, and their teachings were adapted to the capacities and circumstances of the recipients, bringing them actual benefits. This can be seen from the following stories.

There was once a Zen Master who cultivated with extreme diligence. He usually slept in a sitting position rather than lying down, and hardly rested much at all. However, despite engaging in ascetic practices for many years, he still had not become enlightened to the Way. One day, a novice of unknown provenance sought permission to join the Order. This novice was habitually lazy, to the point where he would often remain in bed even after the bell announcing the early prayer session had been rung. Informed of this, the Master summoned him and scolded him in the following terms, "How is it that you have joined the Order but are still so lazy as to be always lying down? Don't you remember what the rules of discipline say: 'Remaining in bed and failing to arise after hearing the bell will bring the future retribution of rebirth as a snake?'"

The novice replied, "You said, Master, that I often lie down and therefore will become a snake. How about you, who are attached to the sitting posture? You will be reborn a toad. What can you ever hope to awaken to?"

Immediately after this exchange, the novice disappeared. However, the Master had been awakened. As the story goes, the novice was in fact a Bodhisattva, who had assumed the appearance of a novice in order to enlighten the Master.

There is also a well-known story about a Zen master who sat astride the neck of a Buddha statue and split and burned wooden Buddhas in order to destroy the concept of attachment to the Buddhas. Another anecdote, from the *Platform Sutra*, concerns Master Fa Ta, who, having recited the *Lotus Sutra* three thousand times, prostrated himself only half way and was then reprimanded by the Sixth Patriarch for not having severed his attachment to merit and virtue. Yet another story concerns Master Pei T'a, who, upon achieving the Great Freedom Samadhi, wrote the names of the Bodhisattvas Manjusri and Samantabhadra on his underpants, to destroy the concept of attachment to transcendental beings.[34]

Enlightened Masters of the past, with their high level of practice and achievement, could teach the Dharma according to the times and conditions. Moreover, the practitioners of the time included individuals of the highest capacities, so that the teaching of Emptiness was often fruitful. Today, the majority are of limited and moderate capacity.[35] Therefore, in our teaching, we should harmonize theory and practice, nature and marks, so as not to engender doubts, and to keep the Bodhi Mind of the cultivators from retrogressing. Since the majority of practitioners cannot enter directly into the sphere of True Emptiness in one step, rejection of external forms would bring on the calamity of "prematurely destroying the boat before stepping onto the shore." How, then, could they escape drowning?

***

One more point to bear in mind: if we speak about the Truth of Emptiness without having attained that stage or at least reached a certain level of achievement in our practice, we certainly cannot convert others, but will only end up in useless arguments and disputes.

A few years ago, this author witnessed the following occurrence: a young monk versed in the Dharma was staying at a certain temple to lecture on the sutras. The abbot, who was advanced in age, was diligent in his daily recitation, but accustomed to traditional ways of worship. He took a dislike to the young monk and his free, progressive ways and said to him, "You are teaching and urging people to follow the Way, yet you yourself have never been seen to recite a single sutra or the Buddha's name. Under these circumstances, how can you be a model of cultivation for the Four-Fold Assembly?"

The young monk replied, "There are many ways to cultivate. It is not necessary to follow appearances, reciting the sutras and the Buddha's name day and night, as you do, Master, to qualify as a cultivator. The *Diamond Sutra* states:

Who sees Me by form,
Who sees Me in sound,
Perverted are his footseps upon the Way;
For he cannot perceive the Tathagatha.
(A. F. Price, tr. "The Diamond Sutra," p. 65. In *The Diamond Sutra &*

The Sutra of Hui Neng.)

"Take the Sixth Patriarch, who recited neither the sutras nor the Buddha's name, yet attained Enlightenment and became a Patriarch." The abbot at a loss for words, remained silent.

In truth, the abbot was guilty of attachment to appearances and forms; the young monk, on the other hand, while citing abstruse principles, actually practiced neither meditation nor recitation. Therefore, he not only failed to enlighten the abbot, he irritated him unnecessarily.

Of the two types of attachments, to Existence and to Emptiness, the latter is the more dangerous. Both the *Lankavatara* and the *Esoteric Adornment Sutras* warned:

It is better to be attached to Existence, though the attachment may be as great as Mount Sumeru, than to be attached to Emptiness, though the attachment may be as small as a mustard seed.[36]

Attachment to Existence leads to mindfulness of cause and effect, wariness of transgressions and fear of breaking the precepts, as well as to such practices as Buddha and Sutra Recitation and performance of good deeds. Although these actions are bound to forms and not liberated and empty, they are all conducive to merit, virtue and good roots. On the other hand, if we are attached to Emptiness without having *attained* True Emptiness, but refuse to follow forms and cultivate merit and virtue, we will certainly sink into the cycle of Birth and Death.

This author, knowing himself to be filled with karmic obstructions and being of limited capacity, has no desire to discuss lofty doctrinal questions, lest his practice not be in accord with his words, thus creating the karma of false speech. However, with a sincere mind, wishing people to eliminate doubts and believe in Buddha Recitation, he has reluctantly provided some explanations. He always compares himself to a handicapped person sitting at the crossroads; although he himself cannot walk, he strives to show others the way, reminding passersby to avoid the dangerous paths and follow the wide, even and peaceful way. He certainly would never entertain the ambition to engage in discussions designed to separate the important from the trivial or the true from the false.

4

Vows

Earnest Vows: Main Force Behind Rebirth in the Pure Land

21) The Importance of Vows

As indicated earlier, the essential elements of the Pure Land method are Faith, Vows and Practice.

To practice this method, the cultivator should first believe that the Land of Ultimate Bliss does exist and that Amitabha Buddha always extends his protection, ready to welcome and guide all sentient beings who earnestly seek his help. Such belief is called Faith.

Having developed a mind of Faith, the practitioner should eagerly seek escape from this Saha World full of suffering and obstructions, and rebirth in the peaceful Land of Ultimate Bliss, filled with countless pure adornments. Once there, he can progress in his Practice and achieve the goal of rescuing both himself and others. This is called Vows.

Having made such Vows, he should earnestly recite

the Buddha's name to the point where his mind and that of Amitabha Buddha are in unison -- thus achieving rebirth in the Pure Land. This is called Practice. The previous chapter dealt with Faith. This chapter covers Vows, while the following chapter will explain Practice.

Faith, Vows and Practice are called the "three provisions" of the Pure Land method. Just as travellers embarking on a distant journey must make provisions for medicine, food, clothing and funds sufficient to cover their needs en route, so, too, Pure Land practitioners require Faith to make firm Vows. However, Faith and Vows are hollow without Practice. Likewise, even if Practice is adequate, without Faith and Vows, that Practice will go astray, lacking criteria and direction. Therefore, Faith, Vows and Practice are the "provisions" of those returning to the Pure Land from afar.[37]

***

The eminent Pure Land master Ou-I once said:

To be reborn in the Pure Land or not depends entirely upon Faith and Vows; the grade of rebirth (high or low) depends on whether one's Practice is deep or shallow.

He further added:

Without Faith and Vows, you cannot be reborn in the Pure Land, even if you recite the Buddha's name to the point where neither the blowing wind nor the falling rain can penetrate and your recitation is as solid as a bronze wall or an iron gate.

Those who practice Buddha Recitation assiduously but lack Faith and Vows will merely obtain the merits and blessings of the human and celestial realms, according to their level of cultivation. When their blessings are exhausted, they are once again subject to Birth and Death, as exemplified in the following account.

During the Later Lê dynasty in Vietnam, there was a certain monk at the Temple of Light who diligently practiced Buddha Recitation, but had not vowed in earnest to achieve rebirth in the Pure Land. After his death, so the story goes, he was reborn as a prince in Ch'ing dynasty China. At his birth, he had certain red spots on his shoulders pointing to his previous incarnation. A hermit summoned to the palace prophesized that these spots would disappear only if they were washed away with water taken from a well at the Temple. Years later, while scrubbing the red spots with water taken from the well, the prince was moved to compose a poem with the following lines:

> I was originally a disciple of Amitabha Buddha in the *West*,
> Why have I now strayed into a royal household?
>
> ["West" means Vietnam, west of China, and also the Pure Land.]

Although the prince was aware of his previous life as a novice practicing Buddha Recitation at the Temple of Light, in his high royal position, enjoying countless blessings and pleasures, he could not, in the end, pursue his cultivation. Such are the unhappy results of reciting the Buddha's name while lacking Faith and Vows!

***

Thus, carefully re-examining the words of Elder Master Ou-I, we can see that the real issue is not the grade at which we will be reborn, but rather, *whether we will be reborn in the Pure Land or not*. To achieve rebirth there, both Faith and Vows are required, with Vows being the crucial factor. The Master insisted further:

> If Faith and Vows are strong and firm, uttering the Buddha's name just ten times, or even only once, at the time of death, will ensure rebirth in the Pure Land. On the other hand, though our Practice may be as solid as walls of bronze or gates of iron, if our Faith and Vows are weak, we will merely succeed in obtaining the merits and blessings of

the human and celestial realms.

This discussion makes it quite clear: it is preferable to have firm Faith and Vows, for even though our Practice may be deficient, we will still achieve rebirth in the Pure Land and emancipation. From this we can see how important true and firm Vows are!

22) Sutra Passages on the Making of Vows

The guiding force of the Vow for rebirth can be seen from the following excerpt from the "Vows of the Bodhisattva Samantabhadra":

> Further, when a [king] is on the verge of death, at the last instant of life, when all his faculties scatter and he departs from his relatives, when all power and status are lost and nothing survives, when his Prime Minister, great officials, his inner court and outer cities, his elephants, horses, carts, and treasures of precious jewels can no longer accompany him, these [Great] Vows alone will stay with him. At all times they will guide him forward, and in a single instant he will be reborn in the Land of Ultimate Bliss. (Hsuan Hua, tr. *Flower Adornment Sutra [Avatamsaka Sutra]*, Ch. 40, p. 125.)

The *Amitabha Sutra* repeatedly reiterates the importance of making Vows, as in the following passages:

> Moreover Shariputra, all those born in the Land of Utmost Happiness never fall back. Among them are many whose next birth will be in Nirvana. The number of them is extremely large; there is no reckoning that can tell it. Only in measureless, unlimited, innumerable kalpas could it be told.

> Shariputra, the beings who hear this ought to make a vow -- a vow to be born in that land. Why should they? Having succeeded thus, all are then persons of the highest virtue; all are assembled in the same circumstances.

> Shariputra, I see this gain and therefore speak these words;

if any beings hear them, they ought to make a vow to be born in that land.

Shariputra, if there are persons who have already made a vow, are presently making a vow, or shall in the future make a vow, desiring birth in Amida Buddha's land, all these persons obtain nonretrogression in Highest Perfect Knowledge in that land, whether already born, now being born, or yet to be born. Therefore, Shariputra, all good men and good women, if they have faith, ought to make a vow to be born in that land. (Hozen Seki, tr. *Buddha Tells of the Infinite: the ("Amida Kyo")*, p. 47, 54, 69, respectively.)

It can thus be seen that Buddha Sakyamuni repeatedly reminded us, in the most earnest terms, about the principle of making Vows. Even toward the very end of the *Amitabha Sutra*, he repeatedly enjoined us to make a Vow for rebirth in the Pure Land. Why is this so? It is because if we are reborn in the Pure Land, we will be dwelling in a realm of infinite splendor and adornments, radiating vigor and health, replete with the thirty-two marks of greatness, completely rid of the sufferings of birth, old age, disease and death. We will always be near Amitabha Buddha and various Bodhisattvas, in the company of "persons of the highest virtue" and endowed with spiritual powers and samadhi. We will also be free from retrogression. Sakyamuni Buddha, realizing in his wisdom the many benefits to be derived, compassionately enjoined sentient beings to seek rebirth in the Pure Land. His compassion is truly immense!

23) A Brief Examination of the Vow for Rebirth

In the *Longer Amitabha Sutra*, Buddha Sakyamuni succinctly listed the number of Bodhisattvas in various realms or lands (including our Saha World) who would be reborn in the Pure Land of Amitabha Buddha:

Then Bodhisattva Maitreya asked the Buddha, "World-Honored One, how many nonregressing

Bodhisattvas in this Buddha-land will be born in the Land of Utmost Bliss?"

The Buddha told Maitreya, "In this Buddha-land, seven billion two hundred million Bodhisattvas, who have planted good roots in incalculable hundreds of thousands of [millions of] billions of myriads of Buddha-lands and have become nonregressing, will be born in [the Pure Land]. The Bodhisattvas who will be born in that Buddha-land [the Pure Land] because of fewer roots of virtue are countless ...

"Ajita [Maitreya], if I enumerate the names of the Bodhisattvas in other lands who have been, are being, and will be born in the Land of Ultimate Bliss to make offerings to, pay hommage to, and worship [Amitabha] Buddha, I will not be able to finish doing so even if I spend an entire kalpa." (Garma C.C. Chang, general editor. *A Treasury of Mahayana Sutras*, p. 357.)

***

As seen above, countless sentient beings will be reborn in the Pure Land, their numbers exceeding even the innumerable raindrops. However, they can be divided into three categories, according to the nature of their Vows.

The First category comprises ordinary beings who are of limited capacities but true and sincere. They may not understand what constitutes the virtues or adornments of Buddha lands; nevertheless, realizing that life is full of hardship and suffering, and that the Saha World abounds in worries and troubles, they vow to be reborn in a pure and happy land.

The Second category: is composed of individuals who, although ordinary beings, possess great aspirations and a certain degree of wisdom. They seek rebirth in the Pure Land to ensure escape from transmigration, swift attainment of Buddhahood and fulfillment of their Vows to rescue themselves and others.

The Third category ranges from the lesser saints who have escaped Birth and Death to the greatest Bodhisattvas (those at the Equal Enlightenment stage). They vow to be reborn in the Pure Land in order to progress swiftly to the ultimate "Bodhisattva ground" and study the wonderful Dharma leading to Buddhahood.

Thus, we can see that seeking rebirth in the Pure Land is not limited to those weary of the sufferings in the realm of the Five Turbidities (first category). It also includes those who compassionately wish to save sentient beings in the Saha World (second category). Rebirth in the Pure Land is also for the *sages and Bodhisattvas* who look "upward" to the goal of Buddhahood and "downward" to the salvation of deluded sentient beings throughout the worlds of the ten directions (third category). Whether their Vows and aspirations are low or high, once they are reborn in the Pure Land, all derive the same benefits; none will ever retrogress and all will ultimately achieve Buddhahood and help sentient beings.

An ancient master once said:

The Pure Land method is extremely lofty, profound and wonderful; only the Buddhas can really fathom its depth. This is why even those great Bodhisattvas who have reached the level of Equal Enlightenment still vow to be reborn there. Even "One-life Bodhisattvas" (those who will become Buddhas in their next lifetime) must remain there to study and practice. Such Mahayana texts as the *Avatamsaka Sutra*, the *Lotus Sutra*, the *Maharatnakuta Sutra*, etc. all extol the Pure Land and discuss rebirth there.

Furthermore, to demonstrate the supreme value of the Pure Land method, Buddha Sakyamuni stated in the *Longer Amitabha Sutra:*

Ajita [Maitreya], if Bodhisattva-Mahasattvas wish to cause

numerous sentient beings to be rapidly and securely established in nonregression from [the pursuit of] supreme Enlightenment, and wish to see the magnificent adornments of that superb Buddha land and to embrace its perfect merits, then they should strive vigorously to learn this Dharma-door. They should not back away or become pretentious in seeking the Dharma, even if they have to go through a raging fire that fills a whole billion-world universe. They should read, recite, accept, retain, and copy this sutra, and make use of every moment to explain it to others and persuade them to listen to it without worry or annoyance. Even if they are thrown into a fire for doing so, they should entertain no doubt or regret. Why? Countless billions of Bodhisattvas seek, esteem, learn, and obey this subtle teaching. Therefore, all of you should seek this teaching too. (Garma C.C. Chang, general editor. *A Treasury of Mahayana Sutras*, p. 358.)

Given the value and beneficial nature of the Pure Land method, Buddha Sakyamuni repeatedly warned His followers against developing doubts about Pure Land teachings after His demise. Alas, however, a number of Buddhists who are not thoroughly conversant with the Dharma find it difficult to believe Him. Attempting to explain this Sutra, they become unduly attached to noumenon and ignore phenomena, thus misrepresenting the Dharma. What a pity!

An ancient master once said:

Only two types of people can benefit from the Pure Land method. First are those completely ignorant and deluded but truthful and sincere individuals who, upon hearing the teaching, wholeheartedly believe, accept and begin to practice it. Second are those persons with deep wisdom and good roots in the Pure Land method who clearly understand noumenon and phenomena and the virtues achieved through Buddha Recitation and who therefore resolve to believe and practice it. On the other hand, those with ordinary intelligence can neither understand profoundly, nor do they have the simple belief of the completely deluded. Therefore, it is difficult for them to receive benefits.

However, everything stems from causes and conditions. I only hope that reading these explanations will help those with affinities for the Pure Land method to strengthen their Faith and Vows.

Texts of the Vows Made by Ancient Masters

24) The Vow for Rebirth in the Pure Land

In each Buddha Recitation session, after the recitation itself, the practitioner immediately pays respect to Amitabha Buddha, seeking His guidance. He then kneels down and recites verses of repentance, Vows and dedication (transference) of merit. This last part is very important, because it is the time when he concentrates his mind to direct merits and virtues toward the desired goal. This is similar to a boat which moves by human strength or engine power but whose direction is determined by the person at the rudder. The Vow for rebirth is the part of Pure Land cultivation in which the practitioner uses his mind to steer the boat of Buddha Recitation toward the Western Pure Land.

However, many cultivators, missing this point, recite compositions which exhort cultivation rather than repentance and Vows. I am referring to the compositions beginning with such lines as "the thatched hut is a place of peace to nurture our Self-Nature ..." or "the universe of dust is spinning out of control; this ephemeral life comes together and dissolves itself hundreds of times ..." *Such recitation is not in line with Pure Land practice.*

As far as the form of the Vow for rebirth is concerned, some cultivators prefer long compositions through which they can develop an earnest mind.

Others prefer a shorter version that includes the desire to achieve rebirth in the Pure Land. These ideas are succinctly expressed in the "Prayer to Amita[bha] Buddha," as follows:

> Of Buddhas in all places and at all times, Amita[bha] Buddha is the foremost. He delivers sentient beings of all nine grades. His glory and power are unlimited. We now are taking complete refuge in him, and repent our physical, oral and mental sins. If there is any blessing or good action, we sincerely apply it as parinamana [transference of merit]. May we, as fellow Amidists, enjoy miraculous manifestations from time to time. At the end of our lives, the scene of the Western Paradise will manifest clearly in front of our eyes. What we see and hear will contribute to our good progress toward rebirth in Paradise. We shall see the Buddha and end further births and deaths, just like Buddhas who deliver all beings. May boundless klesas [afflictions] be severed. May countless approaches be practiced. We vow that we wish to deliver all sentient beings and that all may achieve Buddhahood. Even if the Void is finite, our wish, however, is infinite ... (Sutra Translation Committee of the United States and Canada, tr., *The Buddhist Liturgy*, p. 271-273.)

25) Vows Should be Made in Earnest

In addition to the above composition, there is another text, which is considered quite effective. It has been reported that when reciting it, some cultivators see auspicious marks while others, in their dreams, view Amitabha Buddha emitting illuminating rays. Such responses are too numerous to be recounted here. Excerpts from the composition follow below:

> I vow that at the moment of death, there will be
> no obstacles,
> The Lord Amitabha Buddha will welcome me from afar,
> Avalokitesvara will shower sweet dew upon my
> head,
> Mahasthamaprapta will bring a lotus blossom
> [for my feet].

In a split second, I will leave the turbid world,
Reaching the Pure Land in the time it takes to
extend my arms;
When the lotus blossom opens, I will see Amitabha
Buddha, the Compassionate,
Hearing the profound Dharma, I will be enlightened
and reach Tolerance of No-Birth.

I will then return to the Saha World, without
leaving the Pure Land,
Through all kinds of expedients, I will benefit
sentient beings,
Always taking earthly toil as Buddha-work.
This is my Vow, please accept it and help me
fulfill it in the future.

If the cultivator is of limited capacity or failing memory and is unable to recall long involved sentences, he should simply memorize the following short form of the Vow for rebirth in the Pure Land:

On .... (date), this disciple, (name) ... vows that through the virtues just accumulated, he will, at the time of death, be welcomed and guided by Amitabha Buddha to the Land of Ultimate Bliss, so that he may achieve Buddhahood and save sentient beings.

This short Vow, accompanied by its exact date, has the effect of strongly focussing the practitioner's mind at all times on the Pure Land and on rebirth there. This small detail is an expedient that renders the Vow that much more powerful and firm.

When making the Vow for rebirth in the Pure Land, we should do so from the depth of our earnest mind. If we merely recite pro forma at our convenience, without earnestness, our practice of Buddha Recitation will not be true and sincere. Elder Master Yin Kuang has said:

Deep sincerity is a major element that leads to

one-pointedness of mind. One part of deep sincerity destroys one part of bad karma and yields one part of merit and wisdom. Ten parts of deep sincerity destroy ten parts of bad karma and yield ten parts of merit and wisdom.

The ancients have also said:

The power of deep sincerity focussed in any direction can explode mountains and melt gold in that direction.

Determination has great power indeed!

***

This author remembers the story of a French physician. Young and widowed, he travelled to the countryside to allay his sorrow. One day, when he was staying at a blacksmith's house, he was touched by the beauty of his host's daughter. He told her about his widowhood and, seeking her hand in marriage, obtained the consent of her parents. However, before the wedding could take place, he began to co-habit with her. Shortly thereafter, he left for the city. Seeing his daughter pregnant and growing heavier and heavier by the day, with the culprit no more in sight than the wings of a redbird in flight, the blacksmith reflected on the fact that he was too poor and isolated to sue successfully. He therefore tried to relieve his anger and frustration by striking his hammer against its iron stand each evening, while shouting the name of the physician, wishing to blow his head apart. Unbeknownst to him, in the faraway city, each evening at five o'clock, the physician would grab his head and scream in pain. He tried every known remedy without success.

Some time afterward, a friend of the doctor, on a visit to the countryside, happened to pass the blacksmith's shop one evening and overheard the striking hammer and the swearing. He went in to inquire and having understood the whole story, deduced the cause of his friend's predicament. Upon returning to the city, he urged the physician to make amends by marrying the blacksmith's daughter. As might be expected, after the wedding, the physician's strange symptoms disappeared.

Thus, we can see the unseen power of the mind. If we realize the significance of the above story and sincerely vow to recite Amitabha Buddha's name, why worry about failing to get a response?

***

In short, Faith and Vows are "wisdom practice," while Buddha Recitation is "action practice." "Wisdom practice" is like the two eyes, "action practice" is like the two feet. Feet and eyes should complement one another, Vows and Practice must be in earnest. Only then can we achieve rebirth in the Land of Ultimate Bliss.

5

Practice

The Four Realizations and the Four Practices

26) Intensive Practice is Indispensable

As indicated above, a cardinal element of Buddha Recitation is the Vow for rebirth in the Pure Land.

Some people may think, "As long as I keep reciting the sacred name and the myriad virtues of Amitabha Buddha over and over, I will naturally accumulate countless virtues. Even if I do not achieve rebirth in the Pure Land, those merits and virtues will not be lost."

Such thoughts are not only erroneous and dangerous, they show a lack of wisdom. This is because the virtues accumulated through cultivation without a Vow for rebirth in the Pure Land will become merits and blessings in the next life. In that next life, while enjoying these delusive blessings,[38] we are likely to create bad karma; in the following (third) lifetime we will surely sink and be lost along the three Evil Paths. Failing to seek rebirth in the Pure Land is therefore a dangerous mistake! For this reason, Faith and Vows were referred to earlier as "wisdom practices."

***

Still, Faith and Vows without Practice are like a boat with a rudder but no oars; they cannot result in rebirth in the Pure Land.[39] Some people, hearing that "only earnest Faith and Vows are necessary, for at the time of death ten utterances or even one will ensure rebirth in the Pure Land," may immediately think: "If this is so, there is no need to hurry -- reciting the Buddha's name on our deathbed is good enough." Such thinking is also erroneous and trivializes the practice of Buddha Recitation. We should be aware that the main condition for rebirth in the Pure Land, according to the *Amitabha Sutra*, is that a person on his deathbed have an *undisturbed mind*. If the cultivator truly has no aberrant, topsy-turvy thoughts at the time of death, then one thought or ten thoughts of Amitabha Buddha will ensure rebirth in the Pure Land.

However, who among us can be certain that he will not have disturbed thoughts at the time of death? If we do not concentrate on recitation in our daily lives, at the time of death the four constituents of the body (earth, water, wind, fire) will come apart, the power of karma will intensify, our bodies and minds, gripped by suffering, will be overwhelmed by fear and dementia -- at that time, even one thought of Amitabha Buddha will be impossible, let alone ten thoughts!

If we want some assurance at the time of death, we should practice Buddha Recitation assiduously in our daily lives, striving for "one-pointedness of mind." While it is possible in theory to wait for the time of death to recite the Buddha's name, in practice this is not a simple matter. Therefore, Pure Land cultivators should strive to practice steadily and should not be indifferent to or contemptuous of Practice -- lest they fail to achieve rebirth in the Pure Land.

27) Buddha Recitation and the Four Realizations

Reciting the Buddha's name seeking rebirth in the Pure Land is a "perfect sudden" method in the Mahayana tradition, because the cultivator takes Enlightenment in the "effect stage" as his point of departure for awakening the mind in the "causal stage." If it were not taught by Buddha Sakyamuni Himself, who would believe that a common mortal of the "Four Ways of Birth and Six Paths" could reach the stage of non-retrogression, equal to the higher level Bodhisattvas, thanks to Amitabha Buddha's power of "welcoming and escorting"? After all, cultivators following other methods would have to spend ten thousand eons in diligent, continuous cultivation to obtain such results. With the Pure Land method, since the cultivator has put his faith in "other-power" in addition to using all his "self-power," every single cultivator will be reborn in the Land of Ultimate Bliss, escape the cycle of Birth and Death and achieve non-retrogression.

If we were to use Buddha Recitation to discover the Mind-Ground and awaken to our Original Nature, the Pure Land method would be no different from other methods. However, when we rely on Buddha Recitation to seek rebirth in the Pure Land, this method has unique characteristics.

Ancient masters have said:

1. Birth [in the Pure Land] is definitely birth; however, return [to the Pure Land] is, in truth, no return. This is True Realization of realms, not of beings.

2. Return is definitely return; however, birth is, in truth, No-Birth. This is True Realization of beings, not of realms.

3. Return is, in reality, no return; birth is also, in truth, no birth. This is True Realization of both realms and beings.

4. Return is definitely return; birth is definitely birth. This is *not* True Realization of realms and beings.

These four statements explain the Four True Realizations of Pure Land teachings. *True Realization* means thorough comprehension of essence, or noumenon. Since the whole Dharma Realm (cosmos) is only Mind, sentient beings and realms are illusory [see Glossary, "Illusion"]. If we conceive that there are sentient beings achieving rebirth in the Pure Land and that there are realms to go back to, we are still attached to beings and dharmas and are still making a distinction between here and there. This is not True Realization, i.e., not a complete understanding of essence and noumenon. The reverse is called True Realization. The ancients have summarized the idea in the following stanza:

Recitation is equal to non-recitation, No-Birth is Birth,
[Having reached that stage] do not bother to move even half a step,
You have arrived at the Enlightened capital city.

True Realization of beings and realms [No. 3] is the ultimate goal of Pure Land practitioners. Nevertheless, the doctrine taught in the Three Pure Land sutras and the *Commentary on Rebirth* is No. 4 ("not True Realization of realms and beings"), which is consonant with seeking rebirth in the Pure Land. This is because Buddha Sakyamuni knew that common mortals in this world of the Five Turbidities, especially in this Dharma-Ending Age, would have heavy and deep karmic obstructions; establishing a realm of marks [the Pure Land], enabling them to anchor their minds and cultivate, would be difficult enough -- not to mention abandoning all marks!

If common human beings of this Dharma-Ending Age cultivate while grasping at marks (i.e., the Pure Land), their Practice and Vows will be more earnest and the final result of rebirth in the Pure land easier to achieve. Once reborn in the Pure Land, why worry about not attaining the state of No-Birth and No-Mark?

For those who are not of the highest capacity or endowed with a sharp mind, hastening to achieve lofty goals and engaging in cultivation without marks leaves the mind with no anchor. Earnestness and sincerity are then difficult to develop. If their Vows are not earnest, how can they achieve rebirth in the Pure Land, and without rebirth in that Land, how can they escape Birth and Death? This is an instance of "haste makes waste," climbing high but landing low, wanting to be clever and ending up clumsy and awkward!

***

Many who like to voice lofty principles frequently reject the Pure Land method in these terms: "To recite the Buddha's name seeking rebirth in the Pure Land is to grasp at marks, seeking the Dharma outside the Mind, failing to understand that all dharmas are Mind-Only." These individuals, seeking the subtle and the lofty, are in reality shallow and superficial! This is because they do not understand that if the Saha World is Mind-Only, then the Western Pure Land is also Mind-Only, and nothing can be found outside the True Mind. Thus, to recite Amitabha Buddha's name is to recite the Buddha of our own Nature and Mind; to be reborn in the Pure Land is to return to the realm of our own Mind -- not to an outside realm! Since neither the Saha World nor the Pure Land is outside the Mind, how can remaining in the Saha World, enduring samsara, scorched and burned by the fire of the Five Turbidities, be compared with returning to the tranquil and blissful Pure Land -- the pure and cool realm of freedom?

We should realize that the ones truly in a position to honor the Mind-Only Pure Land are those who have attained the Dharma-Nature-Body, always free and at ease in all circumstances. At that time, whether in the Saha World or in the Land of Ultimate Bliss, they are in a "pure land," in the state of Mind-Only -- in the state of liberation. Otherwise, though they may discourse endlessly on the mystery and loftiness of the Pure Land, they cannot escape bewilderment and delusion in the "bardo stage," and, following their karma, revolving in the cycle of Birth and Death!

28) Buddha Recitation and the Four Practices

Sentient beings usually differ in preferences and innate capacities. Therefore, although they may engage in the common practice of Buddha Recitation, they are bound to differ somewhat in their practice. For this reason, ancient masters have summarized four types of practice: Zen-Pure Land; Sutra Recitation-Pure Land; Esotericism-Pure Land; Exclusive Pure Land Practice.

1. The first category of cultivators comprises those who engage primarily in Buddha Recitation but practice Zen as well. They are said to practice Zen-Pure Land, also called dual practice of Zen and Pure Land. Here, rebirth in the Pure Land is the principal goal, while seeing the True Nature and becoming enlightened to the Way is a secondary matter which depends on the individual practitioner's good roots and conditions.

2. The second category comprises those whose main practice is Buddha Recitation with Sutra Recitation as an ancillary practice. They are said to practice Sutra Recitation-Pure Land. As for the sutras chanted, some prefer the *Diamond Sutra* or the *Amitabha Sutra*, while others prefer the *Avatamsaka Sutra* or *Lotus Sutra*, or else individual chapters, such as the "Avalokitesvara Chapter" (*Lotus Sutra*, ch. 25) or the Chapter on

"Samantabhadra's Practices and Vows" (*Avatamsaka Sutra*, ch. 40).

3. The third category is composed of those who engage in Buddha Recitation as their primary practice and Mantra Recital as an ancillary one. They follow the practice of Esotericism-Pure Land. The mantras vary with the practitioner and include such dharani as the Great Compassion Mantra, the Thousand-Armed Avalokitesvara Dharani, the Rebirth Dharani, etc.

4. The fourth category of cultivators comprises those who practice Buddha Recitation diligently and exclusively without cultivating other methods. Within this group, those of high capacities practice the Sixteen Meditations as taught in the *Meditation Sutra*, while the great majority only practice oral recitation of the Buddha's name.

***

The Pure Land Patriarch Shan Tao and Zen Master Yung Ming are traditionally believed to be transformation bodies of Amitabha Buddha. However, Master Shan Tao taught diligent Buddha Recitation alone; Zen Master Yung Ming, on the other hand, in addition to reciting the Buddha's name one hundred thousand times each day, also engaged in other practices, totalling 108 in all.[40] The Patriarch Yin Kuang once commented in this regard:

They both teach rebirth in the Pure Land, but the method followed by Master Shan Tao is designed to help those of limited or moderate capacities and belongs to the *exclusive* Pure Land practice. Master Yung Ming's method, on the other hand, aims specifically to encourage those of the highest capacity, and belongs to the *perfect* practice.

People in the Dharma-Ending Age are generally of

limited or moderate capacities. For this reason, among the four methods discussed above, they should, perhaps, choose Exclusive Pure Land practice, in order to ensure rebirth in the Land of Ultimate Bliss. However, each person is different in preferences and innate capacity and cannot be coerced. Therefore, while he may practice several methods concurrently, the Pure Land practitioner must be attentive and clear in his mind as to the two aspects of Practice: principal and subsidiary. The emphasis should always be on the principal aspect, i.e., Buddha Recitation. Only in this way will he follow the path of cultivation without obstacles and without missing the goal of rebirth in the Pure Land.

Buddha Recitation Methods

29) Four Methods of Buddha Recitation

Buddha Recitation does not consist of oral recitation alone, but also includes contemplation and meditation. Therefore, within the Pure Land School, there are, in addition to Oral Recitation, three other methods, namely: Real Mark, Contemplation by Thought and Contemplation of an Image.

1. Real Mark [Self-Nature] Buddha Recitation

This entails penetrating the Mind's foremost meaning -- reciting our own original Buddha Nature. It is to contemplate the Real Mark Dharma Body of the Buddhas, resulting in attainment of True Thusness Samadhi.[41]

This method is really a Zen practice; however, since the realm revealed by the meditational mind is the Pure Land, it also qualifies as a Pure Land practice. This method is not for those of limited or moderate capacities -- if the practitioner is not of the highest capacity, he cannot "become enlightened and enter" into it. For this reason, few Pure Land teachers promote it and the proponents of the method are found chiefly within the Zen tradition.

Incidentally, I would venture to say here that while we are still treading the path of Practice, not having reached the stage of Perfect Enlightenment, all Dharma methods are expedients; Buddha Recitation is an expedient and so is Zen. According to the Three Pure Land sutras, Buddha Sakyamuni provided the expedient teaching of the Western Pure Land, and urged sentient beings to recite Amitabha Buddha's name seeking rebirth there. With this method, they can escape Birth and Death, avail themselves of that wonderful, lofty realm to pursue cultivation, and swiftly attain Buddhahood. Diligent Buddha Recitation also leads to Awakening, as in Zen; however, the principal goal of the Pure Land School is rebirth in the Land of Ultimate Bliss, while the degree of Awakening achieved is a secondary consideration.

Thus, the goal of Real Mark Buddha Recitation falls within Pure Land teachings. However, from the standpoint of an expedient leading to rebirth in the Land of Ultimate Bliss, it does not truly qualify as a Pure Land method within the meaning of the Three Pure Land sutras taught by Buddha Sakyamuni. This is, perhaps, the reason why Pure Land Patriarchs merely referred to it to broaden the meaning of Buddha Recitation, but did not expound it widely.

2. Contemplation by Thought Recitation

This entails meditation on the features of Buddha Amitabha and His Land of Ultimate Bliss, in accordance with the *Meditation Sutra*. (The Sutra teaches a total of sixteen contemplations.) If this practice is perfected, the cultivator will always visualize the Pure Land before him. Whether his eyes are open or closed, his mind and thoughts are always coursing through the Pure Land. At the time of death, he is assured of rebirth there.

The virtues obtained through this method are immense and beyond imagination, but since the object of meditation is too profound and subtle, few practitioners can achieve it. This is because, in general, the method presents five difficulties: i) with dull capacities, one cannot easily succeed; ii) with a crude mind, one cannot easily succeed; iii) without knowing how to use expedients skillfully and flexibly during actual practice, one cannot easily succeed; iv) without the ability to remember images clearly, one cannot easily succeed; v) with low energy, one cannot easily succeed.

Very few can avoid all five pitfalls. Thus, upon reflection, this method also belongs to the category of difficult Dharma doors.

3. Contemplation of an Image Recitation

In this method, the practitioner faces a statue of Amitabha Buddha and impresses all the features of that statue in his memory -- contemplating to the point where, even in the absence of a statue, and whether his eyes are open or closed, he clearly sees the image of Amitabha Buddha.

This method is also difficult, because it requires a great deal of energy, a faithful memory and skillful use of expedients. There are cases of individuals who have practiced it in an inflexible way and have developed headaches difficult to cure. Moreover, upon examination, this method of seeking rebirth in the Pure Land is not mentioned in the sutras. It is merely a technique to assist in the practice of Buddha Recitation, so that the practitioner can harness his mind and achieve right thought. Still, if we practice this method in a pure, devoted frame of mind, we can obtain a response, eradicate our bad karma, develop virtue and wisdom, and, through an "illusory" statue of Amitabha Buddha, awaken to His True Marks and achieve rebirth in the Pure Land.

4. Oral Recitation

In this method, the practitioner recites, aloud or silently, either "Nam Mo Amitabha Buddha" or "Amitabha Buddha." The short form (Amitabha Buddha) has the advantage of easily focussing the cultivator's mind, while the longer version facilitates development of a truly earnest, respectful mind conducive to a response.

This method, taught by Sakyamuni Buddha in the *Shorter Amitabha Sutra*, is the dominant form of Pure Land practice at the present time.

***

A brief examination of the four methods of Buddha Recitation shows that the Real Mark [No. 1] and Contemplation of an Image [No. 3] methods are not mentioned in the Three Pure Land sutras. They are referred to only in the *Buddha Recitation Samadhi Sutra* and a few other sutras or commentaries. Both of these methods are secondary expedients to expand on the true meaning of Buddha Recitation; they are not recognized methods traditionally taught by Pure Land Patriarchs.

The Real Mark method has the unique advantage of teaching the profound and exalted meaning of Buddha Recitation. However, it is too lofty to embrace people of all capacities and "strays" in the direction of Zen. The Contemplation of an Image method is merely a subsidiary technique and is not easy to practice. These two methods, therefore, are not recommended for Pure Land practitioners. Likewise, the Contemplation by Thought method [No. 2], although expounded by Buddha Sakyamuni and leading to immense virtue, is reserved for those of high capacities. In the present

Dharma-Ending Age, few can practice it.

In conclusion, only Oral Recitation [No. 4] embraces people of all capacities, leads to swift results and is easy enough for anyone to practice. Oral Recitation, practiced earnestly and correctly, will bring a response; in this very life, we can immediately see the features of Amitabha Buddha and the adornments of the Western Pure Land and awaken to the Original Mind. Even if we cannot attain True Mark in this life, we will certainly attain it after rebirth in the Pure Land. For this reason, the Thirteenth Pure Land Patriarch, Master Yin Kuang, wrote the following words of praise:

> Exclusively reciting the Name will bring attainment
> of True Mark,
> Without contemplation we will still see the Land of
> Ultimate Bliss.

Ancient masters have also commented:

> Among Dharma methods, Pure Land is the short cut for attaining the Way. Within Pure Land, Oral Recitation is the short cut.

Nowadays, this method is the most popular form of Buddha Recitation.

30) Ten Variants of Oral Recitation

As indicated above, Oral Recitation is the most common Pure Land method at the present time. However, this method has many variants, to accommodate the circumstances and capacities of the individual. A few of these variants are summarized below.

1. Reflecting the Name Recitation

With this technique, the ear catches the sound as the mouth recites, examining each individual word and each individual phrase, to make sure they are clear and distinct, phrase after phrase. There are two ways of hearing, with the ears or with the mind. Although the ears "hear deep inside," the sounds do not reside anywhere. The practitioner gradually forgets everything inside and out -- even body, mind, realm, time and space -- with only the Buddha's name remaining.

This technique of "reflecting the name," makes it easy for the cultivator to filter out deluded thoughts and swiftly achieve one-pointedness of mind. The *Surangama Sutra* expresses this very idea when it states, in the words of the Bodhisattva Manjusri:

> This common method of concentrating the mind on its sense of hearing, turning it inward ... is most feasible and wise. (Wai-tao, tr. "The Surangama Sutra," in D. Goddard, ed., *A Buddhist Bible*, p. 260.)

2. Counting Rosary Beads Recitation

In this method, as the mouth recites, the hand fingers the rosary. At first, thoughts are tied to the rosary beads, but later on they gradually move away from the beads, leading to the state of one-pointedness of mind. This technique increases the power of recitation in the same way that a cane enables a mountain climber with weak legs to ascend higher and higher.

With this technique, we should write down the number of recitations per session or per day. This has the advantage of forcing us to keep an exact count, eliminating the affliction of laziness. However, we should take care not to be too ambitious, attempting to achieve too much too soon, or our recitation will not be clear and distinct. The ancients, while reciting the Buddha's name over and over, did so in a clear, distinct manner thanks to two factors: "correct understanding" and "correct concentration of mind." Elder Master Ou-I, the Ninth Patriarch of Pure Land once taught:

> There is no better or loftier way to reach the state of one-pointedness of mind. At first the practitioner should finger the rosary, keeping an exact count, while reciting the Buddha's name over and over in a clear, distinct manner, 30,000, 50,000 up to 100,000 times each day, maintaining that number without fail, determined to remain constant throughout his life. Such recitation will, in time, become second nature -- not reciting being reciting. At that time, recording or not recording no longer matters. If such recitation, accompanied by earnest Faith and Vows, did not lead to rebirth in the Pure Land, the Buddhas of the Three Periods (past, present and future) would all be guilty of false speech. Once we are reborn in the Pure Land, all Dharma methods will appear before our eyes.[42]

If at the outset we seek too high a goal, are over-confident and eager to show that we are not attached to forms and marks, preferring to study according to the free and perfect method, we reveal a lack of stability and depth in our Faith and Vows as well as perfunctoriness in our Practice. Even if we were to lecture exhaustively on the Twelve Divisions of the Dharma [all the teachings of Buddha Sakyamuni] and become enlightened to the 1,700 Zen koans, these would merely be activities on the fringes of life and death.

This advice is indeed a compass for the Pure Land practitioner.

3. Breath-by-Breath Recitation

This technique consists of reciting silently or softly, with each breath, inhaling or exhaling, accompanied by one recitation of the Buddha's name. Since life is linked to breath, if we take advantage of breath while practicing Buddha Recitation, we will not be apart from Buddha Amitabha in life and at the time of death, when breath has stopped, we will be immediately reborn in the Pure Land. The practitioner should remember, however, that once he has mastered this technique, he should recite aloud as well as silently. In this way, the power of recitation will be strengthened and the will to be reborn in the Pure Land more easily developed. Otherwise, his resolve will not be earnest and he might "stray" into the practice of the "Five Meditations to calm the mind" of the Theravada tradition.

4. Continuously Linked Recitation

With this technique, the practitioner recites softly, each word following the one immediately before, each phrase closely following the previous phrase ...

During this practice, through discretion and patience, there are no empty time frames and therefore "sundry thoughts" cannot intrude. The cultivator's feelings and thoughts are intense, his mind and mouth move boldly forward reciting the Buddha's name; the power of right thought embraces everything, temporarily subduing ignorance and delusive thought. Thus, the light of transcendental samadhi breaks through and shines forth.

From early times, Pure Land practitioners would avail themselves of this method when their emotions and thoughts wandered or were in a state of confusion.

5. Enlightened, Illuminating Recitation

With this technique, the practitioner on the one hand recites the Buddha's name and on the other, "returns the light" and illumines his True Nature. He thus enters into the realm of ultimate transcendental emptiness; what remains is only the consciousness that his body-mind and the True Mind of the Buddha have become one -- all-illuminating and all-encompassing. At that time, meditation rooms, cushions, gongs and all else have disappeared. Even the illusory, "composite body" is nowhere to be found.

With this practice, even while our present "retribution body" is not yet dead, silent illumination is attained. Uttering the Buddha's name, the practitioner immediately achieves the state of samadhi. There is no swifter method for common mortals to enter the realm of the saints.

Unfortunately, we cannot understand or practice this method unless we are of the highest capacity. Therefore, its scope is rather modest and limited.

6. Bowing to the Buddha Recitation

This technique consists of making bows as we recite the Buddha's name. Either we recite once before each bow or we bow as we recite, regardless of the number of recitations. The bowing should be supple yet deliberate, complementing recitation, bowing and reciting perfectly synchronized. If we add a sincere and earnest mind, body, speech and mind are gathered together. Except for the words Amitabha Buddha, there is not the slightest deluded thought.[43]

This method has the ability to destroy the karma of drowsiness. Its benefits are very great, because the practitioner engages in recitation with his body, speech and mind. A lay practitioner of old used to follow this method, and each day and night, he would bow and recite an average of one thousand times.

However, this practice is the particular domain of those with strong mind-power. Lacking this quality, it is difficult to persevere, because with extended bowing, the body easily grows weary, leading to discouragement. Therefore, this method is normally used in conjunction with other methods and is not practiced in exclusivity.

7. Decimal Recording Recitation

This is the inscription technique of Buddha

Recitation, taking each ten utterances of the Buddha's name as a unit. Individuals with short breath spans can divide the ten utterances into two subunits (five utterances each) or three smaller subunits (two three-utterance units and one four-utterance unit). One rosary bead is fingered after each group of ten utterances is completed.

With this practice, the mind must not only recite, it must also remember the number of utterances. In this way, if we are not diligent we must become so; otherwise, it will be impossible to avoid mistakes.

This technique, in general, is an excellent expedient forcing the cultivator to concentrate his mind and is very effective with those subject to many errant thoughts. Elder Master Yin Kuang used to recommend it to Pure Land practitioners.

8. Lotus Blossom Recitation

As he recites, the practitioner contemplates the four colors of the lotus blossom (blue, yellow, red and white), one color after another without interruption. With his first utterance of the Buddha's name, he visualizes a huge, blue lotus blossom before his eyes, emitting a blue light. With the second utterance, he visualizes a yellow lotus blossom, emitting a yellow light. The third and fourth utterances are accompanied, respectively, by visualization of red and white lotus flowers, each color emitting its own light. He then repeats the visualization in the same sequence. As the flowers appear, he imagines a vague, lingering touch of pure, soft lotus fragrance.

Ancient masters devised this method because many practitioners in the T'ien T'ai School, despite using all available techniques, found it difficult to stem their errant thoughts. This method uses various forms and colors to focus mind and thought. These forms and

colors take the marks of lotus blossoms in the
Seven-Jewel Pond of the Pure Land ("one utterance of
the Buddha's name, one jewelled lotus blossom"),
because the lotus blossoms appearing in the Pure Land
are inseparable from the lotus blossoms created by the
virtues of the reciting mind. At the time of death, the
mind-consciousness of the practitioner relies on these
jewelled lotus blossoms to achieve rebirth in the
Western Pure Land.

If the Pure Land cultivator should discover that he
has an affinity with this technique, he should apply it and
quickly enter the Wonderful Lotus Blossom Buddha
Recitation Samadhi.

9. Recitation Amidst Light

This method was specially designed for certain
practitioners who, as soon as they close their eyes to
recite, suddenly see filthy forms and marks (ugly
grimacing faces, for example), or dark forms and colors
swirling around.

With this technique, the practitioner, while reciting
the Buddha's name, visualizes himself seated in the
middle of an immense, brilliant zone of light. Within
that zone of light, when his mind has quieted down, the
practitioner feels bright and refreshed. At that time, not
only have deluded thoughts been annihilated, filthy, evil
forms have also disappeared. After that, right thought is
reinforced and samadhi is, in time, achieved.

Although this is a special expedient to destroy evil
deluded marks, even the practitioner who is not in this
predicament can apply this method to clear his mind and
enter deeply into the Buddha Recitation Samadhi.

10. "Contemplation of the Buddha" Recitation

The methods of contemplation taught in the

Meditation Sutra are very important and lead to immense virtue, but they are not a popular expedient for sentient beings in the Dharma-Ending Age. Nevertheless, since the ancient masters did not wish to see the special benefits of the meditation method go unused, they selected the easiest of the Sixteen Contemplations (Contemplation of Amitabha Buddha) and combined it with Oral Recitation to form the Contemplation of the Buddha-Oral Recitation technique. (Recitation is predominant, with contemplation of the Buddha occupying a subsidiary position.)

Each day, after reciting the Buddha's name, the practitioner reserves a special period of time for concentrating his mind and contemplating the Embellishments and Light of Amitabha Buddha. This method is derived from Contemplation Number Thirteen in the *Meditation Sutra*, in which Buddha Amitabha is visualized as some sixteen feet tall and of golden hue, standing at the edge of the Seven-Jewel Pond. If the practitioner cannot yet visualize the Seven-Jewel Pond, he can picture Amitabha Buddha standing before his eyes in a zone of light, in open space, the left hand held at chest level and forming the auspicious mudra, the right arm extending downward in the position of "welcoming and guiding."

To be successful in this meditation, it is necessary, at the outset, to visualize the body of Amitabha Buddha in general, then concentrate on the urna (white mark between the eyebrows). This mark is empty and transparent, like a white gem with eight facets ... The urna is the basic mark among the thirty-two auspicious marks of the Buddhas. When this visualization is successful, thanks to the affinity thus created between Amitabha Buddha and the practitioner, other marks will appear clearly, one after another. However, to ensure success, the practitioner should read through the *Meditation Sutra*, memorizing the thirty-two auspicious marks of Buddha Amitabha before commencing his practice.

With this method, Buddha Recitation should be primary, because if the practitioner does not succeed at visualization, he can still fall back on recitation to ensure rebirth in the Pure Land. In truth, however, recitation aids visualization and visualization complements recitation, so that these two aspects work in parallel, leading the practitioner toward the desired goal.

Although this technique is somewhat more difficult than the others, if it can be accomplished successfully, immeasurable benefits are achieved. It is therefore described here at the very end, to foster diligent practice.

***

As stated earlier, these ten variants of Oral Recitation are also the ten basic techniques to combat the various mental hindrances faced by Buddha Recitation practitioners. Pure Land books discuss several dozen variants. However, they are merely techniques using, *inter alia*, a loud voice or a low voice at busy moments or at times of leisure. They cannot as such qualify as methods of recitation. For this reason, the author has singled out these ten basic variants of Oral Recitation to combat the obstructions of drowsiness and mind-scattering. They are the methods best suited to the majority of today's practitioners. The cultivator can try them out and select the one that fits his particular case.

Entering into Practice

31) The Four Types of Samadhi

When Pure Land practitioners reach the highest

stage, they all attain one state, called the Buddha Recitation Samadhi. This is the realm of all-illuminating still-emptiness, where deluded consciousness has disappeared and only the practitioner's mind continues to dwell on the auspicious features or the sacred name of Amitabha Buddha. However, although the mind is said to "dwell," it is really "non-dwelling," because sounds, forms and marks are illusory by their very nature -- they are really empty.

What are the marks of this samadhi? According to Elder Master Liu Yu, when the practitioner assiduously recites the Buddha's name with one-pointedness of mind, oblivious to body, mind and the external world, transcending time and space, and when he has exerted the utmost effort and reached the goal, right in the midst of present thought, worldly delusions suddenly disappear -- the mind experiences sudden Awakening, attaining the realm of "No-Thought, no No-Thought." That realm is like empty space, all clouds have dissipated, the sky is all blue, reciting is not reciting, not reciting is reciting, not seeing and knowing is truly seeing and knowing -- to see and to know is to stray towards worldly dusts. At this stage, the silver water and green mountains are all Ultimate Truth, the babbling brooks and singing birds all express the wonderful Dharma. The light of the Mind encompasses ten thousand phenomena but does not dwell on any single dharma, still-but-illuminating, illuminating-but-still, existing and lost at the same time -- all is perfect.

The realm of samadhi is, in general, as just described. It is difficult to express in words, and only when we attain it do we experience it. Buddha Recitation Samadhi is always the same state. However, the ancients distinguished four variants, based on the sutras and on different ways of cultivation. These variants are described below.

1. Pratyutpanna Samadhi

When practicing this samadhi, the cultivator has three powers to assist him: the power of Amitabha Buddha, the power of the samadhi and the power of his own virtues.

The unit of practice of this samadhi should be ninety days. In that span of time, day and night the practitioner just stands or walks around, visualizing Amitabha Buddha appearing as a body standing on the practitioner's crown, replete with the thirty-two auspicious marks and the eighty beautiful characteristics. He may also recite Amitabha Buddha's name continuously, while constantly visualizing Him. When practice is perfected, the cultivator, in samadhi, can see Amitabha Buddha and the Buddhas of the ten directions standing in front of him, praising and encouraging him.

Pratyutpanna is also called the "Constantly Walking Samadhi." As the practitioner walks, each step, each word is inseparable from the name of Amitabha Buddha. His body, speech and mind are always practicing Buddha Recitation without interruption, like a continuous flow of water.

This method brings very lofty benefits, but only those of high capacity have the endurance to practice it. Those of limited or moderate capacities or lacking in energy cannot pursue this difficult practice.

2. Single Practice Samadhi

"Single Practice" means specializing in one practice. When cultivating this samadhi, the practitioner customarily sits and concentrates either on visualizing Amitabha Buddha or on reciting His name. Although he actually cultivates only one practice, in effect, he achieves proficiency in all other practices; consequently, Single Practice is also called "Perfect Practice."

This samadhi, as well as the following two samadhis, can be put into practice by people of all capacities.

3. Lotus Blossom Samadhi

This is one of sixteen samadhis explained in Chapter 24 of the *Lotus ("Dharma Blossom") Sutra*. According to the T'ien T'ai School, the "three truths" (emptiness, conditional existence, the Middle Way)[44] perfectly fused, are "Dharma," while the Expedient and the True, being non-dual, are "blossoms." For example, when the petals (the Expedient) of the lotus blossom are not yet opened, its seeds (the True) are already formed: the seeds and the petals exist simultaneously. Thus, in a single flower, the full meaning of the True and the Expedient is exemplified.

In Pure Land terminology, we would say, "recitation *is* Buddha," "form *is* Mind," and one utterance of the Buddha's name includes the "three truths," encompassing the True and the Expedient. If we recite the Buddha's name while understanding this principle, we are practicing the Lotus Blossom Samadhi. In cultivating this samadhi, the practitioner alternates between sitting and walking while visualizing Amitabha Buddha or reciting His name, to the point where he enters samadhi. This technique is somewhat easier than the Single Practice Samadhi described above.

4. Following One's Inclinations Samadhi

With this technique, we walk or stand, lie down or sit up as we wish, constantly focussing our thoughts and never abandoning the sacred name of Amitabha Buddha, attaining samadhi in the process. This practice is also called "Flowing Water Buddha Recitation." It is like water continuously flowing in a river; if it encounters an obstacle such as a rock or a tree, it simply bounces back and continues to flow around it.

Normally, the practitioner of this method, early each morning, bows forty-eight times to Amitabha Buddha, and seven times each to the Bodhisattva Avalokitesvara, the Bodhisattva Mahasthamaprapta and the Ocean-Wide Assembly. He then kneels down to seek repentance. From then on until nightfall, whether walking, standing, lying down, or sitting up, he recites the Buddha's name, either fingering the rosary or simply reciting. Before going to bed, he bows once more to Buddha Amitabha and dedicates the merits of the whole day's practice toward rebirth in the Pure Land. If he is distracted during practice, he should resume recitation as soon as the circumstances of the distraction have passed.

This method is flexible and easy, but the cultivator should minimize distracting conditions and have a good deal of perseverance.

32) The Three Parts of the Pure Land Ceremony

The actual Pure Land ceremony consists of three parts:

a) praise giving;
b) recitation proper;
c) Vows and dedication of merit.

The "praise giving" ceremony recommended for the majority of today's practitioners consists of bowing three times to Amitabha Buddha and once each to the Bodhisattva Avalokitesvara, the Bodhisattva Mahasthamaprapta and the Ocean-Wide Assembly, at the beginning and end of each session. This is the ideal practice for those very busy with everyday, mundane work or the aged and those in failing health. Alternatively, practitioners of limited capacities can just earnestly make three bows at the beginning and three more bows at the very end of the session, before retiring.

With respect to "recitation proper," the practitioner can select, according to his inclinations and preferences, one of the ten variants of Oral Recitation described in section 30. If he is also reciting mantras and sutras, he should do so before the Buddha Recitation part.

For "Vows and dedications," the short form of the Vow described in section 25 (with date and name of the practitioner) is recommended.

33) How to Combat Drowsiness and Mind-Scattering

The cultivator at times drifts into a dark, heavy mental state, akin to sleep; this is the delusive obstruction of drowsiness. At other times, while he recites the Buddha's name, his mind wanders and is filled with sundry thoughts. This is the delusive condition of "mind-scattering." Drowsiness and mind-scattering are two very dangerous obstacles because they hinder cultivation and prevent the practitioner from entering samadhi.

As the cultivator practices, his delusive thoughts may suddenly be submerged and stilled. He recites the Buddha's name in an even monotone, with calm mind and thought, oblivious even to the weather and insect bites. This state usually lasts from one-half to one hour. Sometimes sweat soaks his clothing without his knowledge, and only when he suddenly awakens does he perceive an uncomfortable sensation of extreme heat. Experiencing this, he should not hasten to rejoice, thinking that his mind has settled, or that his practice is bearing some results. In reality, this is only the state of drowsiness in its subtle, mild form. The ancients have said:

Gently, gently, if drowsiness is not exposed, the demons will have their fill all day.

In this situation, the cultivator should take steps to practice steadfastly, with increased diligence and vigor. As he recites, he should "turn the light around," to subdue and destroy drowsiness.

In general, according to the author's experience, as drowsiness approaches, it is preceded by delusive, scattered thoughts. There are, of course, times when drowsiness and delusive thoughts arise at the same time. However, this is a gross manifestation, easily detectable. When subtle drowsiness approaches, at first subtle errant thoughts arise. The practitioner feels that a dim spot is climbing from the back of his neck to the top of his head, then descending to the eyes, ending somewhere deep in the Alaya consciousness. Wherever drowsiness goes, that part of the body is affected. If it reaches the head, the head droops slightly; if it reaches the eyes, the eyes close; if it reaches the mind, the mind becomes clouded. The practitioner should possess a very keen, discerning mind to detect this subtle form of torpor.

***

Delusive thoughts, as well, have two manifestations: gross and subtle. Everyone can detect gross delusive thoughts, because their manifestations are very clear. The ancients had a saying:

> In the early stage of cultivation, be afraid of delusive thoughts; with time, beware of drowsiness!

This saying, while partly correct, is not entirely true, as it refers only to the "scattering" aspect of "gross" delusive thoughts. Even seasoned cultivators, however, should be wary of "subtle" delusive thoughts. When the practitioner puts all his efforts into reciting the Buddha's name, gross delusive thoughts will certainly be stilled and submerged, but it is very difficult to detect the comings and goings of subtle delusive thoughts.

For example, when the froth rises to the surface of a muddy pond, we can see it easily. However, we would need a very limpid pond to see the tiny bubbles arising from the bottom, breaking on the surface or reaching only halfway to the surface. Likewise, only seasoned practitioners (who have reached the stage where the waters of the mind are calm and still) can detect subtle delusive thoughts.

One morning, a well-known Elder Master, in the short span of three seconds, from the time he left his bed to the time he sat on his chair, detected several dozen delusive thoughts arising in his mind. Only then could he verify the teaching of the sutras:

One thought lasts 90 ksana (instants), one ksana has 900 births and deaths.

This refers to delusive thoughts in their subtle manifestations.

***

In this regard, I would like to recount a well-known story about subtle delusive thoughts, to increase the awareness of fellow-cultivators. Once there were two famous Zen Masters who had been awakened to the Way. One day, as they sat in meditation together, the young master had a thought of lust and desire, which he immediately severed. However, the Elder Master, seated opposite, already knew of the occurrence. After emerging from meditation, the Elder Master composed a poem, intending to tease his friend. The latter, sad and ashamed, immediately "gathered up his vital energy," and expired on the spot. The Elder Master, filled with remorse, called his disciples together and followed his friend in death, leaving these parting words: "My friend, while in meditation, had a false thought of lust and desire and will therefore certainly be entangled in love relationships in his next life. He died while unhappy with me, and therefore, upon rebirth, will cause havoc to the community of monks. I am partly responsible for all of this, so if I do not follow and guide him, I will not escape the consequences ..."

The Elder Master went on to be reborn as a distinguished Zen Master, while the former young master had by then become the famous Chinese poet Su Tung-P'o (T'ang dynasty). Because of his previous cultivation, Tung-P'o was a mandarin, endowed with intelligence and wisdom. However, being amorous in nature, he was entangled in the conflicting demands of seven wives and concubines. Moreover, with his learning and intelligence, he often challenged the Zen Masters of his day. Only after he was vanquished by his former friend did he return to Buddhist practice.

This story shows that subtle delusive thoughts should be feared even by seasoned cultivators. The ancients had a verse:

> Though one's cultivation has reached the stage of no
> excess or want,
> It is not easy to destroy ten thousand eons of greed
> and delusion.

Therefore, when the practitioner has experienced a glimpse of some auspicious realms, he should not hasten to show off or grow vain. He should beware of the example of the younger master. Nor should he grow pretentious and denigrate others, but should take the example of the Elder Master to heart.

***

Cultivators who have practiced a long time know themselves how to eliminate drowsiness and subtle delusive thoughts. I shall merely indicate the way to counteract their gross manifestations.

Normally, when afflicted with numerous scattered thoughts, the practitioner should sit still and gather his mind together to recite the Buddha's name. When drowsiness sets in, he should stand up and recite while circumambulating the altar. Alternating between these two techniques will in time eliminate the two hindrances. In my experience, listening and clearly recording each and every utterance of Amitabha Buddha's name, following the Reflecting the Name technique (section 30-1), is probably the most effective way to counteract scattered thought, while Bowing to the Buddha is the supreme method for overcoming the obstruction of heavy drowsiness (section 30-6).

Nevertheless, each practitioner has his own personal experience and knows what is most appropriate to his particular situation. I have merely made some observations to assist him in his practice.

6

Sever all Afflictions

Discussion on the Affliction of Greed

34) Opening up the Mind

As common mortals, by necessity we remain within the cycle of afflictions, subject to its delusive imperatives. Many times we cannot control ourselves. "Afflictions" means "being stirred up and burning," which is unsettling to mind and thought, an obstacle to the practice of the Way. For this reason, afflictions are considered obstructive. Moreover, as our Wisdom-Life Dharma-Body is disturbed by afflictions, they are also termed "demonic."

Some Buddhists keep the precepts against killing, practice charity, and recite the sutras and the Buddha's name; however, they concentrate mainly on the external aspects of worship and do not pay attention to eliminating delusive conditioning and afflictions. We should realize that if afflictions increase by one notch, the Bodhi Mind retrogresses by one notch; therefore, although we may recite the sutras and the Buddha's name, we cannot achieve calmness and purity. For this reason, the Sixth Patriarch, Hui Neng, stated in the

Platform Sutra:

> The deluded cultivate merit and forget
>   about the Way,
> Thinking that cultivating merit is the Way;
> They practice charity and make offerings,
>   gathering immense merit,
> While continually creating greed, anger and
>   delusion.[45]

The word "Way," as used by the Sixth Patriarch, represents the pure True Mind. All methods of practice are expedients, to return to that True Mind. To attain the True Mind is to recover the Self-Nature and escape the sufferings of Birth and Death. The basic criterion for practice and attainment of the Way is to get rid of delusive thoughts and afflictions.

In the *Sutra in Forty-Two Sections*, Buddha Sakyamuni also taught:

> A novice who practices the way should not be like a buffalo pulling a rotating grain mill; he should practice the Way not with his body, but with his mind. If the Way of the mind is cultivated, where is the need to cultivate the body?[46]

Reciting the Buddha's name, engaging in acts of repentance, sitting in meditation, worshipping and circumambulating are all expedients to eliminate delusive karma and open up the True Mind. If the body and mouth practice these external forms of cultivation but the mind is still full of the karma of greed, hatred and delusion, how can this be called practicing the Way?

On the other hand, even if a person does not engage in these external forms, as long as his mind is always clear and bright, "like the moon reflected in a lake in summertime," this is true practice.

A king once asked the twenty-seventh Indian

Patriarch of Zen, "Other cultivators all recite the sutras; why is it that you do not?"

The Patriarch replied, "This humble monk, when exhaling, is not in contact with mundane conditions, and when inhaling, does not dwell in the 'conditioned world' of the Five Skandas. He has recited that sutra over and over millions of times."

The Patriarch meant that he habitually recited the "Wordless Sutra of the Mind."[47] This "sutra" means, *externally*, not relying on or clinging to the multitude of conditions and, *internally*, remaining silent and still, unperturbed by the Five Skandas (Aggregates) and the Eighteen Elements. Even all marks, internal, external and in-between, are eliminated forever. This is the meaning of "mind cultivation."

Nevertheless, we should not be so attached to the above that we reject vegetarianism, charity, repentance, Buddha and sutra recitation. This is because all of these practices, from the standpoint of wisdom, help the practitioner swiftly eliminate karmic obstacles and become enlightened to his Self-Nature; from the standpoint of blessings and merit, they enable him to attain favorable karma and rebirth in auspicious lands or the Western Pure Land, where he may pursue his practice without retrogression. Only when he has perfected both merit and wisdom can he achieve Buddhahood.

For this reason, the great Bodhisattvas, completely enlightened as they are to the source of the mind, still practice the ten thousand merits to adorn the pure lands. For example, even though the Bodhisattva Maitreya is in his last rebirth before Buddhahood, he still practices repentance continually to rid himself of subtle obstacles and swiftly achieve Supreme Enlightenment. We should realize that the teaching in the *Sutra in Forty-Two Sections* and the words of the twenty-seventh Zen

Patriarch are deliberately one-sided in character, partial examples designed to eliminate attachment to form -- that is, cultivation bereft of the mind.

In summary, in addition to reciting the Buddha's name, mantras and sutras and conducting repentance ceremonies, the Pure Land cultivator should also devote attention to "opening up the mind." For the mind to be awakened, so that Buddha Recitation can lead to swift rebirth in the Pure Land, he must rid himself of afflictions.

Going deeper, while uttering the Buddha's name is "form," it is also "essence," because noumenon does not exist outside of phenomena -- *to recite is Buddha, to recite is Mind.* That is why merit and wisdom are fully encompassed in the sacred words "Amitabha Buddha," perfectly fusing noumenon and phenomena, and swiftly leading the practitioner both to the state of Perfectly Enlightened Wondrous Mind and to the pure karma of rebirth in the realm of Amitabha Buddha.

35) How to Combat and Subdue Lust and Desire

Afflictions stemming from greed, while numerous, are all included within the defilements of the "five desires" and the "six Dusts." From the root of greed stem other evil afflictions, such as stinginess, envy, hate, fraud, deceit ... known as secondary afflictions. The "five desires" refers to the five defilements, that is, the desire for beautiful forms (sexual desire ...), wealth and money, fame and power, exquisite food and elegant attire, [excessive] rest and sleep.[48] The "six Dusts" are form, sound, scent, taste, touch and dharmas [i.e., external opinions and views].

The six Dusts encompass the five desires; however, the term "five desires" was created as a separate expression to stress the five heavy defilements of human beings in the realm of the "six Dusts." The concept "six

Dusts" is used when speaking in general, while the expression "five desires" refers to specific afflictions. I employ the term "six Dusts" here to cover other defilements not included in the five desires, such as excessive fondness for music and songs as well as infatuation with romances, novels, etc ...

When the five desires and six Dusts flare up, the general way to counteract them is through skillful visualization of four truths: Impurity, Suffering, Impermanence, and No-Self.

1. Impurity

This means that the body is impure, the mind is impure and the realm is impure. Impurity of the body means that we should reflect on the fact that beneath the covering layers of skin, our bodies and those of others are composed entirely of filthy, smelly substances such as meat, bones, blood, pus, phlegm, saliva, excrement, urine, etc. Not only that, body fluids are excreted through nine apertures (mouth, ears, nose, anus, etc.). If we stop to think carefully, the physical body of sentient beings is hardly worth cherishing.

Impurity of the mind means that once the mind develops thoughts of greed, it has already become evil and defiled, not unlike a limpid pond that has been polluted with dirt and sludge. The dirty pond cannot reflect the images of trees, mountains, sky, clouds; likewise, a polluted mind has lost all spiritual powers and wisdom. Thus, we have the saying:

> One who knows how to cultivate does not waste
> his efforts;
> A peaceful, still mind will bring spiritual
> powers and wisdom.

Those who are determined to tread the Way should endeavor gradually to sever the mind of afflictions, polluted by greed in its gross and subtle aspects.

The impure realm is the world of the Five Turbidities, full of dirt and mud, rocks and stones, spikes and thorns, which harbors countless sentient beings defiled in body and mind. Therefore, this impure world is not worth craving or clinging to.

2. Suffering

This refers to the fact that the body undergoes suffering, the mind endures suffering and the environment is one of suffering. The suffering of the body means that our body is not only impure, it is subject to birth, old age, disease and death, as well as to heat and cold, hunger and thirst and other hardships that cause us to suffer, preventing us from being free and happy.[49]

The suffering of the mind means that when the mind is afflicted, it is necessarily consumed by the fire of afflictions, bound by the ropes of afflictions, struck, pursued and ordered about by the whip of afflictions, defiled and obscured by the smoke and dust of afflictions. Thus, whoever develops afflictions is lacking in wisdom, because the first person he has caused to suffer is himself.

The suffering of the environment means that this earth is subject to the vagaries of the weather, scorching heat, frigid cold and pouring rain, while sentient beings must toil and suffer day in and day out to earn a living. Tragedies occur every day, before our very eyes.

3. Impermanence

This means impermanence of the body, the mind and the environment. Impermanence of the body means that the body withers rapidly, soon grows old and debilitated, ending in death. The ancients have lamented:

> Oh, that time when we were young and would ride
> bamboo sticks, pretending they were horses,
> In the twinkling of an eye, our hair is now
> spotted with the color of frost.

What happened to all those brave and intelligent young men and those beautiful and enchanting women of bygone days? They ended as in the following poem:

> Rosy cheeks have faded, heros have passed away,
> Young students' eyes, too, are weary and sad.

Impermanence of the mind means that the mind and thoughts of sentient beings are always changing -- at times filled with love or anger, at times happy or sad. Those thoughts, upon close scrutiny, are illusory and false, like water bubbles.

Impermanence of the environment means that not only do our surroundings always change and fluctuate, but happiness, too, is impermanent. Succulent food, once swallowed, loses all taste; an emotional reunion, however sweet and joyful, ultimately ends in separation; a delightful party soon becomes a thing of the past; a good book, too, gradually reaches the last page.[50]

4. No-Self

This means that there is no self, no permanent nature *per se* and that we are not true masters of ourselves. This point, too, is divided into the no-self body, the no-self mind and the no-self environment.

The "no-self body" means that this body is illusory, not its own master.[51] It cannot be kept eternally young or prevented from decaying and dying. Even gods and "Immortals" can only postpone death for a certain period of time.

The "no-self mind" refers to the deluded mind of sentient beings, which has no permanent nature. For example, the mind of greed, thoughts of sadness, anger, love and happiness suddenly arise and then disappear; there is nothing real.

The "no-self environment" means that our surroundings are illusory, passive and subject to birth and decay. Cities and towns are in time replaced by abandoned mounds, mulberry fields soon give way to the open seas, every single thing changes and fluctuates by the second, one landscape disappears and another takes its place.

Visualizing that everything, from body and mind to the environment, is impure, subject to suffering, impermanent and without self, the practitioner can rid himself of the mind of greed. Sentient beings, lacking wisdom, always live upside down; they mistake the impure for the pure, suffering for happiness, impermanence for permanence, no-self for self.[52] They then develop delusions and become degraded and defiled. Therefore, Buddha Sakyamuni taught sentient beings the Four Truths, to sever their delusions.

For example, the human excrement that we consider fetid and dirty is regarded as fragrant, clean and succulent by animals such as insects, dogs and pigs -- because of their deluded karma. They therefore compete and struggle to gobble it up. The defiled desires of this world are considered by humans as lovely and clean. However, the gods and Immortals see them as foul-smelling, dirty and unclean, not unlike the way human beings regard dogs and pigs eating filthy substances. The various desires of sentient beings, defiled and upside down, are generally thus. The practitioner should strive gradually to destroy them.

36) How to Subdue Greed in its Subtle Form

As indicated briefly above, the five desires in their gross forms are easy to detect. The practitioner should, additionally, pay attention to the deep-seated, subtle manifestations of greed. For example, a hundred thousand dollars might not necessarily excite a person's greed, but an amount in the millions could move his mind; ordinary beauty can easily be resisted but heavenly charm has the power to lure people down the path of transgression. Even monks and nuns can be infatuated with exquisitely carved rosaries, beautiful statues or auspicious, peaceful realms; these too are in the category of defiled greed. We should see them as expedients, illusory causes and conditions, and not develop defiled greed. To shed light on this state of mind, I shall cite three stories, as examples ranging from the gross to the subtle.

Once upon a time there was an official who was well-known for his honesty. He would sternly reprimand those who attempted to bribe him with money and gold. One day, however, a rich and powerful person, seeking the resolution of a private matter, offered him the equivalent of a hundred thousand dollars. The official immediately accepted the bribe. Later on, when a friend asked him why, he replied, "A hundred thousand in cash can sway the gods." Thus, this official could only be honest with small bribes, but could not resist huge ones. This is a case of deep-seated greed.

Another story dates from the Ming dynasty. One day, an Elder Master was conversing with a visiting monk. The guest lamented, "The majority of today's monks and nuns are defiled by the desire for fame and profit." The Master replied, "I notice that you are pure and clean, because thus far you have always rejected fame and profit." When the visiting monk heard this, his face brightened for a fleeting moment. This monk, while disliking ordinary fame, was attached to a lofty reputation. This is a case of profound subtle greed.

There is another story [which forms the basis of a well-known koan]. Once there was a devoted old woman who built a place of retreat for a monk, arranging that he would not lack for anything, so that he could concentrate upon his meditation and practice. One day, after twenty years, she instructed her daughter: "Today, after serving the Master his meal, take advantage of the situation to embrace him tightly, asking him at the same time, 'how does it feel to be hugged these days?' Come back and let me know his answer as faithfully as you can."

The daughter dutifully did as she was told, putting her arms around the Master and asking the question. The Master replied, "I am not moved in the very least by sexual desire, no different from a dried up tree leaning against a cold mass of rocks in the middle of winter, when not even a drop of warmth can be found." The young girl repeated the answer to her mother, who said unhappily, "I have really wasted my time and effort during the last twenty years. Little did I know that I was only supporting a common mortal!" Having said this, she went out, evicted the monk, lit a fire and burned the meditation hut to the ground.

In truth, it is rare enough these days for anyone to cultivate to the level of that monk. As far as the old woman is concerned, she is said to be a Bodhisattva in disguise. Her action of burning down the hut was to "enlighten" the Master. Why is this so? It is because, while not moved by sexual desire, *he still saw himself as pure and was still attached to the empty and still aspects of samadhi.* Thus, he had not attained true and complete Awakening.[53]

To further clarify the matter, Zen practice requires the cultivator to pass through three "narrow gates." The practitioner who meditates on his koan until he has destroyed "the Great Doubt" [see Glossary under "Zen"], become fully enlightened to the significance of Patriarch Bodhidharma's arrival from the West [i.e., India], and clearly seen his Original Face before birth, has effectively passed the first gate. At this stage, although he has transcended the ordinary mind, deluded from time immemorial, he is still in the realm of subject-object, the realm of opposites of the contemplative mind and has not completely severed forms or transcended feelings. Therefore, while he has reached the state of No-Mind [non-discrimination, non-grasping] in everyday life, he is still separated from the Great Path of Enlightenment by an endless series of doors (degrees of delusion). The ancients have said, in this regard:

Do not say that No-Mind is inherently the True Path,
No-Mind is still separated from Buddhahood by an
endless series of doors.

Although this Master had reached a fairly high level of attainment, he was still attached to the mark of purity. This is another instance of subtle greed, which the practitioner should sever.[54]

The same is true for the Pure Land practitioner. He should know that all forms and marks are illusory. Even though he may have reached the level of one-pointedness of mind and seen precious lotus blossoms, other auspicious marks, or transformation bodies of Buddhas and Bodhisattvas, he should realize that these are merely instances of good causes leading to auspicious results. He should be calm and still and not greedy for them -- nor should he deny their occurrence. Only then will he understand and be awakened to the principle of Truth-like No-Void of the Mind-ground.

Preliminary Discussion on Anger

37) How to Combat and Subdue Anger

Among the various afflictions, only anger manifests itself in a very crude manner, destroying the practitioner in a most effective way. Therefore the ancients said:

> When we allow an angry thought to arise, we open the door to millions of obstructions.[55]

For example, while reciting the Buddha's name, a practitioner may suddenly think of a wicked, ungrateful, stern and evil person who has treated him cruelly; or, he may remember close relatives who are troublesome and unreliable and have caused him grief. He therefore becomes sad and angry, fidgety and uneasy. In that state of mind, his mouth recites the Buddha's name while his mind is saddened and full of delusive thoughts. Some practitioners drop their rosaries and stop reciting; lying down, they put their arms on their foreheads and let their minds wander aimlessly. Others are so afflicted and saddened that they forget about eating and sleeping in their desire to confront the culprit and shout at him; or they look for ways to take revenge and get even. The angry mind can harm the practitioner to that extent.

To combat and subdue anger and resentment, we must develop a compassionate mind. The *Lotus Sutra* teaches:

> We should take the mind of great compassion as our house, forbearance as our armor, the Truth of Emptiness as our throne.

We should think: we ourselves and all other sentient beings are common mortals drowning in the sea of Birth and Death, all because of karma and afflictions. However, afflictions by their very nature are illusory and unreal. For example, where does an angry thought come from *before* it arises? Where does it *return to* when it dissipates? When we are angry and resentful, we are the first to suffer, because we have ignited the fire of afflictions, which will consume us. Anger, moreover, can neither convert nor bring a single benefit to anyone. Is it not then a useless case of delusion?

We should think further: those who have harmed us by their wrongful actions have, through delusion, planted evil seeds; they will necessarily suffer retribution. They should therefore be the objects of pity, not anger. This is because, if they were clear-minded and understood the causes of merit and retribution, they would never dare do such things. We are offspring of the Buddhas and should apply their teachings to dissolve our own afflictions -- because the goal of cultivation is to seek liberation and happiness, not to descend upon the path of suffering. We should feel compassionate and forgiving of injurious actions and practice forbearance, understanding that everything is illusory and void. We should remember the words of the ancient masters:

The fire of the three poisons, greed, anger and
        delusion,
Burns up all the forests of virtue;
Those who would tread the Bodhisattva
        Path,
Should be forbearing in mind and body.

Compassion is the pure and refreshing water that can extinguish the fire of afflictions; forbearance is the enduring armor that can block all poisoned arrows; the Dharma of the Void is the light that can completely destroy the somber smoke of delusion. Knowing these three things and relying on them to rid ourselves of anger and resentment is to have "entered the house of the Buddhas, worn the armor of the Buddhas and sat on the Buddhas' throne."

38) How to Do Away with the Judgemental Mind

We ordinary people, not having attained the mind of true equanimity, and still making the distinction between ourselves and others, count life's successes and failures, rights and wrongs, praise and blame, in the tens of millions; no one can escape this condition. Even the Buddhas and Bodhisattvas, who in their compassion appear in this world to save sentient beings, must endure criticism, affection and distaste.

The ancients have said:

No one is immune from criticism and
        blame,
It is just that people refrain from speaking
        openly.

This is an accurate observation born out of experience.

If the practitioner is not clear-minded and calm, criticism can sometimes upset him, giving rise to afflictions, and greatly obstructing his cultivation. I therefore raise this question in an attempt to find a cure.

***

To avoid being judgemental, we should follow three principles.

First principle: we should examine and correct our own mistakes, not watch or discuss the transgressions of others. Take the case of a black buffalo which allows a white heron to perch on his back, but uses his horns to chase away a crow trying to do the same. Little does the buffalo realize that it is much darker than the crow!

Ordinary people, too, are similar, fond of praise, loathing criticism, delighting in exposing other people's mistakes while not realizing that they themselves have many more failings and are nothing to be proud of! For this reason, the main principle followed by practitioners is to reverse the light, observing and correcting themselves, not watching or discussing other people's transgressions. Examining and correcting our own mistakes will develop our wisdom, while watching and discussing the failings of others will certainly create karmic debts and injustice.

Second principle: When we are the object of slander or blame, we should remain calm and forbearing and not necessarily seek ways to justify ourselves. For example, if a sheet of white paper is stained by a spot of black ink, left alone it will be smudged in only one place and the spot will gradually fade away. If, on the other hand, we try to erase the blot, the whole sheet can become dirty.

A well-known commentary states:

> Being the object of injustice, do not always seek to justify yourself, because to do so will create more rancor .

This is because when someone has set his mind upon speaking ill of another, if the latter tries to justify himself, he is in effect saying that the speaker is wrong. Naturally, this leads to hatred, resentment and conflict, and unintentionally makes the dispute known to everyone around, who then begin to harbor doubts about the very person attempting to justify himself.

In general, those who have just begun to cultivate see themselves in the right and others in the wrong. Those who have cultivated for a while see themselves and others as sometimes right and sometimes wrong. Seasoned cultivators only see themselves as being in the wrong. Why is this so? It is because, if those of us who are the object of slander are not wrong in this life, we may have committed transgressions in a previous life for which we must now endure retribution. Even if we have not created "personal karma" by directly committing a transgression, it must have been due to "common karma" that we were born in this world of the Five Turbidities.[56]

Having created adverse karma, let us not blame Heaven for being near or far.

These words by the well-known Vietnamese poet Nguyễn-Du are indeed quietly consonant with the teaching of the Way.

Third principle: The practitioner should be steadfast in his determination, believe firmly in the law of cause ar ¹ effect, and not be moved by words of praise and blame from outside. The *Dhammapada Sutra* teaches:

A high mountain stands immovable in the midst of a raging storm. The upright man is calm and at peace within the swirl of criticism and gossip.

No amount of praise or ridicule from outside can make us good or bad, free from suffering or mired in suffering; everything depends on ourselves. If we create good karma, even though we are despised as evil and full of transgressions, we will still be reborn in the higher realms. On the other hand, if we create bad karma, although we may be honored and praised, we will still be reborn in the lower realms.

A Vietnamese Zen Master once wrote a refreshing stanza along these lines:

Let us not concern ourselves with fame or
      fortune, right or wrong;
Let them drop with the morning flowers, freeze
  with the midnight rain and gradually
      fade away.
There, a bird's song, springtime has passed.
Why not concentrate on practicing the Way?

39) **Some advice on Fault-Finding**

An ancient proverb states:

If even what we see before our eyes is sometimes untrue, how can we possibly believe what is said behind people's backs? Therefore, while our ears may hear talk of right and wrong, our mouths should not repeat it.

Criticism and issues of right and wrong often originate in unfounded doubts, misunderstanding and misinterpretation. What in the house is merely a mouse, past the gate takes the shape of a goat, and outside in the street is transformed into a buffalo. While originally there may have been very little substance to a rumor, by the time it reaches the tenth person, even the one who actually started it may receive quite a shock!

Frequently, disparaging words spring from a contentious or jealous frame of mind, the determination to settle accounts, or the desire to denigrate those who have more advantages or qualities than ourselves. Women, and many men as well, seem prone to this habit of gossip, jealousy and criticism. When they like and respect someone, he is depicted as an Immortal or a Buddha; when they despise or resent him, he easily becomes a demon or a ghost. A respected master once observed, "women tend to have stronger faith than men and are usually diligent and assiduous in their practice. However, the virtues they reap from cultivation often go up in smoke because of their mouths!"

***

To avoid such mistakes and ensure that virtues are not lost, I will relate, for our common edification, the teachings of the Patriarchs and Buddha Sakyamuni Himself.

One leisurely evening, a king asked a certain

courtier, "You appear to be a man of integrity. Why is it that you are the target of so much criticism, slander and hatred?" The official replied, "Your Majesty, when the torrential rains of spring arrive, farmers are elated because their fields are well-irrigated. Pedestrians, on the other hand, are unhappy because the streets are muddy and slippery. When the summer moon is as clear and bright as a mirror, poets and writers rejoice at the opportunity to travel and compose couplets and poems, while thieves and felons are distressed at the brightness of the moonlight! If even the impartial heaven and earth are the object of blame and resentment, love and hate, how can this subject of yours, imperfect and full of blemishes, escape denigration and criticism?

"Thus, I venture to think, we should remain calm in the face of praise or criticism, think it over, and not rush to believe it. If a king believes gossip, his subjects lose their lives; if parents believe gossip, their children are hurt; if brothers and sisters, husbands and wives, believe words of gossip, they experience separation; if relatives, friends and neighbors believe gossip, they sever relations with one another. Fault-finding is really more noxious that snakes and serpents, sharper than swords and knives, killing without spilling a single drop of blood."

According to the judgement of history, this courtier was a disloyal official; however, his answer was sound and reasonable, and a worthy example for later generations. It is therefore still quoted today.

***

The *Lotus Sutra* states:

Then the Bodhisattva Universal Virtue said to the Buddha [Sakyamuni]: "World Honored One! In the latter five hundred years of the corrupt and evil age, whoever receives and keeps this sutra, I will guard and protect him, eliminate his anxieties and give him ease of mind ... If anyone sees those who receive and keep this sutra and *proclaims their errors and sins,* whether true or false, such a person [will receive all kinds of evil karma]."[57] (Bunno Kato, et.al., tr. *The Three-fold Lotus Sutra,* p. 340-343.)

As Buddha Sakyamuni said, slandering and harming those who recite the *Lotus Sutra* constitutes a heavy transgression. So does slandering and harming those who recite the Buddha's name, mantras and other Mahayana texts.

As stated also in the *Brahma Net Sutra:*

A disciple of the Buddha[s] must not himself discuss the offenses of any Bodhisattva sangham, Bodhisattva lay person, bhikshu, bhikshuni, nor may he encourage others to do so, or involve himself in the causes, conditions, methods, or karma of speaking of the offenses of the Four Assemblies ... If instead, a Bodhisattva discusses the faults of those within the Buddha Dharma, he thereby commits a Bodhisattva Parajika [major] offense.

A disciple of the Buddha[s] must not praise himself and disparage others, encourage others to do so, or involve himself in the causes, conditions, methods or karma of praising himself and disparaging others ... Otherwise, he commits a Bodhisattva Parajika [major] offense. (Hui Seng, *Brahma Net Sutra.* Part I, p. 97 and 100, respectively.)

Buddha Sakyamuni, in his compassion, clearly indicated the paths of transgression and merit, but we Buddhists are so deluded that many of us have forgotten all about them. Because of our minds filled with jealousy and criticism, we create immeasurable evil karma of speech!

In the *Great Heap Sutra*, Buddha Sakyamuni said:

If kings and officials beat and scold monks and nuns, whether the latter keep the precepts or not, the bad karma of the kings and officials is as great as if they had shed the blood of millions of Buddhas. If we see someone wearing the yellow robe, whether he keeps the precepts or not, we should consider him a Buddha.

As the *Great Heap Sutra* clearly teaches, if monks, nuns or laymen have committed transgressions, they will suffer retribution. We should feel only compassion for them, rather than disdain or scorn. Respectful and compassionate thoughts increase our good karma; scornful and deprecating thoughts, and looking for the failings of others, can only reduce our stock of merit and virtue, bringing suffering and tears! For this reason, the true cultivator is always concerned with self-examination and self-improvement. On the other hand, if we still have many faults but do not examine ourselves, spending our time unmasking and denigrating others, we cannot be said to have a true understanding of cultivation.

The ancients used to say:

Harming others brings misfortune; to be harmed is to receive merit.

When the cultivator is subjected to criticism and slander, he should think: "that person is bringing me merit." Why is this so? It is because, from time immemorial, we have committed obstructive transgressions. If we are the object of one word of scorn and belittlement, our bad karma has been lightened by one part. Are we not then receiving merit and benefit? Those who engage in scornful speech and slander will certainly suffer retribution; through delusion, they bring calamity upon themselves.

***

In order to demonstrate clearly what true cultivation and the personality of the true cultivator are, I will quote a passage from the No-Mark Stanza of the *Platform Sutra*, by the Sixth Patriarch:

He who treads the Path in earnest
Sees not the mistakes of the world;
If we find fault with others
We ourselves are also in the wrong.
When other people are in the wrong,
    we should ignore it,
For it is wrong for us to find fault.
By getting rid of the habit of fault-finding
We cut off a source of defilement.
When neither hatred nor love disturbs our mind
Serenely we sleep. (Wong Mou-Lam, tr. "The Sutra of Hui Neng,"
p. 34. In *The Diamond Sutra & The Sutra of Hui Neng*.)

Buddhist adherents, whether clergy or laymen, all consider themselves cultivators, concerned with the Way. However, how can we tell the genuine from the sham cultivator? On this issue, the Sixth Patriarch has advanced a simple criterion. He said:

He who treads the Path in earnest sees not the mistakes of the world.

In effect, the genuine cultivator always looks at himself to correct his own mistakes and dwells in empty, still meditation. Having severed the mind of discrimination between himself and others, how can he think about the good and bad points of others? With the sham cultivator, on the other hand, the mind of self and others, right and wrong, jealousy and hate runs rampant; as soon as he opens his mouth, he criticizes others and speaks of the good and bad points of the world. This is very far from the Way.

Therefore, when we continue to see the mistakes of others, denigrating and slandering them, we demonstrate that we are the most awkward and wanting of all, because our minds are still deluded, full of discrimination, lacking in wisdom and compassion. We thus bring retribution upon ourselves in the future. Regardless of whether or not others are in the wrong, let us strive not to be in the wrong ourselves. We should learn from great men and let our minds be as clear and bright as a mirror. Without anticipating or hedging about future events, without regretting or dreaming about things of the past, with the mind filled with brightness and equanimity, we will surely receive a wonderful response!

If we have distracting thoughts of envy and hate and speak words of scorn and blame, then, *internally*, our True Nature becomes defiled and *externally*, we bring rancor and disputes upon ourselves. This results in further errors and transgressions. For this reason, to achieve peace of mind and be free of afflictions, we should not comment on people's shortcomings.

The phrase "by getting rid of the habit of fault-finding" also has the deeper meaning of eliminating the Four Propositions and eradicating the One Hundred Errors.[58]

"When neither hatred nor love disturbs our mind, serenely we sleep" ("reclining with both legs stretched out and resting") describes the state of great liberation, all eagerness for study gone, eating when hungry, sleeping when tired.[59]

***

True cultivators always have a clear and solid position and viewpoint, and pay no attention to the praise and criticism, likes and dislikes of the outside world. As an example, it once happened that a well-known Zen Master, having awakened to the Way under Elder Master Fu Shan, went to reside in a famous monastery. Although living among the Great Assembly, he did not practice meditation or seek guidance in the Dharma; all he did all day was lay sleeping.

Upon hearing this, the abbot arrived at the meditation hall, a big staff in hand. Seeing the guest master reclining with eyes closed, he admonished: "This place does not have surplus rice to allow you to do nothing but eat and rest!" *Reply*: "What would you, High Master, advise me to do?" The abbot said: "Why don't you sit in meditation?" *Answer*: "Succulent food cannot tempt those who have eaten their fill." The abbot continued, "A great many people are unhappy with you." *Answer*: "If they were happy, what would I gain?" Hearing these unusual replies, the abbot inquired further, "Who was your master?" *Answer*: "I arrived here after having studied under the eminent Master Fu Shan." The abbot said, "No wonder you are so headstrong!" They then clasped hands, laughing aloud, and headed toward the abbot's quarters.

One day, many years later, the guest Zen Master, having washed himself, ascended the Dharma seat, bid farewell to the great assembly, wrote a parting stanza, immediately dropped the pen and expired in a seated position. The guest master, as we can see, conducted himself easily and freely, having mastered life and death. Is it not because he had truly internalized the meaning of the passage "when neither hatred nor love disturbs our mind, serenely we sleep?"

Discussion on the Affliction of Delusion

40) General Outline of the Karma of Delusion

When the practitioner cannot thoroughly grasp the noumenal and phenomenal aspects of various events, all kinds of errors and misunderstandings arise, agitating his mind and thought. This is the beginning of the karma of delusion. For example, in the middle of a recitation session, he suddenly remembers that one should recite with one-pointedness of mind to achieve rebirth in the Pure Land. Realizing that he cannot easily reach that level and may be wasting his efforts, he grows perplexed. This is a manifestation of the karma of delusion.

Delusion (ignorance) is the source of all afflictions. Greed and anger stem from delusion, as do pride, doubts and wrong views. For example, when we have such thoughts as: "I have few equals in hard and assiduous cultivation, even among the ranks of monks and nuns" -- this is the affliction of pride and self-love. If, on the other hand, we develop such thoughts as: "the Land of Ultimate Bliss is so well-adorned, while I have heavy karma and few merits; how do I know I will achieve rebirth there?" -- this is the affliction of doubt.

Wrong views consist of seeing and understanding in a wicked and grasping manner. They include five types: Wrong Views of the Body, One-Sided Views, Wrong Views Not Consistent with the Dharma, Wrong Views Caused by Attachment to one's own Erroneous Understandings and Wrong Views (understanding) of the Precepts.

For example, during cultivation a thought suddenly arises: "my health has always been poor, and today I feel tired, worn out; if I continue to recite the Buddha's name, I may fall ill." This is an example of a Wrong View of the Body.

Or else, we think: "death is like a candle which has been extinguished; if there was a previous life, how come I cannot remember it? It is better for me to follow Taoism, to prolong my life and avoid death." This is an instance of a One-Sided View.

Or else, we wonder why someone who had performed only good deeds had a short life and met a violent death, while others who had committed numerous transgressions lived long lives and died peacefully; thus, cultivation brings no benefit whatsoever! These are instances of Wrong Views Not Consistent with the Dharma, and failure to understand that the law of cause and effect spans many lifetimes.

Or else, someone might think, "I used to follow the externalist practice of circulating energy currents, and was achieving results in barely a few months. How is it that I have been reciting the Buddha's name for a long time, but have not yet seen any change?" This is an instance of Attachment to one's own Erroneous Understandings.

Or else, we may think: "In other religions, people who hurt and kill other sentient beings can still be reborn in paradise; therefore, in seeking rebirth in the Pure Land, there is no need to keep the precept against killing." This is an instance of a Wrong View of the Precepts.

The karma of delusion takes numerous forms. The Pure Land practitioner should, first and foremost, follow the sutras and put his entire faith in them. If he fails to understand certain passages, he should seek out good spiritual advisors for an explanation. Delusion can easily lead the practitioner astray when he is challenged by other teachings and ideologies. This is a particularly important point, as the Pure Land method is profound and lofty, difficult to understand and believe in.

**

According to the sutras and commentaries, the Pure Land practitioner should follow three guidelines to consolidate his faith.

1. The Guideline of Reason

This is the reasoning and understanding of human logic. For example, we may reflect: All realms are created from the mind. If there is a world such as ours, where good karma and bad karma are about equal, there must exist other worlds such as the three Evil Paths, with a preponderance of evil karma, as well as celestial realms, where good karma prevails. It therefore stands to reason that the Western Pure Land exists, as a result of the pure, good Vows of Amitabha Buddha as well as the virtues of the Bodhisattvas and other morally superior beings.

2. The Guideline of the Teachings of the Sages

These are the words of the Buddhas and Bodhisattvas in sutras and commentaries. Buddha Sakyamuni, with his pure vision, clearly saw the auspicious environment and superior beings of the Western Pure Land and described them in the Pure Land sutras. The great Bodhisattvas, such as Manjusri and Samantabhadra, all extolled the Land of Ultimate Bliss and enjoined sentient beings to seek rebirth there. If Buddhists are not guided by the words of the Buddhas and Bodhisattvas, whom then should they believe?

3. The Guideline of Actual Seeing and Understanding

This is a method of reasoning based on actual occurrences, verifiable through our eyes and understanding. The commentary, *Biographies of Pure Land Sages and Saints*, has amply documented the stories of individuals who have achieved rebirth in the Land of Ultimate Bliss through Buddha Recitation ... Moreover, those who have practiced Buddha Recitation with a pure mind have been known to witness scenes of the Pure Land during their current lifetimes.

***

I have described above three guidelines that Pure Land practitioners should follow to consolidate their faith. Moreover, according to Elder Master Yin Kuang, Pure Land followers should not seek guidance on Pure Land matters from Zen Masters. This is because the answers of Zen Masters are all directed towards principle and essence, while the Pure Land approach is based on phenomena and marks. This being the case, and considering the different areas of emphasis, beginning Pure Land practitioners who do not yet fully understand essence and marks, noumenon and phenomena, will not only fail to benefit from the answers of Zen Masters, they may develop even greater doubts, perplexity and inconsistent views.

41) Sadness and Discouragement Should Be Eradicated

One minor affliction in Buddhism, caused by the karma of delusion, is a pitfall for many practitioners. I will elaborate on it, to strengthen the resolve of cultivators.

Compassionate individuals, or those who have the interests of the Dharma at heart, generally go through three stages: in the first, they are eager and enthusiastic; in the second, they grow sad and discouraged; in the third and last stage, they achieve the mind of compassion and wisdom, adapted to circumstances. Unfortunately, however, these good and eager individuals usually give up and lose their determination during the second stage; very few reach the third stage. To get past the second stage and reach the third, we must have a mind of great compassion and wisdom, like the mythical dragon which can soar to the blue yonder or hide in the ocean depths.

Confucian followers express this idea as follows: "The true scholar teaches the Way if the world is receptive; if the time is not right, he retreats and lives in seclusion." Confucius himself, at one point in his career, saw his teachings rejected by the local rulers. At that time, he retreated to write books and teach his disciples, his determination to help the world intact. Those who do not understand this principle of timing and conditions are usually discouraged and stricken with sadness!

Let us look at the issue from an everyday point of

view.

We meet numerous individuals in their prime, endowed with good health, seeing life as a flower in a dream, full of enthusiasm and zeal, determined to build an ideal, bright, beautiful life, if not for all humanity, at least for those around them, or for themselves personally. However, after a few ups and downs and some sour, cruel setbacks, having penetrated deeply into real life and witnessed the ingratitude of human nature, they become despondent. The more enthusiastic and eager they were, the more distant and cautious they become! Some even wish to go into seclusion, shunning all contacts and avoiding everything. This state of mind is described in the following couplets:

> It is better not to know,
> The more we know, the more heartrending
>   it becomes!

> The ways of the world are such, we know this;
> Better live in seclusion in the mountains,
>   neither hearing nor knowing!

In general, human resolve is easily shaken and we easily retreat!

We find the same state of mind among monks and nuns. The ancients accurately observed:

> In general, practitioners are assiduous in the beginning; later on, they usually grow lazy and tardy.

The fervent resolve that some possess when first developing the Bodhi Mind resembles that of the great Bodhisattvas. However, with time, because of karmic obstructions *within* and adverse conditions *without*, they grow lazy and arrogant. Their thoughts are then no different from those of ordinary people.

These practitioners, in general, do not yet

understand the world of the Five Turbidities; therefore, they easily regress when faced with reality.   For this reason, many monks and nuns, witnessing errors within their own ranks or seeing the many afflictions and attachments of the laity, develop retrogressive thoughts. From there, they either abandon the Order and return to lay life, or they lose their altruistic determination, preferring to live in seclusion, practicing by themselves, unwilling to teach and save others.

Likewise, many lay Buddhists, discouraged at the number of monks and nuns who commit transgressions, abandon Buddhism and cut off relations with the clergy; or else, they grow scornful and decide to take refuge only in the Buddha and the Dharma, but not in the Sangha.   Still others, hearing rumors that their teacher has committed certain transgressions, hastily abandon all practice, without even taking time to investigate the matter.   These people have only a shallow grasp of the Dharma, failing to realize that we cultivate for ourselves, not for our teachers and that to abandon practice is detrimental to ourselves alone, not to others.

As a general comment, the states of sadness and discouragement described above are all misguided and wrong.   This is because, in life, as within the Order, genuine and honest practitioners, while rare, do indeed exist.   "Sugar cane is eaten by worms only in certain spots; a roof leaks only in certain places."   Just because certain individuals transgress, let us not generalize and think that everyone is bad and wrong.   Moreover,

Human beings are bad and false; the Way is neither bad nor false.

Even if everyone were in the wrong, the Dharma would still be the shining, enlightened Way that leads us to liberation.

Furthermore, before criticizing others, let us look at

ourselves to see whether we are already perfect, or whether, in truth, we are not worse than the person we are criticizing. We should feel compassion and forgiveness, blaming ourselves instead of others, forgiving others as much as we forgive ourselves. Let us not throw stones at others while we ourselves are still full of transgressions.

Again, the goal of cultivation is first of all to save ourselves, finding the way to self-emancipation. If because of some external factors we forget even ourselves, is this not delusion? Therefore, the practitioner who has deep and thorough understanding should always fulfill his duties and obligations. He should develop a loyal, truthful, compassionate and forgiving mind, be ashamed of his many remaining karmic obstacles, take pity on sentient beings revolving in the cycle of afflictions, hold fast to his resolve and vows, and earnestly search for a way to save himself and others.

Loving-kindness, compassion, joy and equanimity are the house; wisdom and expedients are the windows.

We should not let our Bodhi Mind regress just because sentient beings have many afflictions, or because the Way is full of obstacles and difficulties. To come to such a realization is to overcome the obstacles of the second stage and reach the peaceful state of the third stage.

42) General Guidelines for Countering Afflictions

The karmas of greed, anger and delusion manifest themselves in many forms, which are impossible to describe fully. I will discuss, in general, four basic ways to subdue them.

1. Suppressing Afflictions with the Mind

There are only two points of divergence between

the deluded and the enlightened (i.e., Buddhas and Bodhisattvas ...): purity is Buddhahood, defilement is the state of sentient beings. Because the Buddhas are in accord with the Pure Mind, they are enlightened, fully endowed with spiritual powers and wisdom. Because sentient beings are attached to worldly Dusts, they are deluded and revolve in the cycle of Birth and Death. To practice Pure Land is to go deep into the Buddha Recitation Samadhi, awakening to the Original Mind and attaining Buddhahood. Therefore, if any deluded, agitated thought develops during Buddha Recitation, it should be severed immediately, allowing us to return to the state of the Pure Mind. This is the method of counteracting afflictions with the mind.

2. Suppressing Afflictions with Noumenon

When deluded thoughts arise which cannot be suppressed with the mind, we should move to the second stage and "visualize principles." For example, whenever the affliction of greed develops, we should visualize the principles of impurity, suffering, impermanence, No-Self. Whenever the affliction of anger arises, we should visualize the principles of compassion, forgiveness and emptiness of all dharmas.

3. Suppressing Afflictions with Phenomena

Persons with heavy karma who cannot suppress their afflictions by visualizing principles alone, should use "phenomena," that is, external forms.

For example, individuals who are prone to anger and delusion and are aware of their shortcomings, should, when they are on the verge of bursting into a quarrel, immediately leave the scene and slowly sip a glass of cold water. Those heavily afflicted with the karma of lust-attachment who cannot suppress their afflictions through "visualization of principle," should arrange to be near virtuous Elders and concentrate on

Buddhist activities or distant travel, to overcome lust and memories gradually. The saying "absence makes the heart grow fonder," should really read "out of sight, out of mind." This is because sentient beings' minds closely parallel their surroundings and environment. If the surroundings disappear, the mind loses its anchor, and, gradually, all memories fade away.

4. Suppressing Afflictions with Repentance and Recitation

In addition to the above three methods, which range from the subtle to the gross, there is also a fourth: repentance and the recitation of sutras, mantras and the Buddha's name. If performed regularly, repentance and recitation eradicate bad karma and generate merit and wisdom.

For this reason, many cultivators in times past, before receiving the precepts or embarking upon some great Dharma work such as building a temple or translating a sutra, would vow to recite the Great Compassion Mantra tens of thousand of times, or to recite the entire *Larger Prajna Paramita Sutra*, the longest sutra in the Buddhist canon.

In the past, during lay retreats, if a practitioner had heavy karmic obstructions and could not recite the Buddha's name with a pure mind or clearly visualize Amitabha Buddha, the presiding Dharma Master would usually advise him to follow the practice of "bowing repentance with incense." This method consists of lighting a long incense stick and respectfully bowing in repentance while uttering the Buddha's name, until the stick is burnt out. There are cases of individuals with heavy karma who would spend the entire seven or twenty-one-day retreat doing nothing but "bowing with incense."

***

Depending on circumstances, the practitioner can use any of these four methods to counteract the karma of greed, anger and delusion in a general way. If these methods are practiced patiently and in earnest, there is nothing that cannot be accomplished.

7

Seek a Response within A Definite Time Frame

Conducting Periodic Retreats

43) The Great Issue of Birth and Death

Only Buddhism discusses and offers a thorough solution to the religious truth "swift is the wave of impermanence, great is the issue of Birth and Death." Philosophers merely deal with the questions of everyday life -- after birth and before death. They do not thoroughly investigate the issue of Birth and Death -- before birth and after death. Confucius did comment on the after-life, but he did so with the goal of fulfilling filial obligations and conducting rites and ceremonies according to the motto "worship the dead as if they were still alive." Once, when one of Confucius' disciples asked him about death, he replied "You who do not even know about life, how can you know about death?" The Taoist solution to the problem of death is to lengthen the lifespan, attempting to achieve immortality.

However, while we may live longer, we cannot escape death, because all conditioned dharmas are within the cycle of Birth and Death. In the truth of the Twelve Links of Dependent Origination, Buddha Sakyamuni identified the source, demonstrating clearly that "birth, old age, disease, death, worry, love-attachment and unhappiness" are caused by a single, original thought called delusion (ignorance).[60] To destroy delusion and return to the Original Nature is to completely eliminate the source of Birth and Death. Yet, this is only severing attachment to self and *others*; we should also sever attachment to self and *dharmas* to attain the stage of complete Enlightenment. Nevertheless, to be free of attachment to self and others and dwell in Nirvana without Remainder -- escaping the sufferings of the Triple Realm -- is still a very difficult step which is rarely achieved. It is also the first stage for cultivators.

As Sakyamuni Buddha predicted, in the Dharma-Ending Age, those who have *awakened to the Way* are rare enough, not to speak of those who have *attained Enlightenment*. And, if we have not attained Enlightenment, we are, by necessity, subject to Birth and Death. Therefore, to solve the problem of Birth and Death in this very life, in the middle of the Dharma-Ending Age, there is only one expedient, i.e., "to take our karma along to the Western Pure Land." Why is this so? It is because, if we have neither attained Enlightenment nor achieved rebirth in the Pure Land, we are necessarily mired in Birth and Death. As we revolve in the realm of the Five Turbidities, deep in the Dharma-Ending Age, morality and virtue keep declining, bad karma is easy to commit and good conditions are difficult to create. In the end, we cannot escape from the three Evil Paths. Thus, Birth and Death is the big issue. Practitioners seeking rebirth in the Pure Land should bear it in mind day in and day out.

A famous Chinese Master of recent times, when still a young boy at home, saw the flowers wither and die in front of his parents' house and began to ponder and shed tears ... This monk, full of wisdom, had when still young, deeply realized the truth of Birth and Death as the common fate of all sentient beings![61]

44) The Meaning of Conducting a Retreat

As indicated above, if we have not attained Enlightenment, we should recite the Buddha's name seeking rebirth in the Pure Land. To ensure that this occurs, we should recite to the level of one-pointedness of mind. And, in order to practice to that level, we should conduct periodic retreats. To be "in retreat" is to retire to a small house, meditation hut or small room, cut off all outside activities and conditions and concentrate on reciting the Buddha's name for a period of seven days. Why seven days and not six or eight? The *Amitabha Sutra* states:

> Sariputra: if a good man or a good woman hears Amida Buddha preach and firmly holds the Name wholeheartedly and singlemindedly, be it for one day, two days, three days, four days, five days, six days, or seven days, Amida Buddha, together with all the holy multitudes, will appear before that person as the end of life draws near. When death arrives, that person, with mind undisturbed, at once gains rebirth in Amida Buddha's Land of Utmost Happiness. (Hozen Seki, *Buddha Tells of the Infinite: the "Amida Kyo,"* p. 53.)

Since the Sutra does not refer to *six* days only, nor does it speak of *eight* days, Pure Land practitioners, basing themselves on the words of Buddha Sakyamuni, have traditionally taken the period of retreat as *seven* days.

According to the Esoteric School, the number seven is the ultimate number in the cycle of Birth and Death. Therefore, in the bardo stage, the "soul" must undergo changes every seven days, and to be efficacious, mantras should be recited at least seven times. Buddhist texts note this with the words "the Dharma is thus," i.e., according to the law of nature it has to be that way and cannot be explained, just as it is difficult to explain why fire is hot and ice is cold. Starting with the number seven and multiplying it by three or seven, we have twenty-one or forty-nine. Therefore, the Esoteric School teaches that mantras should be recited [at least] seven times to be effective, twenty-one or forty-nine times if the mind is weak and agitated. Thus, basing themselves on this teaching, practitioners arrange retreat periods of seven, twenty-one or forty-nine days.

***

What does it mean to have "one-pointedness of mind"? It means to concentrate the mind on recitation, without sundry thoughts. "One-pointedness" means the mind is devoid of all distractions, thinking about no other realm except the realm of Buddha Recitation. Individuals of high capacities may reach such a state in, perhaps, one day, those of moderate capacities in three or four days, those of limited capacities in seven days. Looking at it from another point of view, individuals of high capacities, ideally, achieve one-pointedness of mind during the entire seven-day period, those of moderate capacities only do so for three or four days, while those of limited capacities may only do so for one day during the whole period of retreat.

However, why did Buddha Sakyamuni estimate that we could achieve one-pointedness of mind within a week, when in fact, some of us may recite for two or three or even many years without ever reaching that state? This situation results from three causes.

1. From the viewpoint of "marks" (phenomena), we fail to follow Buddha Sakyamuni's admonition to conduct periodic retreats for cultivation. When we do so, we engage in several practices at the same time (sundry practices). We should realize that if we would like to achieve one-pointedness of mind, we should

practice Oral Recitation exclusively during the retreat period, and not engage in Mantra or Sutra Recitation or meditation as well.

2. There are various reasons why some practitioners cannot avoid sundry conditions and thoughts or concentrate on cultivation for seven days. These reasons range from lack of external support (the need to prepare their own meals and attend to other miscellaneous activities) to lack of earnestness.

3. The three capacities mentioned above are a rough estimation. For example, within the category of high capacity cultivators, we have "supremely high," "moderately high," and "low high" capacities. Moderate and limited capacities may likewise be subdivided. There are thus a total of nine categories, which may in turn be divided into many more categories.

We should also realize that Buddha Sakyamuni's words are only generalities. For example, the sutras state that individuals of high capacities can achieve one-pointedness of mind for seven days, not eight or nine. In reality, these sages are not only undisturbed for eight or nine days; conceivably, their minds can remain empty and still during their entire lives. Conversely, those of limited capacities, weighed down by heavy karmic obstructions, not only may fail to reach one-pointedness of mind after seven days, they may even recite during their whole lifetime without ever reaching that state. Thus, we should interpret the words and meaning of the sutras flexibly, without being attached to the words and betraying the phrase, or grasping at the phrase and doing injustice to the meaning.

45) How to Conduct a Seven-Day Retreat

In conducting a seven-day retreat, one can either practice alone, to attain purity more easily, or with many other cultivators. In either case, three types of good spiritual advisors are required.

1. Teaching Spiritual Advisor

This is someone conversant with the Dharma and experienced in cultivation. The retreat members can have him follow their progress, guiding them throughout the retreat, or they can simply seek his guidance before and after the retreat. When several persons hold a retreat together, they should ask a spiritual advisor to lead the retreat and give a daily fifteen-to-thirty-minute inspirational talk.

2. Caretaking Spiritual Advisors

This refers to one or several persons assisting with outside daily chores such as preparing meals or cleaning up, so that those on retreat can cultivate peacefully without distraction. Such persons are called "retreat assistants."

3. Common Practice Spiritual Advisors

These are persons who practice the same method as the individual(s) on retreat. They keep an eye on one another, encouraging and urging each other on. These cultivators can either be participants in the same retreat or cultivators living nearby. In addition to keeping an eye out and urging the practitioners on, they can exchange ideas or experiences for the common good. This concept has been captured in a proverb:

> Rice should be eaten with soup,
> Practice should be conducted with friends.

An Elder Master of great virtue in the Zen tradition once taught:

> The practitioner should take the ten directions as his perfect Enlightenment seat, and not set a limit to the length of retreats. If one year is not sufficient to become

enlightened, he should meditate for ten years. If ten years are not enough, then he should meditate for twenty or thirty years, or up to his whole lifetime, always unwavering in his determination.

Pure Land followers should do likewise. Attending a seven-day retreat is the best expedient to reach one-pointedness of mind. If one retreat is not sufficient, then he should cultivate during many retreats, never wavering in his determination.

* * *

Some might ask, "To achieve rebirth in the Pure Land, we should recite to the level of one-pointedness of mind. However, since few practitioners can reach that level today, are we not wasting our efforts?"

Answer: I briefly answered that question earlier and will repeat the answer here for emphasis. The goal of Buddha Recitation is one-pointedness of mind or samadhi. However, the Pure Land method has one particular characteristic, namely:

Those "above" should reach the state of undisturbed mind; for those "below," only ten thoughts will bring success.

In other words, those of high capacities who recite to the level of one-pointedness of mind *in this very life* will be assured of rebirth in the Pure Land. On the other hand, those of limited capacities who can have ten undisturbed thoughts *at the time of death* will also achieve rebirth there. Therefore, the question of an "undisturbed mind achieving rebirth in the Pure Land" applies at the time of death, not during this current life. Moreover, even if we achieve one-pointedness of mind in our usual practice, should we, on our deathbed, change course and practice other methods, we will not achieve rebirth in the Pure Land.

To have ten undisturbed thoughts at the moment of death is, in truth, no easy thing. This is because at that time, we are faced with a karma-power, caused by current and past transgressions, called "near death karma." If we do not practice Buddha Recitation diligently in our daily lives, that near death karma will overpower the mind. Right thoughts cannot then arise and the mind-consciousness will be disturbed at the time of death. Under these circumstances, how can we achieve rebirth in the Pure Land?

There was once a lay Pure Land practitioner who liked to perform Buddhist works, but his daily recitation was only perfunctory. At the time of death, he developed an aversion to hearing the Buddha's name and refused to follow the admonitions of fellow practitioners. Elder Master Yin Kuang concluded:

This was due to bad karma accrued from time immemorial, in particular the karma of stinginess in giving advice, seeing people headed toward death but not warning them. These inauspicious signs are indications of impending rebirth among hungry ghosts.

Buddha Sakyamuni once said to his disciple, Ananda, "Some people perform good deeds all their lives, but at the time of death are reborn in the hells; others create bad karma all their lives, yet at the time of death are reborn in the heavens. Do you know the reason why?" Ananda said, "Great Master, please teach us the causes." The Lord Buddha said, "When those who perform good deeds are reborn in the hells, it is because their good karma in this life has not matured, while their bad karma from time immemorial has come to fruition. Conversely, when those who create bad karma in this lifetime are reborn in the heavens, it is because their bad karma in this life has not reached maturity, while their good karma from past lives has borne fruit. Good and bad karma interact for many lifetimes before emerging. As with debts, the most important is repaid first.

Therefore the cultivator should be diligent in daily life, and not indifferent or lazy."

Thus, upon reflection, we can see that the practitioner seeking rebirth in the Pure Land should, in daily life, diligently apply himself to recitation. This will facilitate the development of one-pointedness of mind at the time of death. For this reason, if we do not routinely achieve pure recitation, we should make it a point to attend many retreats.

· Be Earnest in Seeking a Response

46) Phenomena and Principle

"Noumenon" (principle) is truth, reason, the realm of understanding and Awakening and belongs to the sphere of "essence." "Phenomena" are expedients, practices, deeds, "form," and fall under the heading of "marks." However, at the ultimate level, phenomena are noumenon, essence is mark, and both belong to the same truth-like state, all-illuminating, all-pervading. In cultivation, noumenon and phenomena are the two sides of a coin, interacting with one another and helping one another. With noumenon, we have a basis, a direction, a goal to develop into action. With phenomena, we are able to actualize what we think, demonstrate our understanding, reach our goal and, ultimately, achieve results.

Noumenon is like the eyes that watch the road. Phenomena are like the feet that set out to walk. Without eyes, or with glassy, dim eyes, it is easy to get lost. Without feet, however sharp our eyes, there is no way to reach our destination. To "have" noumenon but not phenomena is like having a map and knowing the way, but refusing to proceed. To "have" phenomena but not noumenon is like setting out on a journey with neither a guide nor a clear itinerary. To have both noumenon and phenomena is not only to know the way perfectly but also to proceed to walk. We cannot fail to reach the City of Lights.

Noumenon and phenomena, essence and marks are thus interdependent. If one factor is missing, success is illusory. However, even though the practitioner may not have experienced Awakening, if he follows the itinerary taught by the sages and cultivates, he, too, can reach the goal and succeed. Sutras, comment.ries, biographies, as well as the writings of ancient masters and advice from today's good spiritual advisors -- these constitute the itinerary. If we follow these teachings and put them into practice, we will surely achieve results. Therefore, practice without theory is not necessarily a cause for alarm. Of more concern are those who understand theory but fail to put it into practice. Verbalizing incessantly, they discourse without end about the mysterious and the wonderful, but they do not progress one step during their entire lives.

In truth, however, those who lack practice are not really in possession of theory either. Why is this so? As an analogy, if a person knows his house is on fire, yet remains inside without trying to escape, is he any different from someone who is not aware of the fire? Therefore, the Dharma can help those who are of limited capacity and understanding, but cannot save those who possess mundane intelligence and eloquence but are lacking in practice.

***

It once happened that a particularly dull-witted disciple of the Buddha named Suddipanthaka was taught only two words, "broom" and "sweep," and was asked to meditate on them. He was so stupid that when he remembered one of the words, he would immediately forget the other. However, thanks to his power of perseverance, never neglecting his cultivation even for a single moment, he ultimately became an Arhat. On the other hand, although Devadatta was more intelligent than most, fully conversant with the Dharma and possessing the five spiritual powers, he ultimately descended to the hells because of his greed for fame and fortune and his lack of true cultivation.

Thus, we can see that even though we may be versed in the Tripitaka, without actual practice, our knowledge and understanding are useless. This is because our karmic obstacles from time immemorial are still intact, not reduced in the slightest. How, then, can we hope to compare with an old, dull-witted kitchen helper, her face covered with soot, who diligently practices Buddha Recitation? One day she will reach one-pointedness of mind and be at peace, ending up seated on a lotus blossom!

Therefore, individuals who spend their entire lives seeking understanding based on reasoning grounded in forms and marks -- hoping to become Buddhist scholars while not truly cultivating -- are surely in the same position as those who can list succulent dishes but must endure hunger pangs, or those who count other people's money while remaining poor and destitute themselves. Buddha Sakyamuni compared those persons to deaf musicians playing violins for the multitude or merchants peddling all kinds of wonderful drugs while forgetting that they themselves are afflicted with many diseases.

Those who are determined to study the Dharma should pay heed to this point.

47) Buddha Recitation -- Essence and Practice

There are two aspects to Buddha Recitation -- essence and practice. According to Elder Master Ou-I:

"Buddha Recitation-practice" means believing that there is a Western Pure Land and a Lord Buddha named Amitabha, but not yet realizing that "this Mind *makes*

Buddha, this Mind *is* Buddha." It consists of resolutely seeking rebirth in the Pure Land and reciting as earnestly as a lost child longing for his mother, never forgetting her for a single moment.

"Buddha Recitation-essence," on the other hand, means believing and understanding that Lord Amitabha Buddha of the West inherently exists in full within our mind, is created by our mind, and making this sacred name -- inherently existing in full within our mind and created by our mind -- the focus of our recitation, without a moment of neglect.

In other words, "Buddha Recitation-practice" is the method of those who do not understand anything about meaning or essence, who just believe that there is a Land of Ultimate Bliss and a Buddha named Amitabha, and who fervently and earnestly recite the Buddha's name seeking rebirth there.

"Buddha Recitation-essence" is the method of those who practice in an identical manner, but who also deeply realize that the Pure Land and Lord Amitabha Buddha are all in the True Mind, manifested by the pure virtues of the True Mind.

This being so, is there a difference between Buddha Recitation-practice and Buddha Recitation-essence? Of course there is. Those who follow Buddha Recitation-practice see Amitabha Buddha as *outside the Mind*; therefore, opposing marks of subject-object still exist. Thus, such practice is not yet all-encompassing and complete. Those who practice Buddha Recitation-essence thoroughly understand the True Mind and therefore sever all marks of subject-object -- to recite is Buddha, to recite is Mind, reconciling Mind and Realm.[62]

Let me relate an anecdote. One night, a Master who is a friend of this author dreamed that a yellow-robed monk came to ask him, "You practice

Buddha Recitation, but what is Buddha?" *Answer*: "Buddha is Mind." The monk continued, "How about explaining to me what you mean by Buddha is Mind?" In his dream, the author's friend improvised the following stanzas:

> Each utterance of the Buddha's name
> following the rosary is Mind,
> Buddha is clearly Mind, why waste time
> searching for Him?
> The Buddha's sea of wisdom reconciles
> Mind and Realm!
> Mind and Buddha are born equal.

> To abandon Mind and follow the Buddha
> is to be still in a dream,
> To be attached to the Buddha as Mind
> is not yet perfect comprehension;
> Mind and Buddha are both originally
> illusory and dreamlike,
> To transcend both Buddha and Mind is to
> arrive at the perfect City of Lights.

The Master understood the essence of Buddha Recitation, reconciling the Buddha's name with the realm of the Mind.

***

There is one erroneous idea, prevalent among those who lean toward the subtle and the mysterious, which requires clarification. Many of them, emphasizing theory over practice, tend to be attached to the concept of "Amitabha as the Self-Nature, Pure Land as Mind-Only," and reject the existence of the Western Pure Land or rebirth there. These individuals explain the sutra teachings on Pure Land from the viewpoint of principle or essence, saying "Amitabha is our Buddha Nature, the Pure Land is the pure realm of the Mind, why seek it on the outside?" This is the great mistake of those who emphasize mundane, conventional reasoning.

They cling to theory (essence) while neglecting practice, prefer essence to marks, and rely on Ultimate Truth to reject the manifestations of mundane truth -- failing to realize that the two are inseparable.[23]

According to the *Treatise on the Awakening of the Faith*, the True Mind has two aspects: essence and marks. The aspect of essence is called the Door of True Thusness, the aspect of marks is the Door of Birth and Death. True Thusness is inseparable from Birth and Death; Birth and Death *are* True Thusness. This is why the Patriarch Asvaghosha called True Thusness the "truth-like Emptiness treasury" and Birth and Death the "truth-like Non-Emptiness treasury." True Thusness and Birth and Death have the same truth-like nature.

Take the great ocean as an example. We cannot accept sea water but not waves. If we were to do so, we would be wrong about the manifestations of the ocean and fail to understand truly what the ocean is. Therefore, when we abandon phenomena, noumenon cannot stand by itself; when we reject marks, essence cannot remain stable.

A great many individuals, educated in mundane ways, become afflicted with the disease of grasping at the "Truth of Emptiness" when they study Mahayana sutras, particularly those that expound the Prajna Paramita truth, which they do not fully understand. Thus, they explain sutras which elucidate phenomena and marks, such as the Pure Land Sutras or the *Ksitigarbha (Earth Store Bodhisattva) Sutra*, from the viewpoint of noumenon and principle. They mistake these "marks" sutras as expedients to guide those of limited capacities. However, in truth, they are the mistaken ones! In this connection, I will quote a few passages from the sutras, to destroy this attachment to Emptiness.

As stated in the *Heart Sutra:*

There is no wisdom, and there is no attainment whatsoever. Because there is nothing to be attained, a Bodhisattva relying on Prajna-paramita has no obstruction in his mind. Because there is no obstruction he has no fear, and he passes far beyond all confused imaginations and reaches ultimate Nirvana. The Buddhas in the past, present and future, also, by relying on the Prajna-paramita, "have" attained Supreme Enlightenment. (Sutra Translation Committee of the United States and Canada, *The Buddhist Liturgy*, p. 47)

At first, Buddha Sakyamuni, in accord with Ultimate Truth, said "there is no attainment whatsoever." Then, in accord with conventional truth, He said "the Buddhas in the past, present and future have attained Supreme Enlightenment." Seeing "attainment" is attachment to existence. Seeing "non-attainment" is to err in the direction of attachment to emptiness. Therefore, cultivators should thoroughly understand the deep meaning behind the sutras and enter the Middle Way.

In the *Diamond Sutra*, Sakyamuni Buddha stated:

Who sees Me by form,
Who seeks Me in sound,
Perverted are his footsteps upon the Way;
For he cannot perceive the Tathagatha.
(A. F. Price, tr. "The Diamond Sutra," p. 65. In *The Diamond Sutra & The Sutra of Hui Neng*.)

However, the Lord Buddha then continued:

Subhuti, do not think the opposite either that when the Tathagatha attained Supreme Enlightenment it was not by means of his possession of the thirty-two marks of physical excellence. Do not think that. Should you think that, then when you begin the practice of seeking to attain supreme enlightenment you would think that all systems of phenomena and all conceptions about phenomena are to be cut off and rejected [thus falling into nihilism]. Do not think that. And why? Because when a disciple practices seeking to attain supreme enlightenment, he should neither grasp after such arbitrary conceptions of phenomena nor reject them. (Wai-tao, tr., "The Diamond Sutra," in Goddard, ed., *A Buddhist Bible*, p. 103-4.)

First, Buddha Sakyamuni taught that we should not follow sounds, forms and marks in seeking the Way. After that, he reminded us that at the same time, we should not abandon sounds, forms and marks, nor should we destroy all dharmas. Thus, we can see that the Way belongs neither to "forms" nor to "emptiness." Clinging to either aspect is misguided. A famous Zen monk once said:

Thirty years ago, when this old monk had not yet entered the Order, he perceived rivers as rivers and mountains as mountains. After meeting good spiritual advisors who taught him how to cultivate, he saw rivers as not-rivers and mountains as not-mountains. Now that he has seen the Way and reached the state of still emptiness, he realizes that rivers have always been rivers and mountains have always been mountains.

A Zen poet, Su Tung P'o, expressed the same idea:

The sound of the stream is the Buddhas' vast
long tongue,
The shape of the mountain is intrinsically the
pure Dharma body.

The meaning of the poem is that forms, marks and sounds are intrinsically the Great Way. We should understand them with a non-discriminating mind, neither clinging to them nor rejecting them to seek Enlightenment in the realm of hollow emptiness [which is contrary to True Emptiness]. Therefore, the phrase, "Self-Nature Amitabha, Mind-Only Pure Land" is not a denial of the Pure Land or Amitabha Buddha, but is rather an expression that gathers marks toward essence, brings "function" toward nature, to manifest the ultimate truth of the Void. In this ultimate truth, even Buddhas do not exist, let alone other dharmas.

The ancients have said:

Although theory can be understood in a flash, practice should be carried out step by step.

Even in Zen, which is said to be a "direct method," as long as we have to sit in meditation, or gather our mind, or meditate on a koan or enter and exit samadhi, we are still within the sphere of expedients. Moreover, in the metaphysical realm, there are many levels of attainment. Not until we have reached the stage of non-cultivation can we dispense with expedients and really proclaim that all dharmas are empty. *If we have not reached that stage,* even a small thing like a mote of dust is real; we still feel warm near a fire or cold in the midst of frost and we still feel pain when a small thorn pricks our body -- how, then, can we say that all dharmas are non-existent and void?

Therefore, those who like to advance lofty and wonderful propositions, such as "Amitabha is the Self-Nature, the Pure Land is Mind Only," and go on to reject the actual practice of Buddha Recitation will find themselves in the predicament of "destroying the boat before stepping ashore." There is no way such persons can avoid drowning. On the contrary, since ancient times, those who have thoroughly understood essence have always paid particular attention to practice -- because practice symbolizes essence.

The ancients have said:

Only those endowed with wisdom can reconcile the essence and marks of Buddha Recitation and truly understand it in an exhaustive manner. Otherwise, we had better grasp at marks in our cultivation; the more we do so, the more effective our practice will be.

This is because the more we cling to forms, the more earnest is our determination to achieve rebirth in the Pure Land. Once reborn there, we will surely be awakened to the True Mark. The subject of phenomena and noumenon, essence and marks can be discussed *ad infinitum.* However, if we can understand it, we understand everything. I sincerely hope that fellow cultivators will skillfully reflect on this question to avoid being misled while treading the Way.

***

When the author had reached this point in the manuscript, a visiting lay Buddhist asked, "I have heard a number of fairly accomplished Zen Masters say, 'The intelligent should just concentrate their minds and have pure thoughts, without wasting their time and effort to follow the illusion of Buddha Recitation. Let us leave the vehicle empty so that it can run light, not weigh it down with excess baggage!' I have heard such reasoning but do not know how to reply. I wish you could elucidate the matter."

Answer: The aim of Zen is True Thusness Samadhi. The goal of Pure Land is the Buddha Recitation Samadhi. True Thusness Samadhi is like gold bullion, while Buddha Recitation Samadhi is similar to gold necklaces, bracelets, and other pieces of jewelry. All contain the basic metal gold. Therefore, when we have attained Buddha Recitation Samadhi, we have attained True Thusness Samadhi as well. True Thusness Samadhi centers on wisdom; Buddha Recitation Samadhi encompasses not only wisdom but merit and virtue as well. This is because the Pure Land practitioner not only bases himself on pure one-pointedness of mind, he receives the virtues derived from reciting the Buddha's name in addition. However, neither True Thusness Samadhi nor Buddha Recitation Samadhi can be attained in one lifetime; they are the results of many eons of continuous practice. This is particularly true in this Dharma-Ending Age.

Thus, while Buddha Recitation Samadhi is the aim of the Pure Land method, it is not the primary one. The principal and essential goal is to achieve rebirth in the Pure Land within one lifetime so as to reach the stage of non-retrogression. *This is what sets Pure Land apart from other schools and gives it its name.*

This is precisely why many Zen Masters, having awakened to the Way but realizing that Supreme Enlightenment is still far away, change direction and adopt Buddha Recitation seeking rebirth in the Pure Land. Although painstaking, reciting the Buddha's name and bowing to images of the Buddhas bring additional merits and virtues, a result of the cultivation of the two karmas of body and speech.

Take the example of a truck returning to the capital from the mountain town of Dalat. If, after discharging its cargo, the truck returns empty, it will, of course, be lighter. However, if it can load up with vegetables and other produce, the truck will not only be back in the capital, its owners will, in addition, have a cargo of produce. Earning additional merits and blessings through the diligent and painstaking efforts of Buddha Recitation is a natural cause and effect occurrence -- where is the loss? However, any hardship, if it does occur, will only be felt in the beginning stages of Buddha Recitation. When recitation has become second nature, reaching the level of No-Mind, all hardship will have vanished!

48) One-Pointedness of Mind -- Theory and Practice

The practitioner of Buddha Recitation should strive earnestly to achieve a dual goal. *Internally*, he should eliminate all marks of right and wrong, mine and yours, becoming oblivious to body and mind. *Externally*, he should completely sever the marks of Emptiness, form and the Six Dusts, to the point where he no longer grasps at external realms -- only the sacred name of Amitabha Buddha remains before him.

This utmost exertion of effort was best described by the ancients with the following image:

In front of him are ferocious tigers, behind a pack of wolves, on the left a high mountainside, on the right a deep precipice. In such a situation, in which direction should the practitioner escape?

The Pure Land School expresses the same idea with the words:

The seven-jewelled lotus pond is in front of him, the cauldron of boiling oil above the fire pit is behind him; the Buddha Recitation practitioner should proceed straight ahead.

If the practitioner does not see any sign of progress, it is because he himself lacks strong will and is lazy. In this connection, an Elder Master once sternly admonished the assembly:

The way people today seek the Dharma is cause for
                  lamentation,
Still outside the door, they are puzzled in so many
                  ways!
Thinking they have reached the Sage-Emperor's jade
                  city,
They have in fact stopped mid-way, at the mountain
                  pass!

***

If the practitioner exerts the utmost effort without interruption, he will, in time, arrive at the realm of one-pointedness of mind. This sphere of undivided attentiveness has two levels, superficial and subtle, called the level of phenomena and the level of noumenon.

What is one-pointedness of mind at the level of phenomena?

When the practitioner gives undivided attention to the sacred name of Amitabha Buddha, all sundry thoughts are, in time, eliminated. Whether he is reclining or sitting, walking or standing, only the sacred name appears before him. At that point, he has reached the realm of one-pointedness of mind at the level of phenomena. This is the concentration realm of the Pure Land practitioner, equivalent to the level of "phenomena-concentration" in Zen.

What is one-pointedness of mind at the noumenon level?

If we go a step beyond the level of phenomena and exert our utmost efforts, one day our mind will be completely empty, we will completely escape the dust of the senses and become awakened to the True Mark. At that time, the present moment is the Western Pure Land -- and this does not contradict the specific existence of the Land of Ultimate Bliss; our nature is Amitabha Buddha -- and this does not contradict the specific existence of the Lord Amitabha Buddha. This is the realm of "one-pointedness of mind, noumenon level," the realm of "concentration-wisdom being one and thus" of the Pure Land practitioner. This stage is equivalent to the level of Great Awakening in Zen.

Elder Master Ou-I elucidated the question of one-pointedness of mind in the following way:

Regardless of whether we practice recitation at the noumenon or phenomena level, if we recite to the point where afflictions are subdued and Delusions of Views and Delusions of Thought no longer arise, this is the realm of one- pointedness of mind at the level of phenomena. Regardless of whether we practice at the noumenon or phenomena level, if we recite to the point where the mind is awakened and we clearly see the original Buddha Nature, this is the realm of one-pointedness of mind at the noumenon level. At the level of phenomena, we are no longer disturbed by delusions of view and delusions of thought; at the noumenon level we are no longer disturbed by dualities (that is, existence/non-existence, extinction/permanence, etc.).

Thus, one-pointedness of mind is not an easy thing for people today to achieve, even at the level of phenomena, let alone at the level of noumenon. However, thanks to the virtues obtained through recitation and earnest practice, each utterance erases one part of delusion and engenders one part of merit and wisdom, gradually and naturally leading us to rebirth in an auspicious realm. If we practice in that manner over a long period of time, why worry about not reaching the stage where each thought awakens and enlightens, leading to auspicious realms? This idea is expressed in the phrase "each time a new thought arises, a new realm appears."

Therefore, even though we possess only the limited capacities of sentient beings in the Dharma-Ending Age, if we truly exert ourselves, one-pointedness of mind, both at the phenomena and noumenon levels, is not necessarily beyond our reach.

Various Realms Viewed by Earnest Practioners

49) Internal Realms

If we are not diligent and do not exert efforts along the path of cultivation, nothing usually happens; however, if we are diligent and exert a great deal of effort, we will definitely witness different realms. They either come from within the mind or are caused by

outside sources.   I will speak first about the realms
originating from the mind, called internal realms.

Internal realms are also called "realms of the
Self-Mind" because they do not come from outside, but
develop from the mind.   Those who do not clearly
understand the truth that "the ten thousand dharmas are
created by the mind," think that all realms come from
the outside.   This is wrong.   When the practitioner
reaches the stage of mutual interpenetration [of mind
and realms], completely severing external conditions, the
seeds of latent dharmas in the Alaya consciousness
suddenly manifest themselves.   For the Buddha
Recitation or mantra-chanting practitioner, the power of
the Buddha's name or the mantra penetrates deep into
the mind, eliciting a reaction from the wholesome or
evil seeds in the Alaya consciousness. The realms that
result are very complex and usually appear in dreams, or
even when the practitioner is awake and striving to
recite the Buddha's name. In Buddhism, this condition
is called "changing manifestations of the Alaya
consciousness."

Dreaming scenes

If the events or scenes result from evil seeds, the
practitioner, in his dreams, may see various species of
worms crawling out of his body, or witness himself, night
after night, removing from his body six or seven
loathesome creatures with many limbs, such as scorpions
or centipedes. Or else, he may see various species of
wild animals and/or spirits or ghosts. Such realms are
innumerable and cannot all be described!

In general, individuals greatly afflicted with greed,
who are miserly and wicked, usually see marks of men
and women,[63] snakes and serpents and odd species with
white features and forms. Those harboring a great deal
of anger and resentment usually see tigers and leopards
or strange species with red forms and features. Those

who are heavily deluded usually see domestic animals, clams, oysters, snails or different species with black forms and features. The above, however, is merely indicative; it does not mean that everything will be exactly as described.

If the scenes in his dreams come from good, wholesome seeds, the practitioner sees tall trees and exotic flowers, beautiful scenery, brightly adorned with nets of pearls.[64] Or else, he sees himself eating succulent, fragrant food, wearing ethereal garments, dwelling in palaces of diamonds and other precious substances, or flying high in open space.

Thus, in summary, all the seeds of the ten Dharma Realms are found in the minds of sentient beings. If wholesome seeds manifest themselves, practitioners view the realms of Buddhas, Bodhisattvas, human and celestial beings; if evil karma is manifested, they witness scenes from the wretched three Evil Paths. If the cultivator has followed externalist ways in lives past, he usually sees his body emitting electric waves, or his soul leaving the body to roam, meeting demons, ghosts and the like, to discuss politics and the rise and fall of countries and empires.[65] On the other hand, when the practitioner's mind is pure, he will know in his dreams about events that will occur three or four days, or seven or eight months, hence. In general, those who have cultivated in previous lives will immediately see auspicious realms when reciting the Buddha's name. Those with heavy karma, lacking merit and virtue, will usually see evil realms when they begin Buddha Recitation. In time, these evil omens will disappear and gradually be replaced with auspicious omens.

Waking scenes

If the practitioner's efforts have reached a high enough level, there are times during his waking hours when all deluded feelings suddenly cease for a while, body and mind being at ease and free. At other times, the practitioner may recite for four or five hours but feel that the time was very short, perhaps two or three minutes. Or else, at times during recitation, wholesome omens will appear. At other times, unconsciously, his mind experiences great contentment and bliss. Sometimes, he realizes for a split second that mind and realm are both empty. At other times, just by hearing or seeing something once, he becomes awakened to the truth of suffering, emptiness, impermanence and No-Self, completely severing the marks of self and others. These occurrences are too numerous to be fully described!

A layman was once reciting the Buddha's name while seated in the dark. Suddenly, he saw two types of flowers, red ones and white ones, springing up all over the floor, reaching as high as the edge of his bed; meanwhile, other flowers were dropping like rain from the sky. Another layman, while kneeling down to recite the Buddha's name, suddenly saw a red lotus flower appear before the altar, its bud gradually opening up and disappearing after a few minutes.

There was yet another layman who, during recitation, would suddenly see everything around him disappear. In front of his eyes would appear the scene of an immense ocean, calm and still, with no wind or waves whatsoever; countless huge, multicolored lotus blossoms would spring up on the ocean surface. Afterward, the ocean scene would disappear, to be replaced by scenes of mountains, with verdant herbs and flowers, luxuriant century-old trees, and, by and by, a temple complex, sumptuous and magnificent. Then the temple and mountains would disappear, to be replaced by scenes of jewelled nets coming together then drawing apart, drawing apart then coming together again. There are, in general, many such scenes, which the author has heard fellow-cultivators describe and which he has recounted here as examples.

Visionary scenes such as the above, called "internal realms" or "realms of the Self-Mind," have their origin in a thought of peace and stillness, or are caused by wholesome seeds generated by Buddha or Mantra Recitation. They appear suddenly and are lost immediately. The practitioner should not be attached to them, thinking that they are real, nor should he remember them fondly. It is a very great mistake to develop nostalgia for them, thinking how ethereal, calm and peaceful, beautiful and well-adorned they were, then day-dream about them, unable to forget them, longing for their reappearance. The ancients have criticized such thoughts as "scratching in advance and waiting for the itch." This is because these scenes have their origin in diligent exertion and appear temporarily. They have no true existence. We should realize that when the practitioner exerts a certain level of effort, the scenes and features particular to that level will appear naturally.

Take the example of a traveller who views different scenery as he passes along various stretches of the road. If he has not reached home, yet develops such an attachment and fondness for a particular scene along the road that he refuses to proceed, his travel will be impeded. He will then be helplessly lost in the midst of his journey, not knowing when he will finally return home to rest. The practitioner is like that traveller; if he becomes attached to and fond of temporary realms and scenes he will never attain the true realms. Were he to dream of them to the point of insanity, he would be destroyed by demons and waste an entire lifetime of practice!

The *Diamond Sutra* states:

Everything in this world that has marks is illusory; to see marks as not marks is to see the Tathagata.

"Everything that has marks" refers here to compounded, conditioned dharmas. Those marks cannot be said either to exist or not to exist, or to be true or false. Delusions arise precisely because unenlightened sentient beings discriminate, become attached and think that these marks exist or do not exist, are real or are false. Even the fondness which some Zen practitioners develop for samadhi (upon entering concentration and experiencing this immense, empty, still, transparent, peaceful and free realm) falls into the category of "having marks." The same is true when these practitioners, once awakened to a certain lofty, transcendental principle, joyfully grasp at it. Once there are marks, there is delusion.

"To see marks" means to see such marks as auspicious/evil, good/bad, dirty/clean, existent/ non-existent, Buddha/sentient beings, even the realms of the Five Skandas or the Six Dusts, etc.

"As not marks" means seeing but neither becoming attached to nor rejecting them -- just letting everything be. Why should we not reject them? It is because marks, while illusory, are *not* non-existent. This is not unlike the reflection of the moon in the water. Although the reflected moon is not real, this does not mean that there is no illusory mark of moonlight. Therefore, if we see marks appear while we are cultivating, we should disregard them and redouble our efforts, just like the traveller, who views varied scenery en route but must push forward to reach home quickly.

"To see the Tathagata" is to see the original Buddha Nature, to see the Way.

***

In summary, all states of mind, from those described above to the state of one-pointedness of mind, belong to the category of "internal realms." These realms have two aspects: "attainment-like" and "partial attainment." "Attainment-like" realms appear temporarily and disappear immediately. "Partial attainment" realms are those that once achieved, we have forever, because we have actually attained a part of True Thusness. Regardless of whether it is internal or external, if it is "attainment-like" it is not a True Realm; it is merely a full understanding of some of the manifestations of the True Mind.

Practitioners who truly seek liberation should not confuse these aspects, taking attainment-like marks for the True Realm. Attainment-like marks are like a dark, leaden sky which suddenly clears, thanks to the winds which temporarily push away the dark clouds, letting a few rays of sunlight through before the sky becomes overcast again. They also resemble the "mark" of smoke just before the fire, that people used to get when they rubbed two pieces of wood together.

The True Realm can be likened to the bright sunlight in a clear and calm sky. It is like rubbing pieces of wood together and already having fire. However, we should not underestimate attainment-like marks, as they demonstrate the genuine existence of the True Realm. If, from that level, we diligently redouble our efforts, the True Realm is not that far away after all.

50) External Realms

External realms are realms which are not created by the mind, but come from the outside. For example, some practitioners might see Buddhas and Bodhisattvas appearing before them, preaching the Dharma, exhorting and praising them. Others, while reciting the Buddha's name, suddenly experience an awakening and immediately see the Land of Ultimate Bliss. Some practitioners, in the midst of their pure recitation, see deities and Immortals arrive, join hands and circumambulate them respectfully, or invite them for a

Seek Response > 199 <

leisurely stroll. Still other practitioners see "wandering souls of the dead" arrive, seeking to "take refuge" with them. Yet others, having reached a high level in their practice, have to endure challenges and harassment from external demons.

For example, there was once a layman of rather dull capacities who constantly worshipped the Bodhisattva Avalokitesvara. During a dream one night, he saw the Bodhisattva urging him to meditate on the following stanza, and in time he would experience a Great Awakening:

Great wisdom develops from the Mind,
Where in the Mind can it be found?
To realize all meanings,
Is to have neither past nor present.

Another story concerns a nun of the author's acquaintance who was cultivating in the vicinity of Dalat. After her Buddha Recitation session, as she was seated in meditation, she saw two men of noble countenance, dressed like deities or Immortals, respectfully inviting her to scale the mountains and visit their beautiful grounds. In her samadhi, she asked them, "How can I go, when the mountains are so high and I am so weak?" One of the men said, "Do not worry, I have a way." He then touched her lightly with something similar to a willow branch and requested her to follow him. She suddenly saw her body glide effortlessly over the grass, and, in no time, she was scaling the mountains. There she witnessed ethereal scenes, with gigantic trees and a palace and tower in the distance. At that very moment, a companion in the back room dropped something with a bang. The nun suddenly awakened from meditation. All scenes had disappeared but her thighs were still aching from overexertion.

***

The realms and manifestations summarized above are called "external realms." Some might ask, "To see Buddhas and lotus blossoms -- is it not to see demonic apparitions?"

Answer: If cause and effect coincide, these are not "demonic realms." This is because the Pure Land method belongs to the Dharma Door of Existence; when Pure Land practitioners first set out to cultivate, they enter the Way through forms and marks and seek to view the celestial scenes of the Western Pure Land. When they actually witness these auspicious scenes, it is only a matter of effects corresponding to causes. If cause and effect are in accord, how can these be "demonic realms"?

In the Zen School, on the other hand, the practitioner enters the Way through the Dharma Door of Emptiness. Right from the beginning of his cultivation he wipes out all marks -- even the marks of the Buddhas or the Dharma are destroyed. The Zen practitioner does not seek to view the Buddhas or the lotus blossoms, yet the marks of the Buddhas or the lotus blossoms appear to him. Therefore, cause and effect do not correspond. For something to appear without a corresponding cause is indeed the realm of the demons. Thus, the Zen practitioner always holds the sword of wisdom aloft. If the demons come, he kills the demons, if the Buddha comes, he kills the Buddha -- to enter the realm of True Emptiness is not to tolerate a single mark.

A caveat: we are only talking here about novice cultivators. High-level Zen practitioners do sometimes see various marks which are not demonic realms. When their minds become enlightened, Zen Masters who have practiced meditation for many eons can see evil as well as transcendental realms, including the pure and defiled lands of the ten directions. This is because all worlds are within the light of the True Mind. On the other hand, despite what we have said earlier, Buddha Recitation practitioners sometimes see various marks which are "demonic realms," as will be explained later.

In short, when we refer to "internal" and "external" realms, we are speaking at the level of beginning cultivators. For those who have attained the Way, Mind is realm, realm is Mind, the ten thousand dharmas and ourselves have but one common Nature. There is no inside or outside at all.

51) Discussion on Demonic Realms

As indicated above, sometimes the Buddha Recitation practitioner sees marks and forms which could actually be demonic realms. These are instances where cause and effect do not correspond. For example, while visualizing the physical features of Amitabha Buddha, a practitioner may suddenly see the features of a beautiful woman. Another cultivator, diligently reciting the Buddha's name in the hope of seeing auspicious scenes of the Pure Land, may unexpectedly see a slum area, with men, women and domestic animals running back and forth in all directions. Yet another practitioner, hoping to see precious lotus blossoms in the Pure Land, suddenly sees a small cart instead. These are demonic realms, as cause and effect do not correspond.

There are five criteria that can help us determine which events are real and which belong to the demonic realms.

1. Instances where cause and effect do not correspond (such as visualizing one mark but seeing another, hoping to see one realm but seeing another), as well as scenes and realms that do not resemble those described in the sutras, are all demonic realms.

2. Buddhas and Bodhisattvas have pure compassion; therefore, even if they take the appearance of "demons" to test us, we still feel calm, at peace and pure. Demons, on the contrary, are inherently evil and wicked; thus, even when they take the appearance of Buddhas and Bodhisattvas, we feel agitated, angry and uneasy.

3. The Buddhas' light makes us feel calm and refreshed; it has neither shadow nor a blinding effect on the eye. The light of demons, on the other hand, affects our eyes and makes us feel agitated rather than calm and peaceful; it also has shadows. The reference to the Buddhas' light in the *Lankavatara Sutra* illustrates this point.

4. The teachings of the Buddhas and Bodhisattvas are in accord with the sutras and the truth. The words of demons are contrary to the truth and not in line with the sutras' teachings.

5. When an auspicious mark appears, the practitioner who wishes to test it need only concentrate on reciting the *Heart Sutra* with a pure mind, or reciting a mantra or the Buddha's name with one-pointedness of mind. If the mark really is auspicious, the more he recites, the clearer it becomes, because genuine gold is not harmed by fire. If it belongs to the demonic realm, it disappears as he recites, because evil can never withstand the truth.

We should judge events by all five of the above criteria, not just one or two. This is because there are many celestial demons, externalist deities and Immortals who want to lead us their way and therefore falsely take the appearance of Buddhas and Bodhisattvas preaching the Dharma. Although their cultivation is not the ultimate Way leading to liberation, they may have good karma or a fairly high level of samadhi. Thus, their "light" can also make us feel refreshed and peaceful.

Moreover, their teachings at times also encourage the performance of good deeds, keeping the precepts, vegetarianism and Buddha Recitation. However, they diverge from the Buddhist sutras on certain crucial points [such as the need to escape Birth and Death]. Only by exercising careful judgement and understanding the Dharma in depth are we able to know.

For example, certain externalist deities urge vegetarianism and Buddha Recitation, but teach that the sacred words should be visualized as circulating throughout the body -- this, they say, is "turning the Dharma wheel," to release blockages in the energy system. This is the preaching of externalist demons.

There are also demons who take the appearance of Elder Masters and say, "Buddha statues made of bronze or cement cannot vanquish water, because they sink in water; Buddha statues made of wood or paper cannot vanquish fire, because they would burn. Only the Mind-Buddha cannot be destroyed by anything. You need only cultivate the Mind-Buddha, striving to make it pure; there is no need to cultivate body and speech. Therefore, even 'eating meat and drinking wine, lusting and begetting children' [in the case of monks and nuns] are of no consequence. Cultivating body and speech through such restrictive, ascetic practices as precept-keeping, vegetarianism, Sutra, Mantra and Buddha Recitation is of no use and brings no benefit!" This is a typical teaching of some spirits of long years' standing or demons of sexual lust.

There are some types of demon who have reached a fairly high level of attainment and can use their powers of concentration to help the practitioner reach a state of samadhi for a period of seven or twenty-one days. However, their teaching does not lead to ultimate liberation and, in the end, cannot transcend the cycle of ego-attachment.

Ancient masters have said:

> When we see demons yet remain undisturbed, the demons self-destruct; when we see ghosts yet remain undisturbed, the ghosts are vanquished.

This saying means: if we see demons and ghosts but our minds are unmoved and unafraid, holding fast to correct thoughts or singlemindedly reciting the Buddha's name, these demons and ghosts cannot hurt us in any way, and will leave of their own accord.

Not only should we act in such a manner when seeing demons, but even when we achieve some results or see auspicious marks during cultivation, we should not be moved to astonishment, sadness or joy. It is as if we had lost a diamond at the bottom of the lake and because the water was murky, we were unable to recover it despite our best efforts. However, once the water became still and transparent, we found it. Since the diamond had always belonged to us, why should we have been astonished and happy? If the cultivator's mind is not calm and peaceful and is overly given to sorrowful compassion, he will be harmed by the demon of sorrow and cry all the time. If he is given to too much happiness, he will be harmed by the demon of happiness and laugh all the time, as though insane.

Thus, although the Pure Land practitioner may also hope to see transcendental realms and scenes, he should not long for or dream of them too much, because to recite is already to seek. He should be calm and "seek but not seek, not seek but seek," so as to avoid disturbing his mind. He should just earnestly recite the Buddha's name and in time, when the power of his recitation is pure, there will be a response and he will witness auspicious realms. To continuously seek and hope for them is deluded thought which brings harm.

***

Long ago in China there was a layman who had engaged in meditation for some thirty years. One day, he suddenly attained the faculty of transcendental vision. At the beginning, he would see through walls; later on, he could see things within a few dozen miles as clearly as though they were in front of his eyes. Realizing that he had achieved "transcendental vision," he was very astonished and happy! As time went on, he was not only able to "see" but also "hear" the voices of human beings and animals from far away. This is transcendental hearing, which develops after transcendental vision. As time went by, he could see and hear things that occurred within a radius of several thousand miles. Still later, he was able to predict future events. Thus, he "knew" in advance of a war between two neighboring kingdoms and "witnessed" the pitiful sight of countless dead and dying among the populace. He was so moved that he would weep and lament to whomever he met, "A great, violent uprising is going to occur. There will be massacres and utter misery. The people deserve pity and compassion. How can they be helped?"

At the time, everyone who heard him thought he was insane. Later on, however, war and rebellion did occur as he had predicted. Even when the disturbances were over, he continued to go around lamenting. A respected master once commented:

> This is a case of possession by the "demons of sorrow and sadness." The cultivator who has reached a certain high level of practice suddenly develops "transcendental vision." He should reflect it toward the Self-Nature, not letting worldly Dusts move and disturb his mind. He should realize that these psychic powers have always been in his possession and should therefore not be unduly happy or astonished or consider them strange and wonderful occurrences.

Another story concerns the eminent Chinese Zen

Master Nan-Ch'uan:

The master was meditating in a hut next to a river. One night he heard two ghosts conversing. One of them was rejoicing that his term was coming to an end because the next day someone would be replacing him. The second ghost asked, "Who will be replacing you?" He replied, "A man wearing an iron hat." The master wondered to himself who this person could be. The next day there was heavy rain and the river rose to a higher level. The master looked out of his hut and saw a man about to cross the river. He had covered his head with a wok for protection against the rain. Immediately, the master knew that this was the man of the iron hat, so he cautioned him saying, "Don't cross the river today. It's too dangerous." The man asked, "Why?" "Because the water is very deep and running rapidly." The man listened to the old monk's advice and returned home.

You must understand that in Chinese lore, water ghosts are prisoners until another person drowns and takes their place. That night as he was meditating, the master heard the two ghosts again. This time the first ghost was complaining, "I have been stuck here for so many years, and I thought my chance for freedom had finally come. But now the old monk interfered and messed everything up. I'll show him what I can do." (Sheng-yen, *Faith in Mind*, p. 64.)

Upon hearing this exchange, the master immediately entered samadhi. He saw the demons enter, exit and go around his hut, as if searching for someone. However, thanks to the fact that his mind in samadhi was empty and still, "not influenced by the environment, no longer tied to mental objects," the demons could not see him. Discouraged, they finally left.

Of the two stories in this section, the first illustrates the danger of succumbing to the influence of demons while the second points to the way of overcoming their influence. I have recounted them here for the benefit of fellow-cultivators.

52) Various Types of Demons

The author had just finished drafting the previous three sections when he was visited by a Dharma master who requested him to elaborate on the different types of demons for the benefit of fellow-cultivators. In the three previous sections he has, in fact, given a general explanation of the different realms, including those of demons. If the cultivator has understood the main idea, he can keep his mind undisturbed and counteract all harmful occurrences. However, to comply with this request, the author will describe the different types of demons in greater detail, as follows.

"Demons" are called "mara" in Sanskrit. In Chinese, the word has the connotation of "murderer" because demons usually plunder the virtues and murder the wisdom-life of cultivators. "Demons" also represent the destructive conditions or influences that cause practitioners to retrogress in their cultivation. Demons can render cultivators insane, making them lose their right thought, develop erroneous views, commit evil karma and end up sunk in the lower realms.

Those activities which develop virtue and wisdom and lead sentient beings to Nirvana are called Buddha work. Those activities which destroy good roots, causing sentient beings to suffer and revolve in the cycle of Birth and Death, are called demonic actions. The longer a practitioner cultivates, and the higher his level of attainment, the more he discovers how wicked, cunning and powerful the demons are. Although there are numerous demons, they can be divided into three types: demons of afflictions, external demons and celestial demons.

A) Demons of afflictions

These demons represent the afflictions of greed, anger, resentment, delusion, contempt, doubt and wrong views. They also include the demons of the Five Skandas, the Six Entrances, the Twelve Sense Fields [eyes, forms, ears ...] and the Eighteen Elements. These demons are also called "internal" as they are created by topsy-turvy, delusive states of mind. Therefore, they must be overcome by the bright, enlightened mind.

The human mind is easily moved, developing afflictions not only because of personal karma but also because of the common karma of living in an environment filled to a great extent with beings subject to evil karma. Some persons cannot resist the attractions of the five Dusts and thus fall into evil ways. Others, encountering adverse conditions, grow sad and mournful and lose their determination to progress. Such developments, depending on their severity, render the cultivator despondent, indignant and ill, or worse still, cause him to abandon the Buddhist Order or even to commit suicide out of despair. More harmful still, they can lead to loss of respect and good will toward other cultivators, sometimes even hatred and avoidance of clergy and lay people alike. Loss of faith in cause and effect, bad karma and finally, descent upon the three Evil Paths are the end result.

To counteract these demons, the practitioner should reflect that all afflictions are illusory, upsetting, suffocating, binding, evil and conducive only to suffering for both himself and others. To eliminate afflictions is to return to the True Mind, free and liberated, fresh and tranquil, bright and clear, happy and at peace, transcendental and wondrous. The cultivator should also meditate in the same way on all attachments, from the Five Skandas to the Eighteen Elements. In the *Lotus Sutra*, Sakyamuni Buddha said:

You should not be greedy and attached to gross and vile forms, sound, smell, taste, touch and dharmas. If you do, they will burn you up.

The Bodhisattva Manjusri once asked a female deity, "How do you see the Eighteen Elements?" The deity replied, "They are similar to the eonic fire burning up the whole world." These are words of warning, reminding us to eliminate the demons of afflictions.

If the demons of afflictions (internal demons) are not subdued, they will attract "external demons" which wreak havoc. The ancients have said:

If behind the door there are mean-spirited people, mean-spirited people will arrive at the door; if behind the door there are virtuous, superior people, noble superior people will arrive at the door.

Furthermore, when thieves try to enter a house through the side door, if the owner calmly scolds them in a loud voice, they will naturally be frightened and leave. If, on the other hand, he is terrified and panic-stricken, and begs them to desist, he will unwittingly be inviting them into his house.

B) External demons

"External demons" take the form of various spirits, ghosts and deities. Once the cultivator has reached a certain level of attainment, he will be subject to demonic disturbances which will put him to the test. External demons may be divided into three groups.

1. Terrorizing Demons

These are ghosts that like to frighten and terrorize people. They usually take the form of tigers, wolves, deadly serpents, poisonous snakes or other ferocious beasts or hallucinatory, diabolic apparitions to scare the cultivator. Their forms change *ad infinitum*. They may have no head or many heads, many hands, many eyes, or a half-human, half-bestial body. They may brandish weapons or spit fire. If the practitioner is frightened, he loses his right thought and often goes insane.

Faced with these occurrences, we should reflect that all forms and marks are illusory, and that demons can only destroy the illusory body, not the True Mind. Meditating this way, we should remain calm and unafraid of death, peacefully concentrating on Buddha or Mantra Recitation. The demons will then retreat of their own accord.

2. Demons of Lust and Attachment

These are a type of demon which excites a range of emotions, from lust to delusive attachment to the realm of the five Dusts [i.e., this world]. They take the appearance of alluring, nude men and women or of parents, siblings or close relatives, as well as of Buddhas and Bodhisattvas with beautiful, adorned features, in order to entice the practitioner. If he is fond of good food, these demons bring him succulent, fragrant dishes. If he likes diamonds or gold, they take the appearance of strange animals holding precious stones in their mouths as offerings. They cause whatever the practitioner desires to appear. They can also use their psychic power to lead him into evil samadhi, evil wisdom and eloquence, giving him the mystic power to know the past and the future.

Those who do not understand will mistake these occurrences for evidence that the practitioner has attained Enlightenment, and thus believe in and trust him. In reality, however, the cultivator's mind is upside down and he spends all his time engaging in errant, demonic practices to deceive others.

Once there was a Vietnamese monk cultivating at a

deserted temple in Laos. In one of his meditation sessions, he saw a group of beautiful, ethereal women, all naked, holding hands and dancing around. The monk, unable to calm his agitated mind, immediately recited the Buddha's name in all earnestness. Only then did this scene disappear.

Another story: Once, in China, there was a monk seated in meditation. Because he was cold and hungry, the thought of food arose in his mind. He suddenly saw a woman presenting him with an offering of food. The woman knelt, put food in his bowl, and respectfully asked him to eat immediately, before the food grew cold and lost all taste. The monk, being hungry wanted to eat at once but remembering that it was not yet noon [the prescribed mealtime for monks and nuns], he patiently told her to put the bowl aside for the time being. The woman left, appearing angry and upset. Some time later, at noon, he uncovered the bowl to discover that it was full of worms, crawling all around. He then understood that his false thought of food had attracted the demonic apparitions. Thanks to his power of concentration, however limited, he avoided consuming the dirty food and violating the precept against killing.

Yet another story concerns a Zen monk who practiced in a deserted mountain area. Lonely and isolated, he had a deluded thought, wishing to have some fellow-cultivators practicing along with him to make life more bearable. Immediately, an old woman appeared from nowhere, leading two beautiful young girls by the hand, who, she said, lived in the village down in the valley. They had come, they claimed, to seek guidance in the Way. The monk, unsuspicious, immediately gave a Dharma talk to the group. One day, after many such visits over a period of time, the old woman respectfully requested that the two girls be allowed to become attendants to the monk and relieve him of his daily chores. The monk, hearing this, became suspicious. He reprimanded the old woman severely and refused the offer. The three women left, apparently angry and ashamed.

The monk, intrigued, followed them discreetly until they disappeared around a bend in the road. When he reached the spot, he found it was a dead end with no habitation or anything else around, except for three very old trees, one big tree and two smaller ones. He thought it over and realized that he had been "tested." A fleeting thought occurred to him, that he should cut down the trees, start a bonfire, and burn them to the ground. At that moment, the three women reappeared, repentant, begging him to forgive them and spare their lives.

Therefore, the cultivator should remember: when the mind is still, all realms are calm; when delusion arises, demons are born.

3. Nuisance Demons

This type of demon concentrates on harassing and disturbing the practitioner. There is a certain species of spirits and ghosts which can be subdivided into many types, each appearing at a fixed time of the day. In general, each hour has three types of spirits ... For example, during the period between seven and nine in the morning, they take the appearance of dragons, fish and serpent-like creatures.

In his commentary *Samatha and Vipassana for Beginners*, the Patriarch Chih-I mentioned a type of demon with a face like a pear-shaped lute, four eyes and two mouths, which enjoys disturbing cultivators. Waiting for the individual to begin practice, it takes the form of worms or tiny insects and crawls all over his head and face, penetrates into his mouth, nose, eyes and ears, or goes under his armpits or belly to sting him. At other times it shouts loudly into the practitioner's ears, creating a great disturbance and giving him a headache; or it suddenly embraces him tightly. If the practitioner attempts to seize it in return, nothing is there. This type of nuisance demon also causes scenes of the five Dusts to appear, either favorable or unfavorable, or neither favorable nor unfavorable. Such transformations are countless and can cause the practitioner to become agitated. As he does not know what to make of all this, he loses his concentration. The general way to subdue these nuisance demons is to "gather" the mind in correct samadhi, or diligently recite mantras or the Buddha's name -- they will then all disappear.

***

Speaking more broadly, the category of "external demons" also includes demons belonging to externalist cults and other false or quasi-Buddhist sects. According to the observations of this author and many of his colleagues, practitioners who have belonged to cults in this or previous lives but have now converted to Buddhism, as well as those who are themselves Buddhists but who come from families formerly active in other faiths and cults, tend to be bothered by external demons. This is because the cultivation methods of externalists are within the realm of worldly afflictions and are tainted with pride, ego attachment, power and fame. Therefore, they stick together and do not want people connected with them in some way to follow other teachings.

A case in point is a friend of the author, a Buddhist monk of gentle and peaceful disposition, who was continuously disturbed by externalist demons during his cultivation. Unfortunately, because of his "externalist" past seeds, he did not apply the Dharma wholeheartedly, but went instead from place to place, seeking help from externalists. In the end, he strayed completely from Buddhism. While taking the outside appearance of a Buddhist monk, he spent all his time "balancing energy currents" while denigrating such practices as bowing to the Buddhas and reciting sutras as attachments to forms.

Thus, those who were once affiliated with externalist faiths and later returned to the Dharma, should reflect on this example and be cautious.

C) Celestial Demons

This refers to the type of demon that resides in the Sixth Heaven, also called the Heaven of Free Enjoyment of Others' Emanations. This type of demon possesses merits and blessings and enjoys the highest heavenly bliss in the Realm of Desire [of which our world is but a small part]. They then mistake such happiness and bliss as ultimate, and do not wish anyone to escape their influence.[66]

When a practitioner has attained a fairly high level of cultivation, his mind-light develops and shines up to the realm of the Sixth Heaven. It is then discovered by the celestial demons, who seek ways to sabotage his cultivation. Such action can take many forms, threatening or cajoling, or even helping the practitioner attain false samadhi, "wisdom" and spiritual power, with the aim of ultimately deceiving him. These demons take turns watching the practitioner constantly and without interruption, waiting for the opportune moment. If the practitioner has a delusive thought, they pounce on him or steer him toward things contrary to the Way. The practitioner's entire lifetime of cultivation is then over, for all practical purposes.

In his *Awakening of the Faith Treatise*, the Patriarch Asvaghosha admonished:

> There may be some disciples whose root of merit is not yet mature, whose control of mind is weak and whose power of application is limited -- and yet who are sincere in their purpose to seek enlightenment -- these for a time may be beset and bewildered by maras and evil influences who are seeking to break down their good purpose.
>   Such disciples, seeing seductive sights, attractive girls, strong young men, must constantly remind themselves that

all such tempting and alluring things are mind-made, and, if they do this, their tempting power will disappear and they will no longer be annoyed. Or, if they have visions of heavenly gods and Bodhisattvas and Buddhas surrounded by celestial glories, they should remind themselves that these, too, are mind-made and unreal. Or, if they should be uplifted and excited by listening to mysterious Dharanis, to lectures upon the paramitas, to elucidations of the great principles of the Mahayana, they must remind themselves that these also are emptiness and mind-made, that in their essence they are Nirvana itself. Or, if they should have intimations within that they have attained transcendental powers, recalling past lives, or fore- seeing future lives, or, reading others' thoughts, or freedom to visit other Buddha-lands, or great powers of eloquence, all of [these] may tempt them to become covetous for worldly power and riches and fame. Or, they may be tempted by extremes of emotion, at times angry, at other times joyous, or at times very kind-hearted and compassionate, at other times the very opposite, or at times alert and purposeful, at other times indolent and stupid, at times full of faith and zealous in their practice, at other times engrossed in other affairs and negligent.

All of [these] will keep them vacillating, at times experiencing a kind of fictitious samadhi, such as the heretics boast of, but not the true samadhi. Or later, when they are quite advanced [they] become absorbed in trances for a day, or two, or even seven, not partaking of any food but upheld by inward food of their spirit, being admired by their friends and feeling very comfortable and proud and complacent, and then later becoming very erratic, sometimes eating little, sometimes greedily, and the expression of their face constantly changing.

Because of all such strange manifestations and developments in the course of their practices, disciples should be on their guard to keep the mind under constant control. They should neither grasp after nor become attached to the passing and unsubstantial things of the senses or concepts and moods of the mind. If they do this they will be able to keep far away from the hindrances of karma. (Wei-tao, tr., in Goddard, *A Buddhist Bible*, p.402-3.)

***

In summary and as a further generalization, there are only two types of demon, internal and external. Celestial demons are within the category of external demons; however, I have described them separately to alert the practitioner to the dangerous, subtle havoc they can cause. In addition to the demons of afflictions, external demons and celestial demons described above, Buddhist sutras also mention "disease demons" and the "demon of death." A bout of disease will usually wither the practitioner's efforts, while death in the midst of cultivation can make him retrogress. Thus, disease and death are called demons. In general, they represent obstacles to the Way that affect the physical body, but they cannot harm and destroy the Bodhi Mind in the true sense of the word "demon." For this reason, they are only mentioned in passing, but not elaborated upon here.

Considering the level of cultivation of today's practitioners, they generally face harassment only from demons of afflictions or external demons. Such cultivators are not advanced enough to arouse opposition from celestial demons. However, should the latter set their minds to destroying someone, that person has little hope of escaping harm, unless his cultivation is exemplary.

In the *Surangama Sutra*, Buddha Sakyamuni, out of compassion for cultivators faced with many dangers along the Way, advised those who practiced meditation to recite mantras at the same time. This would enable them to rely on the power of the Buddhas to escape harm from demons and achieve correct samadhi. The Patriarch Yin Kuang once said:

> At first glance, it would appear that the *Surangama Sutra* has a different viewpoint from Pure Land. However, upon

closer scrutiny, that Sutra, in its essence, actually praised
and commended the Pure Land School. Why is this so? It
is because, if even those who have attained the third level
of sagehood can suffer retrogression caused by demons, we
can see the crucial importance of Buddha Recitation and
rebirth in the Pure Land: in the "gathering" and helping
light of the Lord Amitabha Buddha, there is no more
danger of demons.

While treading the Way but not yet reborn in the
Pure Land, the practitioner of Buddha Recitation may
also encounter demonic obstacles. However, in most
cases, this is because he does not understand the
Dharma and is not skillful at reining in his mind -- letting
internal demons (afflictions) spring up, which, in turn,
attract external demons. If he can keep his mind empty
and still and recite the Buddha's name, external demons
will be powerless and afflictions will gradually disappear.
Thus, for the Pure Land practitioner, even if demonic
obstacles do appear, they are few in number.

[Advanced] Zen practitioners, on the other hand,
face many demonic occurrences because they rely only
on their own strength and self-power. A Zen follower
should fulfill the following five conditions to be
successful: first, he should keep the precepts strictly;
secondly, his nature and roots should be "quick" and
enlightened; thirdly, he should have a clear
understanding of the Dharma, skillfully distinguishing
the correct from the deviant, the true from the false;
fourthly, he should be firm and stable in his
determination; and fifthly, he should be guided by a
good advisor, who has a thorough understanding of the
sutras and many years experience in meditation. If the
practitioner does not meet these five conditions, he is
very easily subject to harm from demons.[67]

The ancients have said that "in Zen practice, there
are many opportunities to go astray." Therefore, to be
successful in meditation, it is necessary to possess
superior capacities and intelligence. High-level Zen

Masters of the past, in transmitting the Dharma to their disciples, would repeatedly warn them:

Be careful not to accept as a disciple anyone who does not have the deepest good roots and the highest capacities.

These words should serve as proof enough of the above observation.

In the *Awakening of the Faith Treatise* after summarizing the essential points of Mahayana doctrine and explaining the path of cultivation, the Patriarch Asvaghosha added:

Next, suppose there is a man who learns this teaching for the first time and wishes to seek the correct faith but lacks courage and strength. Because he lives in this world of suffering, he fears that he will not always be able to meet the Buddhas and honor them personally, and that faith being difficult to perfect, he will be inclined to fall back.

He should know that the Tathagathas have an excellent expedient means by which they can protect his faith: that is, through the strength of wholehearted meditation-recitation on the Buddha [Amitabha], he will in fulfillment of his wishes be able to be born in the Buddha-land beyond, to see the Buddha always, and to be forever separated from the evil states of existence.

It is as the sutra says: "If a man meditates wholly on Amitabha Buddha in the world of the Western Paradise and wishes to be born in that world, directing all the goodness he has cultivated toward that goal, then he will be born there." Because he will see the Buddha at all times, he will never fall back ... [If a cultivator follows this path], he will be able to be born there in the end because he abides in the correct samadhi. (Asvaghosha, *The Awakening of the Faith*, p. 102.)

As explained above, diligent Buddha Recitation is a wonderful expedient to escape demonic dangers and swiftly attain correct samadhi.

8

Perseverance and Steadfastness in Recitation

Essential Points of Pure Land

53) Remember the Ultimate Aim and Be Diligent

For recitation to be vigorous and steadfast, we should have a firm standpoint. That standpoint is to remember the very goal of cultivation. For example, a farmer who aims for a bumper crop arises early and retires late, endures many hardships and toils all day long. Similarly, an aspiring official, wishing to pass his examinations with honors and make his parents proud, burns the midnight oil in study, tired but not discouraged. The cultivator should do likewise. His current practice is for the goal of ultimate liberation, to save himself and others. Elder Master Ch'e Wu, a master of the highest virtue, versed in both the sutras and the various schools, once wrote a stanza which can be considered the kernel of Pure Land:

Because of Birth and Death,
Develop the Bodhi Mind;
With deep Faith and Vows,
Recite the Buddha's name.

We who are in the cycle of Birth and Death, subject to endless suffering, should urgently seek to escape that cycle. I have already dwelled briefly on this urgent matter. However, self-liberation alone is a limited and narrow goal. We should seek Buddhahood to help ourselves and others reach the realm of ultimate liberation. Our Master, Sakyamuni Buddha, preached the Dharma for forty-nine years and elaborated upon it in more than three hundred assemblies precisely and for no other reason than to reach that goal. Once we have developed the Bodhi Mind, seeking to escape Birth and Death, there is no easier or safer way to go about it than "to recite the Buddha's name with deep Faith and Vows."

Those who are ignorant of the Dharma are, of course, helpless. However, those who know the Pure Land teaching but fail to cultivate diligently are ungrateful to the Buddhas and are wasting a unique opportunity to realize their wonderful Self-Nature.[68] Thus, we should persevere with increased effort in reciting the Buddha's name over an extended period of time, rather than doing so in a perfunctory, haphazard manner, with constant interruptions. The ancients have said:

> If we do not plan to save this body
> in this life,
> When, then, will we do so?

Promising ourselves to cultivate in the next life is no different from a deluded person speaking of a dream-like event. Let us take two examples from ordinary life: a lover sometimes has to travel long distances and endure many hardships just to get to the rendezvous; a gambler, desiring to win, can give up food and sleep, sometimes playing for several days in a row. If ordinary people can endure such hardship over a little bit of worldly lust, how much more should a cultivator endure while pursuing a lofty goal? Therefore, if we are indolent during cultivation, subject to lapses and interruptions, afraid of difficulties and hardships and fond of fleeting pleasures and sleep, it is because we are not firm in our determination or earnest in our will to liberate ourselves and others!

Time flies, the God of Impermanence does not wait, this body is easily lost, the Dharma is difficult to encounter. The practitioner should remember these points and keep the two words "suffering" and "death" constantly before his very eyes, thus urging himself on.

54) A Method for Escaping Birth and Death in One Lifetime

The ocean of worlds throughout the ten directions can be divided, in general, into two types: pure lands and defiled lands. *Pure lands* are the pure and adorned realms of the Buddhas; once reborn there, we have escaped Birth and Death forever and will gradually progress to become sages and saints. *Defiled lands* are realms where everything, from the environment to the bodies and minds of sentient beings, is defiled; their inhabitants must revolve along the Six Paths, subject to the sufferings of samsara.

If sentient beings in this defiled Saha World merely keep the Five or the Ten Precepts and perform other good deeds but do not practice Buddha Recitation, they will have little affinity with the Buddhas. As they lack affinity with the Buddhas, the transcendental seeds in their Alaya consciousness cannot develop. Therefore, although they may perform good deeds, they can at most be reborn in the celestial realms, but not in the Western Pure Land. The lifespan in these realms, while long, is still limited. When their merits and blessings are exhausted, they will undergo rebirth once more, according to their stock of transgressions and merits.

222 < Buddhism of Wisdom & Faith

With attachment to the self as the cornerstone, sentient beings begin to create more good or bad karma; therefore, they continue to revolve in the cycle of Birth and Death. In that cycle, transgressions are easy to commit, while good deeds are difficult to perform. Thus, the time spent on the evil realms is very long, while the periods of stay in the celestial realms are limited. Buddha Sakyamuni once lamented:

Sentient beings usually take the three Evil Paths as their homeland.

For this reason, we can predict that sentient beings who are not reborn in the pure lands of the Buddhas are bound to remain in the defiled lands. In these defiled lands, in the midst of an evil environment full of obstructions and weighed down by their limited capacities and conditions as sentient beings of the Dharma-Ending Age, they will sooner or later descend onto the Evil Paths. Thus, to achieve rebirth in the pure lands of the various Buddhas, they must recite these Buddhas' names.

***

Some might ask: "There are many methods leading to liberation; why should we recite the Buddha's name?" The answer to this question should be obvious, but I will reply all the same, to make it clearer.

In ancient times, even though Sakyamuni Buddha had passed away, the True Dharma still flourished. Sentient beings then had light karma and their minds were intrinsically good. Therefore, they could succeed with whatever Dharma method they chose. With the passing of time, in the Dharma Semblance Period, a long time after Buddha Sakyamuni had entered Nirvana, the environment and the minds of people had gradually grown complicated. Out of hundreds of thousands of practitioners, perhaps one or two would attain the Way.

This is even more true now that we are deep into the Dharma-Ending Age, when virtues and morals have broken down. True cultivators are rare enough; why talk about those who have attained the Way? This is because sentient beings today have heavy obstructions, their minds are confused, and their lives and social organization are more complex and troublesome than in earlier times. Added to this are constant threats of war and strife, poverty, shortages and disasters, one after another. Furthermore, pornography and violence are condoned, while religion and morality are considered anachronisms. With so many obstacles from within our minds and from the environment reinforcing one another, no wonder it is difficult to reach Enlightenment by reliance on self-power alone, as taught in most Dharma methods.

We should know, furthermore, that to escape Birth and Death, we must sever Delusions of Views and Delusions of Thought. However, according to the ancients:

Blocking Delusions of Views is as difficult as blocking a raging stream coming from forty miles away.

Why, then, even mention eliminating all Delusions of Thought?

Thus, if we want to achieve liberation in this Dharma-Ending Age, the most appropriate method is Buddha Recitation. Through this method, the cultivator, after utilizing his self-power to the utmost, receives additional assistance from other-power. Even though his karma and delusions are not yet extinguished, he can, through the power of Amitabha Buddha's Vows, "take his residual karma along" to the Pure Land. Once reborn, he will no longer retrogress and will have transcended Birth and Death forever!

***

As discussed earlier, in the *Great Heap Sutra* and the *Longer Amitabha Sutra*, Sakyamuni Buddha, in His profound wisdom and compassion, predicted the limited capacities and evil conditions of people in the Dharma-Ending Age as well as the efficacy and appropriateness of the Pure Land method. Therefore, in this degenerate age, when Enlightenment "in this very lifetime" can seldom be attained through other methods, only Pure Land can prolong the turning of the Dharma wheel and liberate sentient beings. In a letter to a fellow monk, Elder Master Yin Kuang expressed it this way:

> Deep into the Dharma-Ending Age, when practicing methods other than Pure Land, we may speak of sowing good seeds and creating favorable conditions for Enlightenment in the future, but we cannot speak of attaining the fruit of liberation in this very lifetime.

For these reasons, we can conclude that in the Dharma-Ending Age, only Buddha Recitation brings liberation from Birth and Death in one lifetime.

55) Do not Procrastinate

We should know that Pure Land is a Perfect and Sudden Mahayana method. Why Mahayana? Because this method takes Buddha Recitation as "cause" and complete Enlightenment as "effect." Why "Perfect"? Because this Dharma door, as the ancient masters have said, completely encompasses the Five Periods and Eight Teachings. Why "Sudden"? Because this expedient can guide everyone from the level of an ordinary being completely bound by greed, anger and delusion to the stage of non-retrogression, and from the beginning levels of Bodhisattvahood to Supreme Enlightenment, via a straight and swift shortcut.

Therefore, this method is extolled by all of the

Buddhas of the ten directions, while Bodhisattvas such as Manjusri and Samantabhadra, and Patriarchs such as Asvaghosha and Nagarjuna, all vow to achieve rebirth in the Pure Land. Thus, to recite the Buddha's name is to practice personally according to the Perfect Sudden Mahayana method.

***

When seeking liberation, we should consider Buddha Recitation to be most essential and urgent and put this method into practice immediately, without procrastination. Buddha Sakyamuni taught on many occasions that human life is only as long as one breath, because if we exhale but do not inhale, we have already died and stepped over into a new lifetime. Therefore, death awaits us at all times; behind each year, each month, each day, each hour and even each and every second lurks our impending demise. No one can predict the length of his own lifespan, as reflected in the following stanzas:

Yesterday, at the crossroads, he still rode
        his horse;
Today he lies still in his coffin!

Do not wait until old age to recite the Buddha's
        name,
In abandoned cemeteries can be found the graves of
        many youths.

These stanzas reflect the facts of life. Thus, to avoid being surprised by the God of Impermanence, let us at all times apply ourselves to earnest recitation of the Buddha's name. Only then will we escape bewilderment and confusion in our last moments.

To prevent and discourage laziness and laxity in cultivation, Sakyamuni Buddha carefully taught:

There are, in general, eight occasions when a monk tends to be lax. For instance, whenever he does not receive enough food on his alms rounds, he may think, "I do not have enough food today. Therefore I lack nutrition and good health. Let me postpone cultivation for one night." Whenever he receives ample food, he may think to himself, "today I am full and feel heavy and tired. Let me postpone cultivation for one night and continue tomorrow." He may engage in similar reasoning on such occasions as: preparing to do a great deal of work, having just completed some heavy physical task, feeling ill, recovering from illness, readying himself for a long trip, or having just returned from a long trip. In all these instances, he always has one excuse or another to stop cultivation and rest. On the contrary, when a diligent monk is faced with these same situations, he always sets his mind on the truth of Impermanence and never avoids assiduous cultivation.

If even monks and nuns are that indolent, lay people can be assumed to be worse. A well-known Master once urged a close friend to recite the Buddha's name. The latter wrote back complaining that he was currently too busy, and promised to take the Master's advice into account as soon as his affairs were temporarily settled. The Master penned a stanza on the letter before returning it. The verse reads as follows:

If we have decided to stop, let us stop at once;
Why promise to wait for our cares to end -- as they
never will.

Truthfully, the preoccupations and worries of this world will never end, not even when it comes time for us to close our eyes and depart.

A well-known Master once advised a lay friend to recite the Buddha's name. The latter replied, "There are three things I have not yet attended to: one, my father's coffin is not yet entombed; two, my son does not yet have a family; three, my youngest daughter is still unmarried. Let me take care of these three things and then I will follow your advice." A few months later, the layman was struck by a grave illness and suddenly passed away. After the memorial, the monk offered a stanza in lieu of condolences:

My friend, the wise official,
When I advised him to recite the Buddha's name,
    he countered with three things;
The three things have not been accomplished,
Yet impermanence has already snatched him away.
Lord of Hell, how inconsiderate can you be!

Reading this stanza, who among us dares claim he is not another wise official? Therefore, those who are determined to cultivate should take advantage of every single instant, and recite the Buddha's name at that very moment. They should avoid stepping in the doomed footprints of those who have erred before them -- with cause for regret for a thousand autumns to come.

How to Ensure Perseverance

56) Cultivate Step by Step

If the Pure Land practitioner wishes to cultivate in a lasting way, he should establish a timetable and, depending on his inclinations, health and particular situation, grow progressively more diligent. He should not be over-ambitious at the very beginning, reciting too much for too long. Like a pedestrian who should not walk too fast lest he stumble and trip, those who do not know their limits and go overboard in practice can be discouraged by fatigue and stress and abandon all cultivation.

In general, the Buddha Recitation practitioner should have two periods of practice: fixed and unfixed. "Fixed period of practice" means that each day we should have a pre-determined period of recitation during which we record the number of utterances.

"Unfixed period of practice" means that outside the fixed period, we should always silently recite the Buddha's name whether walking, standing, reclining or sitting, but no recording is necessary. The main point to remember about Buddha Recitation is that whether reciting slowly or fast, we should do so distinctly and deliberately, the mind closely paralleling the utterances, mind and utterances in unison. Reciting in that way over a long period of time makes recitation second nature, and the practitioner can go from one thousand to over one hundred thousand utterances per day.

57) Recitation Should be Pure and Unmixed -- the Number of Utterances is Secondary

Certain practitioners do not like to finger the rosary as they recite the Buddha's name; they just decide in advance the duration of each recitation session. This method has the advantage of "sustaining" the mind, each utterance clearly registering in the Alaya consciousness. However, if the practitioner lacks strong power of mind and determined will, he will be prone to languid, dilatory recitation (making it difficult to achieve results), boredom, fatigue and frequent glances at the clock. On the other hand, fingering the rosary and reciting the pre-determined number of utterances reinforces the power of diligent recitation, just as a weak person leaning on a cane can climb mountains. However, if the practitioner does not follow the cardinal principle of Buddha Recitation (i.e., to recite distinctly and deliberately, with mind and recitation in unison) he will fall into the error of reciting too much too fast, thus becoming sloppy.

We should know that as soon as the practitioner begins to recite, each utterance penetrates deeply into his Alaya consciousness. As the utterances accumulate, the Buddha's name will eventually emerge, whether he is awake or asleep. This is called the "state of non-recitation being recitation." If the cultivator recites clearly and distinctly in daily life, the utterances emerging from the Alaya consciousness will be clear and distinct; if he recites perfunctorily in an unclear manner, the utterances will not be clear.

Cultivation usually fails in this particular area and therefore, practitioners should be cautious from the very beginning. If reciting many utterances swiftly is motivated by the desire for fame and the reputation as someone who recites tens of thousands of times a day, we will be better off reciting less and concentrating on the quality of the recitation.

***

This author knows of a laywoman who practices Buddha Recitation regularly. She has great faith in the Triple Jewel; however, she likes to socialize a lot. Every evening, when she returns home and is invited to the dinner table, she says, "I have promised my master to recite ten full rosaries every day. If I do not keep my promise, I will commit a transgression against the Triple Jewel. Please wait while I fulfill my promise, and then we will sit down to dinner." So saying, she hastily dons her Dharma robe, recites the Buddha's name at top speed, as though she were trying to put out a fire, and is done in about fifteen minutes. How can such recitation lead to rebirth in the Pure Land? Like this laywoman, many practitioners recite the Buddha's name in such a manner "to fulfill the required number." We should know that there are two areas crucial to Buddha Recitation: a true, earnest mind and clear, distinct recitation. Only in this way can we hope to achieve results.

Another anecdote concerns a laywoman who once approached a well-known Elder Master and asked: "I have recited the Buddha's name for some time now, but have not seen any sign of progress. Can you explain to me why this is so?" The abbot said, "*Reciting the*

Buddha's name is not difficult; the difficulty lies in perseverance. Perhaps you have not recited regularly and in a persevering manner." The laywoman replied, "You are entirely right. I am usually interrupted in my recitation and have not been persevering, because of family obligations. From now on, I will put aside all distractions and vow to keep reciting exactly as taught."

Some time later, she returned and asked, "Since receiving your instructions last time, I have put aside all external distractions and recited the Buddha's name regularly, every day. Why is it that I still do not see any results?" The abbot replied, "*Reciting the Buddha's name is not difficult; the difficulty lies in perseverance. Persevering is not difficult; the difficulty lies in being singleminded.* Although, on the surface, you may have put all distractions aside, in your mind you still worry about possessions and property and are still attached to children and family. You have neither discarded worry nor eliminated the root of love-attachment. How can you achieve one-pointedness of mind and see Amitabha Buddha?" Hearing this, the woman sighed aloud "That is so true, Master! Although I have seemingly abandoned all distractions, my mind is still preoccupied with them. From now on, I vow to disregard everything and recite the Buddha's name singlemindedly."

Thereupon she went home and, from that time on, each time her children or anyone else sought her advice or confided in her, she would invariably reply, "I want peace of mind, and do not wish to be bothered by anything." For this reason, everyone referred to her as "the woman who is above all worry and care." A few years later, she went to bow to the abbot at his temple, saying, "Thanks to your advice and teaching, I have now achieved one-pointedness of mind and seen Amitabha Buddha. I have come to pay my respects and take leave of you, Abbot, because I will soon be reborn in the Pure Land."

The laywoman in our story achieved liberation because she was enlightened to two principles: perseverance and singlemindedness. Thus, to be successful, the Pure Land practitioner should consider everything, from personal possessions and property to family and friends, to be illusory and phantom-like, coming together temporarily and then disintegrating. If we care about family and friends, we should ensure our own rebirth and liberation and then rescue them. This is true affection! Therefore, to recite the Buddha's name effectively, we should not only ignore one hundred distractions, we should discard all distractions, be they one thousand or tens of thousands!

58) Let Us Not Lose our Place within the Lotus Grades

When a practitioner recites the Buddha's name seeking rebirth in the Pure Land, a lotus blossom grows there, in the Seven-Jewelled Pond. If he perseveres in his efforts without interruption, the lotus blossom will continue to grow. Otherwise, it will, of itself, wither and die. If the practitioner later resumes recitation, becoming diligent once more, another lotus blossom appears. The flowers come into being as a consequence of the practitioner's power of cultivation and vary according to his deeds. There are nine grades of lotus blossoms, corresponding to the nine grades of rebirth, from low to high *(Meditation Sutra)*. These grades, in turn, comprise an infinite number of subgrades.

Pure land practice differs with each cultivator, as such practice depends on his capacities and circumstances. There are some cultivators who utter the Buddha's name from a few hundred to tens of thousands of times each day. However, regardless of how busy a cultivator may be, he should practice at least ten recitations per day.

"Ten recitations" refers to the Ten Recitations method taught by a well-known Master, which is based on the lowest grade of rebirth described in the *Meditation Sutra*. It is reserved specifically for those who are busy with mundane activities, so that they, too can practice Buddha Recitation and achieve rebirth in the Pure Land. The method consists of uttering Amitabha Buddha's name approximately ten times each time one inhales or exhales. The real intent behind this practice is to use the breath to concentrate the mind. Depending on the cultivator's breath span, he may recite more than ten utterances or fewer. After ten inhalations/exhalations (or some fifty to one hundred utterances in total) the cultivator may proceed to recite the Transference of Merit stanza:

> I vow to be reborn in the Western Pure Land,
> The nine lotus grades are my parents.
> As the lotus flowers bloom, I will see Buddha Amitabha
>   and reach No-Birth,
> Liberating all sentient beings ...

After reciting the stanza, the practitioner bows to the Buddhas three times before retiring. This practice has its roots in the boundless compassion of Buddha Sakyamuni and the Patriarchs. However busy a practitioner is, he can engage in this method and step onto the path of liberation.

There is one caveat about the Ten Recitations method. While inhaling and exhaling, the practitioner should recite the number of utterances with which he feels most comfortable, without trying to lengthen or shorten his normal breath span. Otherwise he might develop a respiratory ailment.

On one of his lecture tours, a respected Chinese Master was told by an elderly layman, "It is because of Buddha Recitation that I have become hard of hearing, and at times cannot hear anything." When the Master inquired further, the old man said, "A junior monk once secretly transmitted a method of Buddha Recitation to me. He said that 'nowadays, high-ranking Masters do not really know the Ten Recitations method because there is a little known oral tradition within the method which is now lost.' I sincerely sought his guidance and he taught me to recite the Buddha's name one hundred and eight times with each breath [corresponding to the number of beads in a long rosary]. I did as I was told, exerting myself until I began to hear a continuous, rumbling noise. My hearing loss dates from that time. Please, tell me whether or not such a method is in keeping with the Buddhas' teaching."

The Elder Master, hearing this, immediately rejected what the young monk had taught, blaming him for subverting the Dharma and converting it into an externalist practice detrimental to health. The Elder Master then gradually taught the layman the Buddhist method of Ten Recitations.

Pure Land cultivators should pay heed and learn from this anecdote.

Pure Land, A Special Door to Liberation

59) Buddha Recitation, an Easy-to-Practice Method

Everyone can appreciate why Pure Land, particularly Oral Recitation, is an easy method. However, the word "easy" has many meanings, with which not everyone may be familiar.

This is because when practicing other methods, for example, Sutra Studies, we encounter an immense number of sutras and commentaries, infinitely profound in meaning. In the first instance, the practitioner should fully understand the basic teaching and, from there, penetrate the different shades of meaning. After that, he should reconcile all meanings, extracting their kernel and essence, to discover and choose the method of cultivation that he will follow all his life. All this cannot be done unless he is willing to spend several dozen years of hard work.

Should he decide to seek liberation through the Discipline method, the practitioner must join the Order and become thoroughly conversant with all aspects of the different bodies of precepts. He should also possess the wisdom to distinguish meaning from words and apply the precepts in a flexible manner, according to the environment, the times and the occasion. Thus, to study the sutras is not necessarily difficult, but to study the precepts to the point of knowing how to adapt them skillfully, neither breaking nor being rigidly bound by them, is truly difficult. Once having understood the precepts, the practitioner must exercise patience and fortitude and endure discomfort and suffering in order to achieve success.

If he decides to enter the Way through Zen, he should have previously sown the seeds of wisdom and have suitably high innate capacities. Otherwise, he has no hope of attaining this lofty Dharma and participating in the "transmission of the lamp" (the enlightenment experience). Therefore, a famous Buddhist scholar once said:

> Practicing Zen to achieve Buddhahood is the domain of scholars endowed with wisdom.

This observation is certainly not incorrect or exaggerated.

With Oral Recitation, once the practitioner has developed the mind of Faith and Vows, he can recite the Buddha's name and engage in cultivation regardless of whether his capacities are high, moderate or limited. Moreover, while other methods depend on self-power alone, the Pure Land Dharma Door first relies to the utmost on self-power and then adds the element of "other-power." Other-power is precisely the infinitely great and powerful Vow of Amitabha Budddha "to welcome and escort." As long as a practitioner sincerely repents and recites the Buddha's name with one-pointedness of mind, even though he is not yet free of delusions and is still afflicted with heavy evil karma, he, too, will be welcomed to the Pure Land.

The ancients used to say, by way of comparison:

Practicing other methods is as difficult and laborious as an ant climbing a high mountain; reciting the Buddha's name seeking rebirth in the Pure Land is as swift and easy as a boat sailing downstream, in the direction of the blowing wind.

This observation is very appropriate indeed. Moreover, once reborn there, living in an auspicious and peaceful environment, always in the company of Buddha Amitabha and the Bodhisattvas, the practitioner will swiftly achieve success in whatever Dharma method he chooses. He is like a log rolling down a high mountain, which just keeps going and never stops, even for a moment.

In summary, Buddha Recitation is easy for three reasons: *easy practice, easy achievement of rebirth in the Pure Land, easy attainment of Buddhahood.* Therefore, the results achieved through Buddha Recitation from time immemorial can be compared to the clear and limpid sound of precious stones striking against genuine gold, or the sight of "smiling lotus blossoms with their fresh and fragrant grades of rebirth."

Within these levels and grades, the path from sentient being to Buddhahood contains many ranks, yet is also without rank. This is because, once reborn in the Pure Land, the practitioner has transcended Birth and

Death -- and to recite the Buddha's name is to become Buddha. This is like the silkworm, the chrysalis and the butterfly, which are inseparable; there is very little difference between saying that a butterfly is originally a worm or that the worm is the butterfly.

60) From Scattered Mind to Settled Mind

When the mouth recites Amitabha Buddha's name while the mind is focussed on the Buddha or rests on His name, it is called "Settled Mind Buddha Recitation." When the mouth recites the Buddha's name but the mind is not on Amitabha Buddha and is lost in errant thought, it is called "Scattered Mind Buddha Recitation." The effectiveness of "Scattered Mind" is very much weaker than "Settled Mind" Buddha Recitation. For this reason, since ancient times, good spiritual advisors have all exhorted us to recite with a settled mind, and not let our thoughts wander. Therefore, Buddha Recitation with a scattered mind cannot be held up as an example to be emulated.

However, all external activities must reverberate in the Alaya consciousness. If reciting with a scattered mind were entirely ineffective, where would the sacred name of Amitabha come from? The very existence of the sacred name results from two conditions: first, the existing seeds arising from the Alaya consciousness; second, the power of outside action reflecting back inward. Therefore, we cannot say that "Scattered Mind Buddha Recitation" is entirely without effect, albeit its effectiveness is much more limited than recitation with a settled mind. Thus, while reciting the Buddha's name with a scattered mind has never been advocated, its significance and effectiveness cannot be rejected either. For this reason, the ancients have handed down the following gatha:

The sacred name of Amitabha Buddha is the
supreme method,

Why bother and fret over scattered thoughts!
Though clouds thousands of miles thick hide the
 sun's brightness,
All the world still benefits from its "amber" light.

Upon reflection, the above verse is quite accurate. This is because once the seeds of Buddha Recitation ripen in the Alaya consciousness, they trigger the sixth consciousness [i.e., the mind], leading to the development of pure thought and pure action. However, when the seeds of Buddha Recitation pass through the sixth consciousness, deep-seated defiled thoughts encroach upon them. Although these seeds ultimately manage to escape, their power has been greatly weakened. They are like the rays of the sun, which, although radiant, are hidden by many layers of clouds and are seen in the world only as "amber" light. This residual light, however, comes from the sun.

Realizing this, the Pure Land practitioner need not be unduly worried or concerned about sundry thoughts. He should continuously recite, content with whatever number of utterances he manages to produce with right thought. As he recites in such a manner over an extended period of time, the horse-like mind will return to the stable, the monkey-like mind will gradually return to the den.[69] With further recitation, right thought will emerge clearly without any special effort on the practitioner's part. Thus, we should emphasize the continuity of recitation, without worrying whether it is done with a settled mind or not. Like muddy water which, with constant decanting, becomes clear and pure, a person afflicted with many sundry thoughts, through extended recitation, can convert them into right thought. We should know that ancient masters would always recite the Buddha's name, whether walking or standing, asleep or awake or working. If they constantly recited with a settled mind, they would trip and stumble while walking and could not succeed in drafting commentaries or performing other tasks. Therefore, at times they recited with a scattered mind, but they never stopped reciting because even though their minds were scattered, not all benefits were lost.[70]

***

At this juncture, I would like to recount a story. Once there was a layman who came to inquire of a monk: "I have to confess to you, Master, that I have been reciting the Buddha's name for over ten years, but I still have innumerable deluded thoughts; I do not know how to get rid of them. I have sought guidance in many places, with many teachers. One master would tell me about this technique, another would teach me a different one. There was even a junior monk who advised me to recite the Buddha's name twenty-one times without breathing and then to swallow all the saliva at once. I have tried all available techniques, but only succeed in reining in my mind at the beginning. Afterward, perhaps because I get used to the technique, deluded thoughts reappear as before. I wonder if you have any effective method to teach me?"

The Elder Master replied: "You have failed because you were not persevering, and constantly switched methods. You should know that ordinary people like us have created immeasurable deluded karma, from time immemorial. How can we be pure after a short period of practice? The main thing is for us to persevere over an extended period of time.

"Let me cite a few examples. Suppose you pour clean, fragrant water into a container filled with dirty and foul liquids. The container being already full, the clean water will, naturally, spill out, except for a few drops sticking to the container. If you persevere and continue to pour clean water in, one day the dirty container will turn into a clean one, filled with pure water.

"Similarly, suppose you have a severe stomach ailment that makes you throw up whatever medicine you ingest, but you persist in taking the prescribed medicine. Each time you take it, even though you may vomit, some of the ingredients will be absorbed, gradually curing you of the ailment. The afflictions of sentient beings are the same. It is fitting and proper to treat them with the medicine of Buddha Recitation, but if we constantly change techniques and methods, how can we expect to achieve results?

"Again, suppose someone is purifying water with alum, but, out of impatience, before the chemical has time to react, starts pouring in salt and then powdered lime. If he continually changes in this manner, how can the water ever become clear?

"Therefore, to rid ourselves of deluded thoughts, we should not keep changing from one method to another, but should select an appropriate method and practice it with perseverance until results are achieved."

The practitioner, hearing these explanations, nodded in agreement.

***

As indicated earlier, the key to a settled mind is to practice with perseverance. However, if we dread scattered thoughts and need an expedient to calm the mind, we should use the Decimal Recording method explained earlier (section 30-7). With this method, we use all of our mind-power to record and remember from one to ten utterances, which easily leads to pure concentration.

If the mind is still unsettled and we cannot use the Decimal Recording method, we should, with each utterance, concentrate firmly on the letter "A" in Amitabha Buddha. When the letter "A" is present, all the other letters are also present. If, because of delusion and forgetfulness, the letter "A" is lost, all the other letters are also lost. Moreover, the letter "A" is the key and fundamental letter of the Sanskrit alphabet and is therefore considered the mother of all other letters. Through concentration on reciting the Buddha's name while simultaneously holding fast to the letter "A," in time, mind and environment both dissolve and amalgamate into one bloc, as great as space itself. Buddha Amitabha and the practitioner will then both disappear. At that time, naturally, the letter "A" will have ceased to exist as well. However, it was lost earlier because the mind was unsettled and scattered, while it no longer exists now precisely because of the harmonious state of "perpetual concentration." This is the manifestation of emptiness of Mind and environment -- the entry point into the Buddha Recitation Samadhi.

61) The Pure Lands of the Ten Directions and the Tushita Heaven

In the realm of the ten directions, there are innumerable beautifully and purely adorned Buddha lands, such as the Pure Lapis Lazuli Land mentioned in the *Medicine (Healing) Buddha Sutra*, or the Land of Many Fragrances and Sublime Joy found in the *Vimalakirti Sutra*. This being so, why should we restrict ourselves to seeking rebirth in the Western Pure Land? There are basically three reasons, namely:

1. Because of the teachings of Sakyamuni Buddha, who exhorted us to seek rebirth in the Land of Ultimate Bliss. Buddha Sakyamuni did not wish to expound at length on the other pure lands, lest sentient beings develop a mind of discrimination, become undecided and have no focal point for their aspirations. Moreover, thanks to the ideal conditions for teaching and transformation in the Western Pure Land, not only do sentient beings from the Saha World seek rebirth there,

but sentient beings in countless other worlds do so as well.

2. Because Amitabha Buddha has adorned the Western Pure Land with forty-eight lofty Vows. These Vows [particularly the eighteenth Vow of "welcoming and escorting"] embrace all sentient beings, from Bodhisattvas to common beings full of evil transgressions.

3. Because sentient beings in the Saha World have great affinities with Amitabha Buddha and the Bodhisattva Avalokitesvara. As proof, when Buddhists meet, they usually greet each other with the words "Amitabha Buddha" and when faced with accidents or disasters, they usually recite the sacred name of Avalokitesvara.

For these reasons, it is more advantageous to seek rebirth in the Land of Ultimate Bliss than in the other pure lands of the ten directions, particularly the Tushita Heaven (the realm of Maitreya, the Buddha of the future).

Among the reasons cited are, *first*, that it is difficult to be reborn in the Tushita Heaven, as the Bodhisattva Maitreya does not have the "welcoming and escorting" Vow of Amitabha Buddha; sentient beings must rely solely on their own self-power to achieve rebirth there. *Second*, and more important, the Tushita Heaven is still part of the World of Desire (of which the Saha World is an infinitesimal part), not outside of it as is the Western Pure Land. Thus, sentient beings in the Tushita Heaven remain subject to retrogression. The difficulty of achieving rebirth in the Tushita Heaven is illustrated by the following anecdote.

Some nine hundred years after Sakyamuni's demise, there were three Indian Patriarchs who cultivated together, Asanga, Vasubandhu, and Simhabhadra.

These three all had the same determination in being born in Tushita Heaven and in desiring to see Maitreya. They vowed that if one were to die first, and obtain a look (at Maitreya), he would return and inform the others. Simhabhadra died, but once he had gone he did not return. Later, when Vasabhandhu was nearing his death, Asanga said to him, "If you see Maitreya, come and tell me." Vasabhandhu died, but returned only after a period of three years. Asanga asked him, "Why did it take you such a long time to return?" Vasabhandhu said that he had arrived there (in Tushita Heaven), had heard the bodhisattva Maitreya preach but one sermon, had circumambulated him ... and had come back immediately; but days are long there (in Tushita), and here (on earth) three years had already elapsed; Asanga again asked, "Where is Simhabhadra now?" Vasabhandhu replied that because Simhabhadra had received such heavenly pleasures, he was enjoying the five desires, and so ... from that time to the present he has never seen Maitreya! (Leo Pruden, tr. "The Ching-t'u Shih-i-lun.")

If even a Patriarch like Simhabhadra finds it so difficult to achieve rebirth in the inner court of Maitreya, common people with ordinary capacities have little hope indeed.[71] This author recalls a stanza by the eminent T'ang dynasty poet Po Chu-I. He was a Taoist early in life, but converted to Buddhism in his later years.

> Preferring the Dharma of Emptiness, I have left
>   the Immortal Way,
> As I fear it, too, has been corrupted during
>   transmission;
> The Immortal Island is not my abode,
> I long only to return to the Tushita Heaven!

The poet-mystic early in life aspired for immortality; later on, he began to practice Buddhism, seeking rebirth in the Tushita Heaven ... In his later years, however, he took up Buddha Recitation, vowing to be reborn in the Pure Land. This shows that the more an intelligent person ponders and chooses, the more he reaches toward the profound and subtle!

9

Tolerance of Adversity

General Discussion of Testing Conditions
62) Causes of Adversity

Elder Masters of the past have made this observation:

> When vowing to perform lofty, virtuous deeds or to begin cultivation, the practitioner usually encounters many obstacles that test his will and challenge his endurance.

There are four stages in the lives of monks and nuns when they can usually expect to face obstacles: when cutting their hair and entering the monastery, when receiving the precepts, when studying the sutras, particularly Mahayana sutras, and when setting everything aside to devote themselves to cultivation. Some, because they have created good conditions in the past or are especially diligent and persevering, may easily pass through the first three stages to reach the fourth. However, it is difficult to avoid obstructing conditions when cultivation reaches a fairly high level.

For example, while an Elder Master of the recent

past was diligently engaged in meditation, his evil karma suddenly manifested itself, making him blind, deaf and mute for three long weeks. Reviewing accounts of the past, this author recalls the story of a layman who built a hut in a quiet, out of the way place to practice meditation. He brought along a helper to relieve him of daily chores. At the beginning, he sat in meditation for periods of one to two hours. Then he progressively increased the time, until toward the end, he could sit up to three full days and nights, remaining all the while in deep concentration. At one point, he was in samadhi for twenty-one days without food or water. The helper, noticing that the layman had been seated for such a long time, approached him and saw that his breathing had "stopped." His chest, moreover, showed no sign of movement, as it had on previous occasions. Not realizing that this was the state of profound samadhi and thinking that the layman was dead, he buried him alive.

Another case: there was a Pure Land Master who practiced assiduously, reciting the Buddha's name up to one hundred thousand times each day. Thanks to such diligence, auspicious signs would appear wherever he went. One day, a vagrant appeared, requesting permission to stay overnight at the temple. The monk glanced at the man and told his young assistant, "This man has the features of a criminal; let him eat his fill and tell him to go elsewhere." However, the novice, being compassionate, was swayed by the man's repeated supplications and did not have the heart to follow his Master's instructions. Sure enough, a few days later, the man slipped furtively into the master's room in the middle of the night, broke his arms and legs and killed him. He then stole a few things from the temple and disappeared.

The ancients have commented that such occurrences are the result of "fixed karma" and are virtually unavoidable. Cultivators usually face three types of obstacles -- the Obstacle of Afflictions, the

Obstacle of Karma and the Obstacle of Retribution -- with the Obstacle of Karma being the most dangerous. Yet, nothing usually happens when the practitioner first begins to cultivate, while the deeper his cultivation, the more obstacles he is bound to encounter. Why is this so? It is because as common people living in the Dharma-Ending Age, most of us, naturally, have heavy obstructing conditions. If not, we would have been reborn in the Dharma Semblance Age or the Perfect Dharma Age. However, it is not cultivation that gives rise to obstacles but rather a phenomenon known as "reshuffling of karma." Heavy karma is commuted into light karma, future karma is "reshuffled" into current karma. Let us suppose that we have ten parts of bad karma but that through cultivation we manage to eradicate seven parts, so that only three parts remain. Instead of having to repay that karma in the future, thanks to our cultivation we may only have to endure light retribution in this very life, and thus be free to attain liberation swiftly.

For example, in one of his previous lives, an Elder Precept Master had been a monarch, who had waged many wars to conquer neighboring kingdoms. Having committed such great karma of killing, he was destined to descend into the hells once his residual merits were exhausted. However, thanks to the Master's earnest cultivation and propagation of the Dharma, his evil karma was commuted into daily bouts of seizures, which made him feel as though many invisible swords were stabbing and slashing his body. This went on for two years before the disease disappeared.

Buddhist treatises also mention the case of a layman who had also committed the karma of killing and was due to suffer rebirth as a hog for seven lifetimes. However, thanks to the fact that he was a vegetarian diligently practicing Buddha Recitation, he was, in his old age, stabbed seven times and killed by marauding soldiers. Thus he repaid his evil karma all at once. In summary, these occurrences are commonly referred to as the state of "bunching together of karma."

However, this does not mean that all cultivators have to suffer retribution for their past karma. In some cases, the more they practice, the more they witness auspicious signs and the more they are at peace and in harmony, with no obstacles in their way. This is because these practitioners did not commit very heavy transgressions in their past lives, or else they have already cultivated for some time and possess many good roots. The majority of practitioners, however, are likely to stumble over some obstacles, major or minor.

***

Apart from the obstacles caused by external factors, there are three other causes of karmic obstructions:

1. According to the Mind-Only School, various evil and wholesome karmic seeds are stored randomly in our Alaya consciousness. When we recite the Buddha's name or meditate, we accumulate the seeds of transcendental virtue, and therefore, evil karmic seeds have to emerge. For example, if a dense forest full of wild beasts is cleared for habitation, trees and shrubs are cut down, causing these beasts to flee out of the forest. The development of afflictions and obstacles from evil karmic seeds is similar. This is called "the reaction of evil karmic seeds."

2. There are cultivators who practice without fully understanding the Dharma, not realizing that the manifestations of the mind and the environment are illusory nor discovering what is true and what is false. They therefore have wrong views. Because of this, they develop thoughts of attachment, happiness, love, worry and fear, creating obstacles for themselves when they are faced with objects and conditions within themselves

or in the outside world.

3. Take the case of a man who follows a map, hoping to find a gold mine. The path that he takes crosses high mountains, deep ravines, empty open stretches and dense forests, an itinerary naturally requiring much labor, hardship and adversity. If his mind is not steady, and he does not adapt himself to the circumstances and his own strength, he is bound to retrogress. Alternatively, he may abandon his search, stop at some temporary location, or even lose his life en route. The path of cultivation is the same. Although the practitioner may follow the sutras, if he is not flexible and patient, ready to change according to his own strength and circumstances, and if his determination is weak, he will certainly fail. This obstacle, in the end, is created by himself alone.

The above summarizes some of the causes of the obstructions faced by cultivators.

63) Demonic Testing Conditions

The karmic conditions that test and create obstacles for the practitioner have many different manifestations. I will summarize them in six points:

1. Internal "testing conditions"

During cultivation, some people suddenly develop thoughts of greed, anger, lust, jealousy, scorn or doubt. They may also suffer delusion, leading to drowsiness and sleep. These thoughts sometimes arise with great intensity, making the practioner feel annoyed and upset over, at times, trivial matters. Sometimes auspicious and evil events alternate in his dreams. The specific details of these events are too numerous to be described. Faced with these occurrences, the practitioner should realize that these karmic marks have appeared as a consequence of his cultivation. He should immediately understand that all karmic occurrences and marks are illusory and dream-like; he should foster right thought and they will disappear one after another. Otherwise, he will certainly be swayed, lose his concentration and retrogress. The ancients used to say in this respect:

> Do not fear an early manifestation of evil karma, fear only a late Awakening.

Sometimes the practitioner, in the midst of intense cultivation, suddenly becomes confused and weary, which is a state difficult to fight off. At that very moment, he should arise and bow to the Buddhas or circumambulate the altar. Or else, he may take a temporary break, read a few pages of a book or rearrange some flowers, waiting for his mind to calm down before returning to the altar to resume recitation. Otherwise, the more he tries to focus his mind, the more scattered it becomes. This is a case of flexibility in cultivation. It is similar to the situation of a commander-in-chief facing an invading army as powerful as a river overflowing its banks. In such a situation, the general should stay on the defensive, consolidating his position, rather than charging into battle.

Some practictioners suddenly feel solitary and isolated when reciting the Buddha's name like a single-note musical piece, and grow melancholy and bored. In such cases, they should not hesitate to add mantra or sutra recitation or visualization to their practice.

***

By way of illustration, I shall recount a few incidents for the benefit of the reader. One day a laywoman visited the author, crying in anguish as she told him that whenever she engaged in Buddha or Sutra Recitation for more than half an hour, she would fall asleep without realizing it. At times she would even urinate right in front of the altar. Therefore, fearing evil karma, she ceased to practice and abandoned all cultivation. I advised her to concentrate on practicing repentance for a while. As expected, in time she was free of those karmic manifestations. Furthermore, she would view numerous snail shells in her dreams, and, as she broke them open, she would see a lotus seed in each shell. The laywoman was afflicted with heavy delusions and the shells were manifestations of the karma of delusion. Breaking them open and seeing lotus seeds symbolized eliminating delusion and creating the causes and conditions of Awakening and rebirth in the Pure Land.

Another story: A novice once told the author that in his dreams, from time to time he would see some thirty to forty persons armed with knives and spears coming at him, striking and slashing him all over. In his daily practice, he would diligently recite mantras, alternating between the Great Compassion Dharani and the Thousand-Armed Avalokitesvara Mantra, without success, as each time he recited either mantra a few times, he would develop a headache which lasted the whole day. He sought medical treatment to relieve these symptoms, to no avail. Knowing that his karma was heavy, the novice vowed to bow to the three thousand Buddhas in repentance. However, when he entered the main Buddha hall, he saw a huge, tall, fierce-looking man, who approached him and pushed him to the floor, preventing him from bowing. For this reason, he came to see the author, weeping in anguish, and asked, "the sutras teach repentance and cultivation to extinguish bad karma, but if you are prevented from repenting and cultivating, what else are you expected to do?"

The author pondered for a moment. He reflected that the novice must have committed a heavy "killing" karma, and been responsible for many deaths in past lives. Moreover, he knew that the Great Compassion Dharani and the Thousand-Armed Avalokitesvara

Mantra had a powerful, beneficial effect, while vowing to bow to the three thousand Buddhas was an all-encompassing, lofty resolution. In this case, however, the novice had made the mistake of just praying and thinking of himself alone, forgetting those whom he had wronged in past lifetimes. Moreover, he was not being flexible in cultivation. This is not unlike a debilitated person suffering a heavy bout of influenza. He should take a mild analgesic, to recover little by little; instead, he begins to ingest a powerful antibiotic. This, of course, provokes a strong reaction which overwhelms him. Therefore, the author advised the novice to bow each night while reciting the short repentance liturgy, and then kneel to recite the rebirth mantra twenty-one times. After that, he should repeat the Buddha's name some five hundred times, seeking repentance, and transfer the merit to all whom he had wronged in previous existences, so that they, too, could swiftly escape the cycle of Birth and Death. He should continue this regimen for some time, and, if nothing untoward occurred, gradually increase the number of recitations. The novice followed the author's advice and as expected, his predicament was resolved.

These cases reflect internal karmic manifestations. If the practitioner does not understand them and eliminate them with flexibility, they will surely develop into dangerous obstacles.

2. External testing conditions

These are external obstacles creating difficult conditions which can make the practitioner retrogress. These obstacles include heat, noise, dirt and pollution, freezing weather, or an outbreak of mosquitoes and other insects. When faced with these conditions, the cultivator should be flexible and not become attached to forms and appearances. He should just seek tranquillity and peace of mind.

For instance, in sweltering heat, he should not mind donning a light robe to bow to the Buddhas, and then retiring to a shady spot outdoors to recite the Buddha's name. At the end of the session, he can return to the altar to make his vows and transfer the merit. If the practitioner happens to be living in a mosquito-infested area, he can sit inside a net while reciting the Buddha's name. As another example, in northern climes, where the weather can be freezing, monks and nuns must dress carefully in socks, shoes and hats when going to the Buddha hall to recite sutras.

As another example, some destitute laymen, living from hand to mouth, going to work early and coming home late, pursued by creditors, tattered, hungry and cold, with sickly wives and malnourished children, can hardly afford a decent place to practice. In such situations, cultivation is truly difficult. The practitioner should redouble his efforts and have the patience and endurance of the beggar woman in one of our previous stories in order to succeed.

Other people, with heavy karmic obstructions, do not experience untoward occurrences as long as they do not cultivate, but as soon as they are ready to bow before the altar, they develop headaches, grow dizzy, and are afflicted with all kinds of ailments. Or else, they may receive sudden visitors or encounter unusual events. Faced with these occurrences, the practitioner should redouble his efforts and find ways to cultivate flexibly.

These ways depend on circumstances; they cannot all be described. One point, however, should always be kept in mind: when faced with difficult circumstances, pay attention to the mind, and do not cling to appearances and forms. The evil, turbid Saha World has always been full of suffering and tears. Without perseverance and forbearance, it is very difficult to succeed in cultivation.

3. Testing conditions caused by adverse circumstances

Practitioners on the path of cultivation are at times impeded by adverse circumstances. Some are prevented from cultivating or frustrated in their practice by parents, brothers and sisters, wives, husbands or children. Others suddenly develop a chronic disease, from which they never completely recover. Still others are continually pursued by opponents and enemies looking for ways to harm them. Others are slandered or meet with misfortunes which land them in prison, subject to torture, or they are sent into exile. Others, again, victims of jealous competition or calumny, lose all peace of mind. This last occurrence is the most frequent. Such cases occur because of the power of evil karma. The ancients had a saying:

> There are instances of sudden praise and unexpected honors which are undeserved, and other instances, not deserving of blame, which create major opportunities for censure and contempt.

The author will recount a few minor incidents to demonstrate this truth.

Early in this century during the French colonial period, there was an abbot who was honored by the Emperor of Vietnam with the title of High Priest. His temple was also given a special honorific name. Thereafter, he was accompanied by soldiers and banners wherever he went and received special treatment, such as being carried on a hammock on and off ferry boats. A local tramp, seeing this, was greatly chagrined and began to curse the abbot. He then declared that on the occasion of the Ullambana Festival [Bon festival or Vu-lan] he would go to the temple and rail against the Master in front of his entire congregation. On the appointed day, the tramp, having gotten drunk, removed his shirt and went to the temple with torso bared. Right at that moment, however, the abbot happened to be busy praying for a number of turtles which were about to be released in the lotus pond. The tramp, unexpectedly touched by this scene, went home and called upon his friends to meet at the temple to become disciples of the abbot. From that day on, wherever he went, he would praise the abbot as a gentle monk of great merit and virtue. He would even explain away the special treatment accorded the abbot, including the instances of being carried by hammock, as fully justified by his great merit.

Another incident took place not long ago. Two laymen from far away came to visit an Elder Master who was from their village and whom they had known "way back when." They reached the temple about fifteen minutes after the Master had gone out. They questioned his young attendant, who said that the Master had just left. When they inquired of others at the temple, the latter, unaware of the Master's departure, replied that they had just seen him. Because of these contradictory responses, the laymen grew suspicious, thinking that the Master did not wish to meet with them. Thereupon, they left the temple, never to return. From that time on, they would criticize the Master wherever they went, accusing him of lacking virtue.

In truth, the conduct of the abbot in our first story was not praiseworthy, yet he was praised. The inadvertent action of the Elder Master in our second story did not warrant any criticism, but he was misunderstood and slandered. These two occurrences are commonly explained as chance events. In Buddhism, however, they are seen as the results of good or bad karma. If this applies even to minor occurrences, all other adverse events can similarly be traced to past or current karma. When faced with such occurrences, the practitioner should repent and exercise patience and forbearance. He should not grow dejected or complain, lest he retrogress on the Way.

4. Testing conditions caused by "favorable circumstances"

Some practitioners do not encounter adverse circumstances, but on the contrary, meet with favorable circumstances, such as having their wishes and prayers fulfilled. However, such successes belong to the category of "binding" conditions, rather than conditions conducive to liberation. Thus, just as some practitioners set their minds to peaceful cultivation, they suddenly encounter opportunities leading to fame and fortune, "beautiful forms and enchanting sounds." Or else, family members, relatives and supporters seek to follow and serve them on their retreats. For example, a monk who has made up his mind to cultivate in earnest may suddenly be requested to become the abbot of a large temple complex. Or else, a layman may unexpectedly receive a letter inviting him to become a minister heading such and such a government department, or offering him the chance to participate in a business venture which promises a quick profit. These instances, all of which are advantageous under mundane circumstances, are seductive to the cultivator, and may gradually lead to other complications. Ultimately, he may forget his high aspirations and retrogress. As the saying goes, more lives are lost in a flood than in a fire.

Thus, on the path of cultivation, favorable circumstances should be feared more than unfavorable ones. Unfavorable events sometimes awaken the practitioner, making it easier for him to escape thoughts of attachment and redouble his efforts in cultivation. Favorable events, on the other hand, may make him quietly retrogress, without being aware of it. When he suddenly awakens, he may discover that he has slipped far down the slope. The ancients have said:

Even two or three favorable circumstances may cause one

to be deluded until old age.

This saying is truly a ringing bell to wake cultivators up. Therefore, the challenge of favorable events is very subtle -- practioners need to pay close attention to them.

5. Testing conditions of a clear, explicit nature

These are clear "testing conditions" which occur right before the practitioner's eyes, without his realizing their implications. For instance, a monk of relatively mediocre talents and virtues becomes the object of adulation, praised for great merit, virtue and talent. He then develops a big ego and looks down on everyone, giving rise to thoughtless action resulting in his downfall. Or else we have the case of a layman with the potential to progress far along the Way. However he is blocked and opposed by others, who advise him, for example, that vegetarianism will make him sick, or that overly diligent mantra and Buddha Recitation will "unleash his evil karma," causing him to encounter many untoward events. He then develops a cautious, anxious attitude, retrogressing in his determination to achieve the Way.

There are also circumstances in which the practitioner realizes that to advance further is to invite failure and defeat, yet, out of ambition or pride, he continues all the same. Or else, even though the cultivator knows that external circumstances are illusory and dream-like, he cannot let go of them, and thus brings great suffering upon himself. For example, there was once a monk who spent a good deal of effort and money hiring stonecutters, carpenters and masons to build a large temple complex on top of a mountain. As soon as the temple was completed, the monk, by then completely exhausted, became gravely ill. Before passing away, he requested his disciples to carry him around the temple on a hammock, as he touched each and every stone, weeping and lamenting![72]

Another story concerns a Vietnamese monk who was of fairly high rank within the Buddhist hierarchy. He was honest by nature, liberal and broadminded, given to practicing charity. However he had a shortcoming -- pride and conceit. Several local politicians, having noticed this, went to see him along with a fortune teller feigning a courtesy visit. During the ensuing conversation, the fortune teller took a glance at the Master and praised him for his "marks of merit," which would surely bring him many supporters, while his fame and renown would spread far and wide. He added that if the monk enjoyed political and social activities, he would surely become a great leader. For example, he would easily be elected Prime Minister, if he were a layman. Hearing this, the monk replied with a few words of modesty; however, his face exhibited extreme delight. Seizing the occasion, the politicians lamented the current period, expressed compassion for the sufferings of the people and the declining state of the country. They then gradually persuaded him to join a political movement. The result was a great deal of pain and anguish for the monk over an extended period of time.

This story demonstrates that the easy-going and credulous are often duped. When they have not eliminated greed, it is easy for others to deceive them with money, sex and fame. It also applies to those who have a temper and too much pride. Easily aroused, they bring a great deal of trouble and anguish upon themselves. These are the trappings and the pitfalls of the outside world -- which are also encountered within the Order. I bring them up here as a warning to fellow cultivators. If they are not careful, they will become entangled in the cycle of obstructing karma. The practitioner should develop a clear understanding of these adverse conditions and resolve to progress along a path consonant with the Way. Only then will he be able to overcome these obstacles.

6. Silent, hidden testing conditions

This refers to silent challenges, inconspicuous in nature. If the practitioner is not skillful in taking notice, they are very difficult to recognize and defeat. Some people, who may have recited the Buddha's name diligently in the beginning, grow worried and discouraged by deteriorating family finances or repeated failures in whatever they undertake, and abandon cultivation. Others see their affairs quietly progressing in a favorable way; they then become attached to profit and gain, forgetting all about the Way. Others diligently engage in Buddha and Sutra Recitation at the beginning, but because they fail to examine themselves, the afflictions within their minds increase with each passing day. They then grow lethargic and lazy, to the point where they do not recite a single time for months, or even years. Still others, although their lives are progressing normally, see their living conditions continuously fluctuating with changing external circumstances. With their minds always in confusion and directed toward the outside, they unwittingly neglect recitation or abandon it altogether.

All the above are the fluctuating effects of good and bad karma, which have the power to influence the practitioner and retard his cultivation. They are therefore called "trying, testing conditions." When first taking up cultivation, every practitioner has a seed of good intentions. However, as they encounter karmic conditions, one after another, both internal and external, ninety-nine cultivators out of a hundred will fail. The ancients had a saying:

> In the first year of cultivation, Buddha Amitabha is right before our eyes; the second year, He has already returned West; by the time the third year rolls around, if someone inquires about Him or requests recitation [at a funeral, for example], payment is required before a few words are spoken or a few verses recited.

This saying reflects the points just discussed; practitioners should bear them in mind and take heed.

How to Clear up Obstructing Conditions

64) Advice of Ancient Masters

When first entering the Order, the author heard a saying, handed down by word of mouth, which contains many hidden meanings and implications. However, he cannot vouch for its authenticity or provenance. The saying is as follows:

> If the Buddha is one foot tall, the demon is ten feet tall; if the Buddha is ten feet tall, the demon stands just above the Buddha's head. However, if the Buddha grows taller still and exceeds the demon in height, the demon will surrender to the Buddha.

Reflecting on this story, the practitioner should ensure that his own Buddha is taller than the demon. Otherwise, he will be subverted and vanquished. Therefore, those cultivators who fail and retrogress should not fault external circumstances or lay blame on others. They should only blame their own Buddha, for being weaker than the demon. If they persist in holding fast to their vows and determination, demonic obstacles will disappear.

The Patriarch Bodhidharma once outlined four practices which Buddhist disciples should take to heart. They are summarized below.

1. The Practice of Compensating for Previous Wrongs

From time immemorial we have been lost along the six Evil Paths. In each lifetime we have incurred karmic debts, large and small, in connection with either love-attachment or hatred. These are truly countless. Although our efforts in cultivation dissolve part of this karma, it is not entirely eliminated, and must be gradually repaid. Thus, someone who is always ill, or is disabled, has created heavy karma of killing in past lives. Those who are the targets of a great deal of slander and calumny were, in earlier times, intelligent and influential people who, proud of their good fortune, despised others. Or else, they created the karma of vilifying the Dharma or the Order. Those who are always lacking in means lacked compassion and failed to practice charity in past lives. Those who must endure banishment, imprisonment, bondage and torture, were, in past lives, in the habit of chaining, beating or imprisoning sentient beings. Those who are lonely and isolated, lacking supportive friends, did not have bonds of affinity with other sentient beings in the past.

These karmas are countless. If today we encounter animosity and opposition to our cultivation, we should remain calm and forbearing, accepting that we must repay our karmic debts without chagrin or complaint. In the wasteland of Birth and Death, all sentient beings have been related at one time or another, sharing the same table, living in the same house -- as family members or as friends. Therefore, of all karmic obstructions, those of killing sentient beings and of love-attachment are the deepest.[73] The ancients have lamented:

In the vast ocean of karma, love-attachment is the most difficult thing to sever. In the great wide world, killing sentient beings [for food] is the most common transgression!

In East Asian folklore, there is the tale of a famous poet who journeyed to the mountains during the Mid-Autumn Festival in search of inspiration. In the moonlit night, he witnessed the Immortals "mount the wind and ride the fog," as they gathered around a huge marble table laden with succulent fruits and rare wines, playing musical instruments and reciting poetry ... Among the fairies was a maiden by the name of "Mountain Moon," with lovely, ethereal features and a gracious, enchanting voice. The poet, eaveasdropping, was moved to the point of confusion. Suddenly, an elderly Immortal, having savored his cup of wine, began to recite verses:

> Those of common destiny,
> Meet at the Assembly of
>   Immortals;
> I consent to the poet
> Wedding Mountain Moon!

Hearing this stanza, the poet reluctantly emerged from hiding and joined the assembly. The elderly Immortal decreed that the young maiden had a karmic affinity with the earthly poet, and that they should live together for thirteen years. He thereupon ordered that the register of Immortals be brought over, and crossed her name out. After thirteen years of life together, her earthly life having come to an end, Mountain Moon rendered herself invisible and flew back to the mountains to pursue her cultivation. Thus, even Immortals are within the cycle of Birth and Death, causes and conditions.

Regarding the karma of killing, both Elder Master Arya Simha (the Twenty-fourth Indian Patriarch of Zen) and Elder Master Hui K'o (the Second Chinese Patriarch), despite having achieved Enlightenment, still had to repay their debts by calmly submitting to violent death.[74] Take also the case of Maudgalyayana, a well-known disciple of Sakyamuni Buddha, with the highest spiritual power among Arhats. Because he wished to repay his previous karmic debts, he let a group of bandits kill him with sticks and stones and bury his body in an excrement pit. The Buddha, moved by this scene, ordered his disciples to unearth the body, cleanse and bathe it with perfume, then cremate it and retrieve the relics.[75]

On the path of cultivation, no one knows who is really perfect. Thus, we should neither be complacent nor look down on others. Because the karmic debts of sentient beings are countless, sometimes they must repay one layer after another. Some cultivators seem to be free of karmic debts, but this may not be the case. It may just be that the time and conditions for repayment have not yet arrived. To eliminate evil karma, we should be patient, practice repentance, and strive to cultivate. Nguyễn-Du, a famous Vietnamese poet of recent times, had perhaps deeply assimilated the Buddhas' teaching on karma and the possible transmutation of cause and effect when he wrote:

Having committed evil karma,
Let us not blame Heaven for
    being near or far,
While Providence plays a part,
So do we ...

These words are generally recognized as a reflection of the truth.

2. The practice of adapting to conditions

This means that the practitioner should adapt flexibly to his situation and conditions. For example, living in conditions of wealth or poverty, he lives in accordance with conditions of wealth or poverty. The same applies to conditions of underdevelopment or prosperity, adversity or good fortune, loss or gain, right or wrong ...

Contentment with conditions means being wealthy without being arrogant, being destitute and beset by misfortune without being sad and depressed or altering one's determination. Why is this so? It is because instances of prosperity, decline, misfortune, and/or blessings are all illusory.[76] They appear for a while according to our karma and then disappear. It is really not worthwhile to become attached, discouraged or sad.

Confucius and his disciples were once surrounded by rebel soldiers. They had been short of food for seven days, yet Confucius was happily playing the lute. His leading disciple inquired, "How is it, Master, that in the face of death you can still smile happily?" Confucius replied, "Whatever misfortunes befall a man after he has done his best to prevent them, can only be the will of Heaven. Why, then, bemoan them and weep?" Confucius may be considered a sage conversant with the will of heaven and earth -- always calm and clearsighted, never bewildered or wavering, regardless of the circumstances. The practitioner should be likewise, realizing that wealth and property, family and friends, are all the result of illusory, temporary conditions. He should not be unduly attached to or preoccupied with them, if he is to progress along the path to liberation.

3. The practice of being in accord with the Dharma

"Dharma" here means "True Thusness Dharma." For Pure Land practitioners, it represents the Buddha Recitation Samadhi. For Zen followers, whether they are walking, standing, reclining or sitting, the mind should always accord with True Thusness, just as water blends with water and empty space is one with the atmosphere. The Pure Land practitioner is the same: his mind is always focussed on the words "Amitabha Buddha."

The ancients have said:

If a practitioner is not in samadhi for one instant, at that moment, he is no different from a corpse.

This is because if a cultivator's mind is scattered, he

has been effectively "captured" by worldly Dusts. Once captured and dragged away, his "Dharma-Body Wisdom-Life" is lost and gone. On the other hand, if the practitioner is always focussed on the Buddha's name, his mind will gradually become silent, still and illuminated, in unison with Buddha Amitabha. He is thus assured of rebirth in the Pure Land.

4. The practice of non-seeking

This refers to the pure practice of not seeking after anything. All dharmas are illusory and dream-like, born and destroyed, destroyed and reborn. What is there which is true, everlasting and worth seeking? Furthermore, worldly phenomena are all relative; in calamities are found blessings, in blessings there is misfortune. Therefore, those who have wisdom are always calm and unruffled, their minds undisturbed in all situations.

For example, when a monk cultivates alone in a deserted hut, his living conditions are miserable and lonely and he has few visitors. Although his mundane conditions may be wanting, his cultivation is diligent. After a while, if virtuous people learn of his situation and come with offerings, his hut will gradually grow into a large temple, filled with monks and nuns. By then, while his blessings may be great, his cultivation has effectively declined, because his mind is now preoccupied with external events. The truth of misfortunes and blessings, mutually dependent, is similar. Therefore, ideally, the cultivator should seek neither untoward occurrences and rebirth as a sentient being nor auspicious occurrences and Buddhahood.

***

Some may ask, "If we recite the Buddhas's name seeking neither rebirth in the Pure Land nor the ultimate blessings and wisdom of Buddhahood, how can we progress in our cultivation?" *Answer:* It is because Buddhahood is True Emptiness. The more we seek it, the farther we are from it, and the more likely we are to lose it. Thus, the *Lotus Sutra* states:

> Even if countless Arhats, Pratyeka Buddhas, and other sages, up to the level of Non-Regressing Bodhisattvas, were to ponder and seek it for innumerable kalpas, they still would not be able to see or understand the true wisdom of the Buddhas.

As far as rebirth in the Pure Land is concerned, the practitioner's method is *to seek yet not seek, not to seek yet seek.* This paradox resembles the case of a bright and clear mirror. When an image appears before the mirror, the mirror reflects it; when there is no image, the mirror remains empty and still. To cling to sight, knowledge and seeking is to "stray" into deluded thought. On the other hand, not to see, know or seek is to be no different from inanimate wood or stone! Speaking more broadly, the practice of non-seeking encompasses all "three doors of liberation": emptiness, signlessness and wishlessness.

If the cultivator can follow these four practices taught by the Patriarch Bodhidharma, he will be able to remain calm and unruffled in the face of all obstructing conditions.

65) How to Ensure Non-Retrogression of the Mind

A Pure Land treatise on the Buddha Recitation Samadhi has explained the "ten practices of non-seeking" to eliminate the ten major obstacles encountered by practitioners on the path to Enlightenment. These ten major obstacles encompass all obstructions and impediments. Therefore if we follow the ten non-seeking practices, all obstacles will disappear. These ten practices are:

1. We should not wish that our bodies be always free

of diseases and ailments, because a disease-free body is prone to desire and lust. This leads to precept-breaking and retrogression.

2. We should not wish that our lives be free of all misfortune and adversity, lest we be prone to pride and arrogance. This leads us to be disdainful and overbearing towards everyone else.

3. We should not wish that our mind cultivation be free of all obstacles because, in such a case, our knowledge would be exceptional. This leads to the transgression of thinking that we have awakened, when in fact we have not.

4. We should not wish that our cultivation be free of demonic obstacles, because our vows would not then be firm and enduring. This leads to the transgression of thinking that we have attained Enlightenment, when in fact we have not.

5. We should not wish that our plans and activities meet with easy success, for we will then be inclined to thoughts of contempt and disrespect. This leads to the transgression of pride and conceit, thinking ourselves to be filled with virtues and talent.

6. We should not wish for gain in our social relations. This leads us to violate moral principles and see only the mistakes of others.

7. We should not wish that everyone, at all times, be on good terms and in harmony with us. This leads to pride and conceit and seeing only our own side of every issue.

8. We should not wish to be repaid for our good deeds, lest we develop a calculating mind. This leads to greed for fame and fortune.

9. We should not wish to share in opportunities for profit, lest the mind of delusion arise. This leads us to lose our good name and reputation for the sake of unwholesome gain.

10. When subject to injustice and wronged, we should not necessarily seek the ability to refute and rebut, as doing so indicates that the mind of self-and-others has not been severed. This will certainly lead to more resentment and hatred.

Thus, we can see that life, while full of obstacles and impediments, can be summarized in ten points:

1. Sickness of the body
2. Misfortune and adversity
3. Hindrances and impediments to cultivation
4. Demonic obstacles to fulfillment of vows
5. Failure in activities and undertakings
6. Indifferent or treacherous friends
7. Opposition from many quarters
8. Hostility in return for good deeds
9. Loss of wealth and reputation
10. Subjection to injustice and wrongs.

Thus, in merit there is misfortune, in misfortune there is merit, in freedom there are obstructions, in obstructions there is freedom. Realizing this, cultivators in the past have used "obstacles as conditions for progress." They have said, "If others do not bother and disturb us, success in the Way is difficult to achieve." This is because contempt, slander, calamity, injustice and all other obstacles are the "yardsticks to measure the practitioner's level of attainment." Remaining patient and calm in the face of such impediments, the cultivator demonstrates that he has reached a high level of practice. If it were not for these obstacles, how could his level of attainment be measured?

In truth, it is not that the practitioner seeks

obstacles and impediments, but that he must be
ever-vigilant, for the Way is full of dangerous and
unforeseen events. He should prepare himself for all
eventualities so that when faced with actual obstacles, he
can remain calm and unruffled. An Elder Master once
said:

> Only those with wisdom and strong determination can
> apply these ten practices. As long as they meditate, are
> enlightened and hold steadfastly to these ten practices,
> even if they enter the realms of the demons, the demons
> cannot make them retrogress. Even though they may be in
> the realms of form, sound, fame, fortune, love, hate, right,
> wrong, prosperity, decline, success, failure ... they will still
> be calm and at peace.

Thus, if we are deluded, all good and favorable
circumstances can become conditions obstructing the
Way. If we truly understand that all disease, suffering
and demonic obstacles are inherently empty and false,
lacking true substance, they cannot harm us in any way.
The wise should apply the above ten points in the
following way:

1. Turn suffering and disease into good medicine
2. Turn misfortune and calamity into liberation
3. Turn obstacles into freedom and ease
4. Turn demons into Dharma friends
5. Turn trying events into peace and joy
6. Turn bad friends into helpful associates
7. Turn opponents into "fields of flowers"
8. Treat ingratitude as worn-out shoes to be
   discarded
9. Turn frugality into power and wealth
10. Turn injustice and wrongs into conditions for
    progress along the Way.

***

We can see, then, that good or bad, success or
failure always depends on the mind. Therefore, while

beginning cultivators are very leary of obstacles, high-level masters are at times eager to face them. I will relate a few anecdotes in this regard.

The Second Patriarch Hui K'o, having experienced Awakening under the Patriarch Bodhidharma, left for an undisclosed destination to work as a hired hand, cutting wood, pounding rice, guarding other people's homes. When he was asked, "Why are you lowering yourself by performing such menial tasks, you who are next in succession as Patriarch?" he replied, "I want to subdue my mind; what difference does my occupation make?"

Another anecdote: A famous Immortal, having achieved success through self-effort, "escaped" his mortal body and went to visit the Heavens. Once there, his mind was moved at the sight of fairies with exquisite, ethereal features, beyond human description. The Fairy Queen reprimanded him sternly, "Although you have attained the Immortal Way, you have not purged your thoughts of lust and desire. How can you be worthy of joining the ranks of True Immortals?"

Ashamed, our protagonist returned immediately to the human realm. He then used his spiritual powers to transform stones into gold. After filling his pockets with the precious metal, he entered a brothel to consort with six or seven of the youngest and most lissome prostitutes. For two years, he would lie next to their nude bodies, training himself to overcome all thoughts of lust and desire. When he knew that he had succeeded, he asked the ladies to prepare a cake batter and place it on his stomach. He then proceeded to bake it, using his internal body heat concentrated at a point just below the navel. He then treated them to the cake and went on to expound the Immortal teachings, before "riding the clouds" back to the Heavens.

I shall next recount a few more stories, by way of comparison.

A certain nun vowed to hold a three months' retreat, to rid herself of transgressions. She followed the cultivation practice of "purifying speech" by taking a vow of complete silence. One evening, as she was seated by the window fingering the rosary and reciting the Buddha's name, a young novice saw her. He immediately turned toward his companion and told him that the nun had heavy karma and numerous character flaws. When she heard this, her face reddened in anger, but she remained calm and continued her recitation. A moment later, the novice added, "I have been watching her and saw her in bed with a neighbor." The nun, no longer able to contain her anger, shouted "Be sure to get the neighbor's name, as I am not going to let you get away with this story." The novice laughed loudly and replied, "I purposely wanted to test you. You have taken a vow of silence. Why are you speaking now? Moreover, the aim of purifying speech is really to purify the mind. Since you cannot purify your mind, what is the point of purifying speech?" The nun was suddenly awakened. Ashamed, she kept silent.

Another anecdote was related to the author by an abbot, when they met on the grounds of the Institute of Higher Buddhist Studies in Vietnam. There was once a Zen Master who was fairly diligent in his meditation practice. At each sitting, he would remain in concentration for six or seven hours without a break. The Master, perhaps out of fear of attachment to worldly conditions, would, as a rule, shun the company of women, to the point where at the end of their visits, he would fetch water and wash the spot where they had sat. After a while, he moved to the Ten Stupa Temple, located in a sparsely populated, mountainous area of Central Vietnam. One morning, he suddenly let out a scream and ran from the meditation hut. The abbot inquired and was told, "I was deep in samadhi when, suddenly, a beautiful woman grabbed me by the neck."

That same evening, the monk became ill. He remained in bed and asked to see the abbot. When the latter arrived, the monk said to him, "You had better get me a wife in a hurry; otherwise, starting from tonight I will not accept any food and will starve to death." The abbot sent for a trusted laywoman, to discuss the matter with her. "Let me go home and tell my young housemaid to pretend to become the Master's wife," she suggested. "After he begins to eat again and recovers, we will see what to do next."

Morning came and the abbot, accompanied by the maid, visited the sick monk and said, "I have settled the issue. This young woman has agreed to become your wife." Upon hearing this, the Zen monk opened his eyes, looked at the maid, held and caressed her hands for awhile, and expired.

***

From the above stories, we can see that the nun wanted to eliminate afflictions, but she followed external forms only. In the case of the Second Zen Patriarch, he understood that all afflictions were empty, grounded in attachment to the self.[77] Therefore, he took the appearance of a poor and lowly laborer accepting orders and insults, to test his mind and cultivate further. As far as the Immortal is concerned, wishing to eliminate thoughts of attachment and lust, he courageously entered a brothel to cultivate and still his mind. As to the Zen monk in our last story, because he had not yet realized that form is emptiness and emptiness is form, he was unduly fearful of female allurements. Still heavily attached to forms and appearances, in the end he was harmed by the "demon of lust."

In conclusion, practitioners endowed with wisdom not only do not avoid obstacles, they use impediments to progress in cultivation. Those cultivators are no longer attached to forms and appearances, because appearances are merely expedients, while the mind represents the Ultimate.

66) Afterthoughts

In the Dharma-Ending Age, many people recite the Buddha's name, but few achieve results. This is because they lack earnest vows and deep faith. In a discourse on the character of the ideal gentleman, Mencius once wrote:

Wealth and power do not make him proud or lustful; poverty and want do not cause him to alter his resolution; force cannot make him yield and submit.

Even the ideal gentleman should be thus -- not to mention those who cultivate the Dharma and practice Buddha Recitation, seeking to transcend this world and enter the "stream of the sages ..."

The Pure Land method stems from the great compassionate Vows of the Tathagatas; with determination, no one will miss the boat of liberation. This author was moved to ask himself: the wonderful Nature in all sentient beings has always been equal and the same; why is it that some of us are reborn in the Pure Land, while others keep revolving within the cycle of Birth and Death? The music of the *high mountains* reverberates down to us; how many listen intently to the sound of the *flowing stream?* The author has, therefore, penned a few thoughts for the edification of others -- as well as himself.

10

The Last Rites

Required Preparations on the Eve of Death
67) Preparation of External Conditions

The ancients had a saying:

We see others die, and our hearts ache. We ache not because others die, but because soon it will be our turn!

There is no greater sadness, no greater tragedy in the world than the separation of death. However, it is something no one in the world can escape. Therefore, those who aspire to be of benefit to themselves and others should be prepared and ready for it. In truth, the word "death" is a misnomer, because it is merely the end of a period of retribution. When we leave this body, because of the connecting undercurrent of karma, we will be reborn into another body. Those who do not know the Dharma are resigned to being under the sway of karma. Those who know the Pure Land method should practice Buddha Recitation with Faith and Vows and prepare their "personal provisions," so that they may be reborn in peace and harmony. Only in this way can they hope to achieve an early escape from the illusory suffering of Birth and Death and attain the true joy of ever-dwelling Nirvana.

Furthermore, the Pure Land practitioner should not be concerned about himself alone, but should be filial and compassionate toward parents, relatives and friends as well, enjoining them all to practice Buddha Recitation. He should also assist them when they are seriously ill -- and at the time of death. These altruistic practices also create merits and good conditions for himself in the future.

There are many details connected with the last rites. I will first speak about external conditions. The Pure Land practitioner should, while still in good health, prepare himself and seek friends of like practice, particularly among neighbors, for mutual devotional help in cases of serious illness and at the time of death. Such preparations are crucial because we generally have heavy karma and even if we have striven to the utmost, it may be difficult to maintain right thought at such times.[78] This is due to the emergence of karma accumulated from time immemorial, which weakens the body and perturbs the mind. Without the assistance of others, it is difficult to escape the cycle of Birth and Death. Is this not wasting an entire lifetime of cultivation? This is the first important point.

Secondly, when a Pure Land practitioner sees his strength ebbing, he should settle all his worldly affairs, so that he will not be preoccupied at the time of death. If he is a monk, he should turn over the affairs of the temple to his disciples and designate his successor. If he is a layman, he should divide his wealth and property in a suitable manner and make all other necessary arrangements. He should also instruct his family and relatives that should he be gravely ill or on the verge of death, they should not weep and lament or otherwise show their grief. Rather, if they care for him, they should calmly recite the Buddha's name on his behalf, or

assist him in other ways to achieve rebirth in the Pure
Land. This would be true concern and love.

68) Spiritual Preparations

In addition to the external preparations just
described, the Pure Land practitioner should prepare
himself spiritually. What do these preparations entail?
On the way to liberation, the practitioner should have a
transcendental bent of mind, realizing that wealth and
property, as well as family, relatives and friends, are all
illusory conditions. Relying in life on an illusory realm,
he will die empty-handed. If he fails to understand this
truth, family and possessions will certainly impede his
liberation. In extreme cases, he may even be reborn in
the animal realm -- as a dog or a snake, for example, to
watch over his former houses and properties.[79] There
are many instances of individuals unable to let go of
family and possessions, who experience difficulty at the
time of death. They cannot close their eyes and die
peacefully.

***

When this author was still a novice, attending to his
Master and serving him tea late at night, he overheard
an elder monk relate an anecdote. The main lines of the
story are as follows.

Once, in times past, there were two monks who
cultivated together. One liked the high mountain
scenery, while the other built himself a hut on the banks
of a brook, near a forest. Years went by. The monk who
resided by the brook passed away first. Learning the
news, his friend went down to visit his grave. After
reciting sutras and praying for his friend's liberation, the
visiting monk entered samadhi and attempted to see
where his friend had gone -- to no avail. The friend was
nowhere to be found, neither in the heavens nor in the
hells, nor in any of the realms in between. Emerging

from samadhi, he asked the attending novice, "What was your Master busy with every day?" The novice replied, "In the last few months before his death, seeing that the sugar cane in front of his hut was tall and green, my Master would go out continually to apply manure and prune away the dead leaves. He kept close watch over the cane, and seemed so happy taking care of it."

Upon hearing this, the visiting monk entered samadhi again, and saw that his friend had been reborn as a worm inside one of the stalks of sugar cane. The monk immediately cut down that stalk, slit it open and extracted the worm. He preached the Dharma to it and recited the Buddha's name, dedicating the merit to the worm's salvation.

This story was transmitted by word of mouth; the author has not found it anywhere in sutras or commentaries. However, if we judge it in the light of the Dharma, it is not necessarily without foundation. Buddhist sutras actually contain several similar accounts.

For example, there is the story of a novice who was greedy for buttermilk and was reborn as a worm in the milk pot. There is also the anecdote of a layman who was a genuine cultivator, adhering strictly to the precepts, but, being overly attached to his wife, was reborn as a worm in his wife's nostrils. As she cried her heart out by the side of the coffin, she tried to clear her nose, and the worm was expelled onto the floor. Greatly ashamed, she was on the verge of stamping it with her foot. Fortunately, the whole scene was witnessed by an enlightened monk, who stopped her and told her the causes and conditions of the worm. He then preached the Dharma to the worm, seeking its liberation.

There is also the story of a sea merchant's wife so attached to her own beauty that upon her death, she was reborn as a worm crawling out of her nostrils and wandering all over her own pallid face.

Thus, the Pure Land cultivator should keep his mind empty and still and meditate day in and day out, severing the mind of greed rooted in attachment and lust. He should resolutely direct his thoughts to the Pure Land, so that at the time of death, he will not be hindered and led astray by his evil karma.

Elder Master Tzu Chao once said:

The Pure Land practitioner on the verge of death usually faces Three Points of Doubt and Four Narrow Passes which obstruct his rebirth in the Pure Land. He should be prepared, reflecting on them in advance to eliminate them.

The Three Points of Doubt are:

1) Fearing that his past karma is heavy and his period of cultivation short, and that therefore, he may not achieve rebirth in the Pure Land;

2) Fearing that he has not yet fulfilled his vows and obligations or severed greed, anger and delusion, and that therefore, he may not achieve rebirth in the Pure Land;

3) Fearing that even though he has recited the Buddha's name, Buddha Amitabha may not come, and that therefore, he may not achieve rebirth in the Pure Land.

The [two main] Narrow Passes are:

1) Because of suffering due to illness, he may come to malign the Buddhas as ineffective and unresponsive;

2) Because of love-attachment, he may chain himself to his family, unable to let go.

Once aware of the doctrine of the Three Doubts and the Four Narrow Passes, the wise can ponder and find a solution. The author shall merely summarize a few points below. Fellow cultivators can expand on them according to their own backgrounds and understanding.

a) Overcoming the Three Doubts

1. Previous heavy karma, present perfunctory practice.

Amitabha Buddha is renowned for his Eighteenth Vow: not to attain Buddhahood unless sentient beings who sincerely desire to be reborn in the Pure Land, and who singlemindedly recite His name, are reborn there. The Buddhas do not engage in false speech, and therefore the practitioner should believe in them. Ten utterances or thoughts represent a very short cultivation period, yet the practitioner can still achieve rebirth in the Pure Land. We who have recited the Buddha's name many times over should, therefore, eliminate all doubts.

Moreover, no matter how heavy the karma of sentient beings is, if they sincerely repent and rely upon Amitabha Buddha, they will all be welcomed and guided back to the Pure Land. Do we not recall that the *Meditation Sutra* teaches:

> If anyone who has committed the Five Grave Offenses or Ten Evil Deeds sees an evil omen appear as he is on the verge of death, he needs only recite the Buddha's name one to ten times with all his heart, and Buddha Amitabha will descend to welcome and escort him back to the Pure Land.

In the commentary *Accounts of Rebirth*, there are cases of individuals who throughout their lives were slaughtering livestock, breaking the precepts and engaging in all manner of evil conduct. Nevertheless, on their deathbeds, when the "marks of hell" appeared and, desperate, they singlemindedly recited the Buddha's name, they immediately saw Amitabha Buddha arriving to welcome them. Why should we, who are not that sinful or deluded, worry about not achieving rebirth in the Pure Land?

2. Unfulfilled vows; non-severance of greed, anger and delusion.

Cultivators' vows can be divided into two categories: religious and mundane.

Religious vows: Some practitioners have vowed to build a temple, practice charity or recite various sutras or mantras a certain number of times, etc. However, they have not completely fulfilled their vows when it is time for them to die. These cultivators should think: reciting the Buddha's name in all earnestness will earn them rebirth in the Pure Land, where they will have ample opportunity to achieve immeasurable merits and virtues. Their present vows to build temples and recite sutras are merely secondary matters. The fact that they may not have fulfilled them should be of no great concern.

Mundane vows: These include family obligations such as caring for sick, aging parents or helpless wives and young children, as well as business debts to be paid or certain other commitments to be fulfilled. Faced with these worries, the practioners should think: on our deathbed, there is nothing that can be done, whether we worry or not. It is better to concentrate on Buddha Recitation. Once we are reborn in the Pure Land and Buddhahood is achieved, all vows, wishes and debts can be taken care of, as we will be in a position to rescue everyone, family and foes alike.

The *Questions of King Milinda Sutra* contains the following parable:

A minute grain of sand, dropped on the surface of the water, will sink immediately. On the other hand, a block of stone, however large and heavy, can easily be moved from place to place by boat. The same is true of the Pure Land practitioner. However light his karma may be, if he is not rescued by Amitabha Buddha, he must revolve in the cycle of Birth and Death. With the help of Amitabha Buddha, his karma, however heavy, will not prevent his rebirth in the Pure Land.

We can see from this passage that thanks to "other-power," the Pure Land method can benefit the practitioner, however heavy his karma may be. The huge block of stone represents the weight of heavy karma, the boat symbolizes the power of Amitabha Buddha's Vows. Therefore, the cultivator should not think that residual greed, anger and delusion will prevent him from achieving rebirth in the Pure Land. This example should also resolve doubts concerning past heavy karma, as in doubt number one above.

3. Despite recitation, Amitabha Buddha may not come, after all.

At the time of death, the Pure Land practitioner will see, depending on his virtues, Amitabha Buddha, the Bodhisattvas or the Ocean-Wide Assembly come to welcome him. Sometimes he may not see anything, but, thanks to the power of his vows and the "gathering in" power of Amitabha Buddha, he will be reborn in the Pure Land all the same. The difference lies in his level of cultivation, whether subtle or gross, transcendental or mundane. What is most important at the time of death is to recite the Buddha's name in all earnestness and not worry about anything else. Any doubts at that time will give rise to obstructions and impediments.

In summary, at the time of death, the practitioner should not be concerned about whether or not he witnesses auspicious signs. He should just concentrate on reciting the Buddha's name in all earnestness until the very end.

b) Overcoming the Narrow Passes

These "passes" can be described as follows:

- Slandering the Buddhas because of suffering and disease;
- Binding and chaining oneself to family and friends through love-attachment.

Sincere practitioners who meet with accidents, disease and disaster should reflect that these are sometimes due to virtues accrued through cultivation. Either the heavy karma (which he should have endured) has been commuted to light karma (which he is now enduring), or else, future karma has been transformed into current karma, giving him the opportunity to repay karmic debts before achieving rebirth in the Pure Land. Should he doubt this and speak ill of the Dharma, he would lack faith and understanding, display ingratitude toward the Buddhas and bring evil karma upon himself.

Among the rebirth stories, we find instances where this "bunching and compressing of karma" has allowed cultivators to hasten their rebirth in the Pure Land. Therefore, when Pure Land cultivators encounter such instances, they should be aware and understand them thoroughly.

Furthermore, this body is illusory and provisional. Depending on his merit or bad karma, the practitioner's life will be long or short, happy or filled with hardship. He should systematically rely on the Buddhas and firmly believe in the law of cause and effect.

When ill or in bad health, the practitioner should direct his thoughts toward Amitabha Buddha exclusively. He should not seek the help of externalist gurus, shamans or healers. Nor should he listen to those who do not yet understand the Dharma and revert to a non-vegetarian diet, drink alcoholic beverages, etc. Our bodies are truly full of filth; the sooner we return to the Pure Land, the better. It is like casting off a smelly, ragged garment and donning a beautiful, fragrant outfit. What is there to worry about?

***

Concerning the danger of love-attachment at the time of death, as indicated earlier, the practitioner should think thus: family members, including parents, brothers, sisters, husbands, wives and children, are temporarily gathered together in this life as a result of previous causes and conditions, such as karmic debts or love and hatred, accumulated from time immemorial. When these causes and conditions come to an end, we all part and go our separate ways. If we truly care for them, we should endeavor to be reborn in the Pure Land, so as to be able to save everyone, friend and foe alike.[80] Although we may have attachments to family and friends, when death approaches, there is nothing we can bring along or do, as even our very body disintegrates and returns to dust. If we harbor thoughts of attachment and love, not only will we fail to achieve rebirth in the Pure Land, we will not escape the endless cycle of Birth and Death.[81]

The practitioner should ponder and clearly recall the Three Doubts and Four Narrow Passes to prepare himself. His mind will then be calm and undisturbed at the time of death.

Critical Importance of the Moment of Death

69) Seeking Guidance from Spiritual Advisors

The Pure Land practitioner should take medicine when he falls ill and his condition is not desperate, but he must persevere in reciting the Buddha's name. When his condition is hopeless, he may refuse further medication. A well-known Elder Master, gravely ill, responded with the following gatha, when his disciples sought his approval to send for a physician:

The Honored Amitabha Buddha
Is the foremost king of physicians.
If we forget this and fail to heed Him,
We are indeed deluded!
One utterance of the Buddha's name
Is the wonderful panacea,
If we forget this and fail to take it,
We are truly and greatly mistaken!

We must remember that when death is impending, the practitioner should let go of everything around him, including his own body and mind, and concentrate singlemindedly on reciting the Buddha's name, earnestly seeking rebirth in the Pure Land. By so doing, if his life span has come to an end, he will surely achieve rebirth there. On the other hand, if his life span is not yet over, even though he seeks rebirth, his condition will improve, thanks to his sincere and steadfast mind (as part of his bad karma will have been dissipated in the process). Acting otherwise, he will forfeit rebirth in the Pure Land if his lifespan has come to an end (as he was only seeking recovery, not rebirth). If his lifespan is not yet over, he will aggravate his illness through worry and fear.

When they fall gravely ill, some Pure Land practitioners are not encouraged to practice Buddha Recitation, as their family members lack understanding of Buddhism. On the other hand, their kin spare no time or effort seeking out all kinds of charlatans and quacks. Some families even go to such lengths as making offerings to various deities in the hope of obtaining a quick cure. Thus, the patient not only does not receive the benefit of "supportive recitation," his mind is divided and disturbed. He cannot, therefore, be reborn in the Pure Land. The entire process is sometimes motivated by a sense of filial obligation or the desire for a good name, aimed at neighbors and friends. Little do they know that the Buddhas and sages are not deceived, and that a filial, sincere mind does not depend on external factors! Such behavior only makes the wise smile in pity.

When the patient is gravely ill but still conscious, his close family members should invite good spiritual advisors to preach the Dharma and enlighten him. If no monk or nun can be found, a knowledgeable lay person should be invited over to comfort the patient and preach the Dharma to him. The spiritual advisor should remind and enjoin the patient's relatives to be compassionate and ensure that everything is conducted according to the Way, so that the patient may enjoy the benefit of rebirth in the Pure Land.

***

In general, the spiritual advisor should follow the guidelines set out below.

1. Remind the patient of the sufferings of the Saha World and the joys of the Pure Land, so that he may develop a mind of devotion and attraction to the Pure Land. The good advisor should also enumerate and praise the patient's good deeds, merits and virtues in cultivation. This will make him happy and free of doubts, certain that when the time comes to die, he will, thanks to his good deeds, be reborn in the Pure Land.

2. If the patient has any doubts, the advisor should, depending on the circumstances, explain the Three Points of Doubt and the Four Narrow Passes discussed earlier. A critical detail to bear in mind here: the dying person should be reminded to eliminate all regret over wealth and property, as well as attachment to close family and relatives.

3. If the patient has a will, so much the better, but if not, the advisor should counsel against all inquiries in

this regard. He should also advise everyone to refrain from useless chitchat that could rekindle the patient's love-attachment to the world, which is detrimental to rebirth in the Pure Land.

4. When relatives and friends come to visit, they should be discouraged from standing before the patient, inquiring about his health in a sad, piteous way. If they come out of true concern, they should merely stand on the side, reciting the Buddha's name aloud for a moment. If, lacking understanding of the Dharma, the visitors act conventionally [crying, etc.], they are in effect pushing the dying person into the ocean of suffering -- a most regrettable occurrence indeed!

5. The patient should be counselled to practice charity and give away his personal effects to the needy. Or, better still, in accordance with the *Ksitigarbha (Earth Store Bodhisattva) Sutra*, he should use the proceeds from the sale of his personal possessions to purchase Buddhist images or sutras for free distribution.[82] All this helps the patient increase his stock of merits and eliminate bad karma, thus facilitating rebirth in the Pure Land.

The good advisor should keep these general guidelines in mind, but be ready to improvise according to the situation.

70) Conducting "Supportive Recitation"

Family members and relatives of a dying patient should remain calm, without weeping or lamenting, from the time he becomes gravely ill until his last moments. Some people, while not crying, still show sorrow and emotion on their faces. This, too, should be avoided, because, at this juncture, the dying person has reached the crossroads which separate the living from the dead, and the mundane from the transcendental. The critical importance and danger of this moment can be compared to standing under a sword -- his fate is determined by a hair's breadth![83]

At this time, the most important thing is to practice supportive recitation. Even though a person may have set his mind on rebirth in the Pure Land, if family members weep and lament, thus arousing deep-seated feelings of love-attachment, he will certainly sink into the cycle of Birth and Death, wasting all his efforts in cultivation!

When a patient on the verge of death wishes to bathe, dress in different garments, or change his position or sleeping quarters, we may comply, while exercising caution and acting in a gentle, careful manner at all times. If the patient refuses, or cannot give his consent because he has become mute, we certainly should not go against his wishes. This is because the patient on the verge of death is generally in great physical pain. If he is forced to move, bathe or change clothing, he may experience even greater pain. There are numerous cases of cultivators who had sought rebirth in the Pure Land but failed to achieve this goal because their relatives moved them around, disturbing them and destroying their right thought. This unfortunate development occurs very often.

There are also cases of individuals who might have achieved rebirth in the higher realms. However, out of ignorance, others made them suffer physically (by rearranging the positions of their hands and feet, for instance), making them irritated and angry. Because of this one thought of anger, they immediately sank into the evil realms. As an extreme example, King Ajatasatru[84] had earned numerous merits and blessings through cultivation. However, at the time of death, one of his attendants dozed off and inadvertently dropped a paper fan onto the king's face. He became so furious that he expired on the spot -- to be reborn, it is said, as a python! This example should serve as a warning to us all.

At the time of death, the cultivator himself should either lie down or sit up, according to what comes naturally, without forcing himself. If he feels weak and can only lie down, forcing himself to sit up, for appearances' sake, is dangerous and should be discouraged. Likewise, even though, according to Pure Land tradition, he should lie on his right side facing west, if, because of pain, he can only lie on his back or on his left side facing east, he should act naturally and not force himself. The patient and his family should understand all this and act accordingly.

* * *

Supportive recitation by family members or Dharma friends is most necessary when a patient is on the verge of death. This is because, at that time, he is weak in body and mind and no longer master of himself. In such trying circumstances, not only is it difficult for those who have not cultivated in daily life to focus on Amitabha Buddha, even individuals who have regularly recited the Buddha's name may find it difficult to do so in all earnestness -- unless there is supportive recitation.[85]

Such recitation should closely follow the guidelines set out below.

1. Respectfully place a standing Amitabha Buddha statue in front of the patient, so that he can see it clearly. Place some fresh flowers in a vase and burn light incense with a soft fragrance. This will help the patient develop right thought. A reminder: the incense should not be overpowering, to avoid choking the patient and everyone around.

2. Those who come to practice supportive recitation should take turns ... It should be remembered that the patient, in his weakened state, requires a lot of fresh air to breathe. If too many persons come and go or

participate in the recitation session, the patient may have difficulty breathing and become agitated, resulting in more harm than benefit. Therefore, participants should consult their watches and silently take turns reciting, so that recitation can continue uninterrupted. They should not call to one another aloud. Each session should last about an hour.

3. According to Elder Master Yin Kuang, the short recitation form (Amitabha Buddha) should be used, so that the patient can easily register the name in his Alaya consciousness, at a time when both his mind and body are very weak. However, according to another Elder Master, we should ask the patient and use the form he prefers (short or long), to conform to his everyday practice. In this way, the patient can silently recite along with the supportive recitation party. To go counter to his likes and habits may destroy his right thought and create an offense on our part. Furthermore, we should not practice supportive recitation in too loud a voice, as we will expend too much energy and be unable to keep on for very long. On the other hand, neither should we recite in too low a voice, lest the patient, in his weakened state, be unable to register the words.

Generally speaking, recitation should not be too loud or too low, too slow or too fast. Each utterance should be clear and distinct so that it can pass through the ear and penetrate deep into the patient's Alaya consciousness. One caveat: if the patient is too weak [or is in a coma], he will not be able to hear "external" recitation. In such a case, we should recite into the patient's ear.[86] This helps the patient keep his mind clear and steady.

4. With regard to percussion instruments, it is generally better to use the small hand bell, instead of the wooden fish gong with its bass tone. The hand bell, with its clear, limpid sound, can help the patient develop a pure and calm mind. However, this may not apply in all

cases. For instance, an Elder Master once taught, "It is best to recite the Buddha's name by itself without musical accompaniment, but since each person's preferences are different, it is better to ask the patient in advance. If some details do not suit him, we should adapt to the circumstances and not be inflexible."

The above are some pointers to keep in mind with regard to supportive recitation.

After Death

71) Between Death and Burial

When a person has just died, the most important thing is not to rush to move him. Even if his body is soiled with excrement and urine, we should not hasten to clean it. We should wait about eight hours -- or a minimum of three hours -- before cleaning the body and changing its clothes. Relatives should not weep and wail immediately before and after the actual death. Doing so is not only useless, it can be harmful, as this can cause the deceased to develop thoughts of attachment, which may prevent him from achieving liberation. To be of true benefit to the patient, we should concentrate on reciting the Buddha's name in all earnestness, without crying until at least eight hours have passed. Why is this necessary? It is because although the patient has stopped breathing, his Alaya consciousness has not yet left his body.[87] If, during this period, we move the body, clean it, change its clothes, or weep and lament, the deceased may still experience feelings of pain, sadness, anger or self-pity, and descend upon the Evil Paths. This is a crucial point -- a critical one -- that relatives should note and remember well.[88]

***

The practice of touching the body of the deceased

to locate the last warm spot and deduce his place of rebirth is grounded in the sutras and commentaries.[89] However, we should not be inflexible. If the patient had sincere, earnest faith and vows in normal times and clearly exhibits right thought at the time of death, this is sufficient evidence of rebirth in the Pure Land. Some persons who are not careful keep "feeling" the body, touching one spot after another, disturbing the deceased. This can cause great harm.

After the patient has expired, the persons who came to recite the Buddha's name should continue doing so for another three hours. After that, the body should be left alone, free of all disturbances, for another five hours (or a total of eight hours), at which time it can be bathed and given a change of clothing. If, during the entire eight-hour period, someone, or a group of persons, can remain near the deceased reciting the Buddha's name, so much the better. Except for recitation, nothing should be done. A reminder and caveat: during this period, the "deceased" may still have consciousness and feelings.

After the eight-hour period, if the limbs have grown stiff and cannot move, we should put a towel soaked in hot water around the joints. After a while, the body can be repositioned.

***

Funeral arrangements should be kept simple, not accompanied by superfluous ceremonies occasioning unnecessary expenses. Another caveat: only vegetarian food should be served. No non-vegetarian food should be provided as offerings or to entertain guests -- for to take life is to sadden the departed with more karmic obstructions and "heavy baggage," making his liberation that much more difficult. Even if he has already been reborn in the Pure Land, his grade of rebirth may be lowered as a result.[90]

Some time ago, this author, along with other monks and nuns, attended an elaborate funeral for the stepmother of one of his friends, a high-ranking Master in Long An province, southern Vietnam. Throughout the funeral, only vegetarian food was served. After congratulating his friend, the author inquired about this and was told, "the serving of vegetarian food is due partly to my recommendation; however, the major impetus was an event which took place not long ago in a nearby village:

"After a prosperous elder had passed away, his son ordered a huge quantity of livestock slaughtered to feed relatives and friends for several days. (In his lifetime, the elder, a good-natured, benevolent man who practiced Buddha Recitation and was vegetarian several days a month, had had many friends and associates.) The very evening after the funeral, his eldest grandson suddenly had a fit in front of everyone. His face all red, he suddenly jumped onto the wooden plank bed in the living room, sat squarely upon it, and slapped his hand against a nearby desk. Calling his father by his given name, he scolded him loudly: *'Right up until my death,* I practiced charity and accumulated merits; without any heavy transgressions, I should have been reborn wealthy and into a good family. Instead, because of you and the heavy karma of killing you created on my behalf, I, as *your father*, am now confined and forced to look after a herd of cows, as well as pigs, chickens and ducks. I have to run back and forth barefoot through mud and thorns. My sufferings are truly beyond description!'"

After recounting the story, the Master smiled and said, "This event, which occurred only a few months ago, is known to the entire village and is believed and dreaded by my relatives. For precisely this reason, when I suggested vegetarian food, the idea was immediately accepted."

The *Ksitigarbha Sutra* [ch. VII] goes into detail about the harm associated with slaughtering animals to serve guests at funerals. Buddhist followers should take heed and bear this in mind.[91]

***

When performing follow-up good deeds on behalf of the deceased, we should dedicate the merit and virtue to all sentient beings in the Dharma Realm.[92] In this way, these merits and virtues will be multiplied many times over, and so will the benefits accrued to the deceased.[93]

These preparations for the time of death have been taken from the teachings of Elder Masters of the past. The last moments of life are the most crucial ones. If the "provisions for rebirth" are not ready and adequate, the patient cannot avoid extreme fright and bewilderment. At that time, too late to seek help and faced with the simultaneous appearance of all kinds of bad karma accumulated over countless lifetimes, how can he achieve liberation?

Therefore, while we may rely on others for support and assistance at the time of death, we ourselves should strive to cultivate during normal times. Only then will we feel free and at peace.

I beg you all, fellow Pure Land practitioners, to take heed and be prepared, so that we may all be reborn in the ocean-wide Lotus Assembly!

72) Success and Failure in Supportive Recitation

1. Story of LCL

The layman LCL was a legislator and an official early in life. As he had affinities with Buddhism, he contributed to such good works as restoring a local temple, donating land to it and inviting an Elder Master to head it. He was also diligent in raising funds to build a statue of the Bodhisattva Avalokitesvara, which was about one hundred feet high.

In 1933 he took refuge with the Triple Jewel under the Patriarch Yin Kuang. He resolved to be a vegetarian six days a month and took up the practice of Buddha Recitation. In the years that followed, however, because of his heavy schedule, his practice, while sincere, was irregular.

In 1938, he fell gravely ill. As time went by and his condition did not improve, he made large donations to worthwhile activities, in the hope of expunging some of his bad karma. He also became a full time vegetarian. The following year, as his illness took a turn for the worse, his wife and sons, realizing the importance of the last moments, hurriedly invited monks from the local temple to recite the Buddha's name at his bedside.

On the 19th of January of that year, LCL, sensing that his end was near, asked to be taken out to the courtyard to breathe fresh air. After speaking to his brothers and sisters, he requested his son to kneel down to hear his will. As he was speaking, LCL's countenance suddenly changed. Seeing this, his wife and son helped him back into the house and placed a statue of a standing Amitabha Buddha before him.[94] They then began to recite aloud, together with the monks. For several months, LCL's left arm had been paralyzed, but when he saw the statue, he managed to regain the use of his arm. With palms joined, he began to recite the Buddha's name, his face radiant and beaming with joy. At that moment, he seemed to have forgotten all pain and suffering, as he recited along with the others for a while, before dying peacefully, at the age of sixty-one.

The layman LCL had practiced Buddha Recitation sincerely during the last part of his life. At his deathbed, thanks to supportive recitation, a number of auspicious signs appeared. These included stable faculties, right thought and a peaceful death, as though in samadhi. We can therefore deduce that he certainly achieved rebirth in the Pure Land.

While the layman's rebirth was due to his maturing good roots, it was also helped by the supportive recitation he received when on his deathbed. Thus, Pure Land practitioners should recognize the particular importance and urgency of supportive recitation just before death.

2. Story of DH

The laywoman DH was the wife of a certain man in the city of Yangchow. As she could not bear children, her husband took a concubine, which made it difficult for her to remain in the conjugal home. Therefore, she went to live with her stepmother, another lay Buddhist, who loved her as her own daughter. They supported and relied on one another, and two years passed as though they were but one day.

The laywoman DH was a vegetarian who earnestly practiced Buddha Recitation day and night. She and her stepmother realized that they had scant merits and few good conditions in this life, and no one else to rely on in case of need, as their relatives were dead or far away. They therefore wholeheartedly helped one another, as Dharma friends along the Way. From the point of view of faith and daily cultivation, DH far surpassed LCL of our previous story. Unfortunately, however, because of heavy residual karma and unfavorable conditions, she always met with adverse circumstances and her mind was never at peace.

In 1938, sensing that a major upheaval was impending, mother and daughter immediately left Hong Kong, where they had been staying, to seek refuge back on the mainland. At that time, the cost of living was skyrocketing. Renting a place to live was dificult, while staying in hotels for any length of time was both costly and inconvenient. Fortunately, a local abbot took pity on the women and set aside a small area of his temple for them and three other refugees.

Around March of the following year, DH suddenly contracted typhoid fever. The illness lasted for over a month, with no signs of recovery. At that time, the temple was very busy and space was at a premium. If she were to die there, it would cause a great deal of inconvenience. Therefore, with great reluctance, her stepmother decided to bring her to the local hospital.

The hospital followed Western medical practice, making it difficult to engage in supportive recitation freely and in an appropriate manner. On the 18th of August, after two or three days in the hospital, with no one practicing supportive recitation at her bedside and in a confused state of mind, the laywoman DH died. She was fifty-one years of age at the time.

We can see that the laywoman DH was truly a woman of faith, who had practiced in earnest. If, at the time of death, she had had the benefit of adequate supportive recitation, auspicious signs of rebirth in the Pure Land should have appeared, no fewer than in the case of LCL. Such was not, unfortunately, the case. Because of adverse circumstances, she died in a coma, unattended by Dharma friends. She probably did not achieve rebirth in the Pure Land, but merely managed to sow the seeds of Enlightenment for future lives. What happened to her was regrettable, but demonstrates that supportive recitation at the time of death is truly of crucial importance.

3. Story of DLH

The layman DLH was from a poor merchant family. Well-mannered and courteous, he had a good grasp of worldly affairs. In 1922, following the example of a friend, he took refuge with the Triple Jewel, and along with others, vowed to develop the Bodhi Mind, to rescue himself and others.

A few years later, because of a serious illness, he abandoned vegetarianism and began to drift away from his Buddhist friends. In July of that year, his illness grew more severe, and everyone feared the worst. Realizing that his end was near, DLH sincerely repented his past transgressions, let go of everything and concentrated all his time and effort on Buddha Recitation. Fellow cultivators, fearing that his practice was still shallow, were continuously at his bedside.

Supportive recitation itself began on the 12th of July. Three days later, the layman DLH suddenly experienced a surge of strength, feeling fresh and well. On the 17th, he told everyone that in a dream, he had seen an aura of light as bright as five or six electric bulbs. That evening, his complexion appeared to be normal. His fellow cultivators continued their recitation until the wee hours and were preparing to leave, when DLH suddenly said, "I have not yet reached the Pure Land. Please continue reciting all day."

The group gladly complied, and recitation went on, with DLH mostly remaining silent. He was smiling calmly, his face radiant, as though he had received some news that was good beyond expectation. This continued for some time, until he became still and immobile, his gaze fixed on the standing Amitabha statue facing him. His eyes then began to cloud over and his breathing subsided. He passed away at five o'clock that morning.

The cultivators took turns reciting, interspersing

recitation with words of encouragement and exhortation, until his body was completely cold. His next of kin had been warned not to weep or wail. At ten a.m., one of the practitioners touched DLH's body and discovered that it was cold all over except for the crown, which was as hot as boiling water.

The sutras contain a stanza:

The crown stands for sainthood, the eyes rebirth in a
celestial realm,
The heart indicates the human realm, the belly stands for
the ghostly,
The knees are tantamount to animality, the soles of the
feet stand for the hells.[95]

When the cultivator's body is completely cold except for the crown, that person has been reborn in the realm of the saints, or of the Buddhas. When his eyes are the last to remain warm, he has been reborn in the celestial realms; warmth in the area of the heart means rebirth among human beings. If the abdominal area retains warmth after the body has grown cold, he has been reborn among hungry ghosts. The knees represent rebirth among animals, while the soles of the feet indicate the hellish realms. Thus, the last warm spot represents the place where the consciousness of the deceased escaped the mortal body.[96]

The fact that DLH's crown was the last warm spot shows that he achieved rebirth in the Pure Land -- his very goal in the last years of his life.

The layman DLH was not above violating the precepts. His cultivation was shallow and wanting as well. His rebirth in the Pure Land, therefore, was largely due to the supportive recitation of his fellow cultivators. Here again, we can see the importance of supportive recitation at the time of death. That time was the 18th of July 1924 -- and DLH was thirty years old!

Epilogue

The ancients had a saying:

We should wait until old age before writing books, because
by then we will have fuller knowledge and experience, and
the books will be more accomplished.

This author has not yet reached old age and his
experience and knowledge must therefore have
deficiencies. Nevertheless, because of his urgent desire
to be of benefit to others, and not knowing when the
ghost of impermanence may strike, he has reluctantly
taken the liberty to offer the reader some preliminary
thoughts. Although this book is meant to be an original
manuscript, most of the ideas contained therein are
taken from Buddhist sutras and commentaries. Thus,
the author believes that it could still bring some benefit
to the reader.

In his seventies, an Elder Master once remarked
sadly:

Although the human life span is supposed to be one
hundred years, seventy is already a ripe old age. However,
when I look back and examine my past actions, I discover
that they were all fraught with mistakes.

If even an Elder Master of high repute judged
himself thus, how many more mistakes must common
mortals like ourselves commit? Therefore, at times this
author feels ashamed and perplexed, reluctant to write
anything, as he realizes that he is still full of
transgressions, unable to save himself, let alone counsel
others. However, he has decided otherwise, just as a

fellow traveller in the sea of Birth and Death may remind others to escape from it along with him. Hopefully, he can gather some merit through such action, and lighten his own heavy karma somewhat.

In this connection, he recalls a certain poem, composed in a bygone era:

> Hurriedly, painstakingly, we hope and seek,
> Spending spring and autumn in the rain and sun;
> Day in and day out we attend to our livelihood,
> Forgetting that our hair has taken on the color
> of snow.
> We should sever thoughts of right and wrong,
> Afflictions and sorrows, as well;
> The Way is so clear and distinct,
> Why do so many refuse to cultivate?

These lines, while deceptively simple and seemingly lacking in depth, clearly describe the various activities and karmic obstructions of the human condition. Only those who stand outside the framework of this poem, and strive to cultivate, can be said to be treading the path of liberation.

The author of the poem wrote these sad words as he realized how easy it is to drown in the ocean of suffering and how difficult to tread the path of liberation. In the *Sutra in Forty-two Sections*, Buddha Sakyamuni said:

> People encounter twenty kinds of difficulties:
>
> It is difficult to give when one is poor.
> It is difficult to study the Way when one has power
> and wealth.
> It is difficult to abandon life and face the certainty
> of death.
> It is difficult to encounter the Buddhist sutras.
> It is difficult to be born at the time of a Buddha.
> It is difficult to resist lust and desire.
> It is difficult to see good things and not seek them.
> It is difficult to be insulted and not become angry.

It is difficult to have power and not abuse it.
It is difficult to come in contact with things and have
    no [attachment to] them.
It is difficult to be greatly learned [in the Dharma].
It is difficult to get rid of self-satisfaction [pride
    and conceit].
It is difficult not to slight those who have not yet
    studied [the Dharma].
It is difficult to practice equanimity of mind.
It is difficult not to gossip.
It is difficult to meet a good knowing advisor.
It is difficult to see one's own Nature and study the
    Way.
It is difficult to [save sentient beings with means appro-
    priate to their situation].
It is difficult to see a state and not be moved by it.
It is difficult to have a good understanding of skill-in-
    means [and apply it well].

(Hsuan Hua, *A General Explanation of the Buddha Speaks the Sutra in Forty-Two Sections*, p. 28-29.)

I shall merely cite a few instances of these twenty difficulties. For example, it is difficult to practice charity when we are poor and destitute because, under such conditions, even if we have the will, we lack the means. To force ourselves to practice charity must entail sacrifices. Likewise, it is difficult to study the Dharma when we are wealthy and eminent, because under such favorable circumstances, we may have the means, but we are pulled away by opportunities for enjoyment and self-gratification.

The difficulty of being born during the lifetime of a Buddha is elaborated in the *Perfection of Wisdom Treatise*: in the town of Sravasti, India, out of a total population of nine hundred thousand, only one-third had actually seen and met Buddha Sakyamuni, another one-third had heard His name and believed in Him but had not actually seen or met Him, while the remaining one-third had not seen, heard or even learned of His existence. Sakyamuni Buddha taught in Sravasti for some twenty-five years, yet a full one-third of the town's population were completely unaware of His existence. Is it any wonder, then, that those who were born during Sakyamuni Buddha's time but did not reside in Sravasti, or those who happened to be born before or after His time, would find it difficult to learn of Him or hear the Dharma?

However, even though we may not be able to meet Sakyamuni Buddha, cultivating according to the Dharma is tantamount to meeting Him. On the other hand, if we do not follow His teaching, even while near Him, we are still far away. Thus, Devadatta, Buddha Sakyamuni's very own cousin, as well as the Bhikshu Sunaksatra who attended Him personally for twenty years, both descended into the hells because they strayed from the Path. There is also the case of an old woman in the eastern quarter of Sravasti who was born at exactly the same moment as Buddha Sakyamuni, yet, because she lacked causes and conditions, wished neither to see nor to meet Him. Thus, not everyone can see the Buddhas and listen to the Dharma. Extensive good roots, merits, virtues and favorable conditions are required. Although Buddha Sakyamuni has now entered Nirvana, good spiritual advisors[97] are taking turns preaching the Way in His stead. If we draw near to them and practice according to their teachings, we can still achieve liberation.

Nevertheless, those who possess only scant and shallow roots must find it difficult to meet good spiritual advisors. Even when they do so and hear the Dharma, if they do not understand its meaning, or merely grasp at appearances and forms, refusing to follow it, no benefit can possibly result.

According to the *Brahma Net* and *Avatamsaka Sutras*, we should ignore appearances and external forms when seeking a good spiritual advisor. For example, we should disregard such traits as youth, poverty, low status or lack of education, unattractive appearance or incomplete features, but should simply seek someone conversant with the Dharma, who can be of benefit to us. Nor should we find fault with good spiritual advisors for acting in certain ways, as it may be due to a number of reasons, such as pursuing a hidden cultivation practice or following an expedient teaching. Or else, they may act the way they do because while their achievements may be high, their residual bad habits have not been extinguished. If we grasp at forms and look for faults, we will forfeit benefits on the path of cultivation.

Thus, when Buddha Sakyamuni was still alive, the Bhikshu Kalodayin was in the habit of moving his jaws like a buffalo; a certain Bhikshuni used to look at herself in the mirror and adorn herself; another Bhikshu liked to climb trees and jump from one branch to another; still another always addressed others in a loud voice, with condescending terms and appellations. In truth, however, all four had reached the stage of Arhatship. It is just that one of them was a buffalo in a previous life, another was a courtesan, another was a monkey, and still another belonged to the Brahman class. They were accustomed to these circumstances throughout many lifetimes, so that even when they had attained the fruits of Arhatship, their residual habits still lingered.

We also have the example of the Sixth Patriarch of Zen. Realizing that the cultivators of his day were attached to a literal reading of the sutras and did not immediately recognize their Buddha Nature, he took the form of an ignorant and illiterate person selling wood in the marketplace. Or else, take the case of a famous Zen Master who, wishing to avoid external conditions and concentrate on his cultivation, took the expedient appearance of a ragged lunatic, raving and ranting. As a result, both distinguished Masters were criticized during their lifetimes. The Sixth Patriarch was faulted for ignorance, while the Zen monk was called insane and berserk. Therefore, finding a good spiritual advisor is a difficult task indeed! Students of the Dharma should realize this, to decrease the habits of attachment and grasping -- thus avoiding the mistake of maligning monks and nuns.

As for other kinds of difficulties, fellow cultivators can draw inferences from the above discussion and understand for themselves.

***

Nevertheless, the words "difficult" and "easy" belong to the realm of opposing dharmas; in difficulty there is simplicity, in simplicity there is difficulty. If we truly understand and are determined, difficult things are not necessarily impossible to accomplish.

During the lifetime of a certain transhistorical Buddha, for example, there was a couple so destitute that husband and wife had but one robe between them. When the husband would leave their shack to seek work, his wife had to shut the door and stay home, nude, and vice versa. However, upon hearing wandering monks teach that charity would extinguish the sufferings of poverty and want, husband and wife discussed the matter between themselves. They decided to donate their only piece of cloth by passing it through the window, determined to remain in the shack, completely nude, resigned to death. This resolute good action came to the attention of the local ruler, who then showered them with garments and riches. From that time on, through each succeeding lifetime, they never again were in want for the necessities of life, and ultimately attained complete liberation.

Thus, although it may be difficult to practice charity when we are destitute ourselves, we should understand that the cause of such poverty and want is our own past stinginess. If we are determined to endure deprivation and suffering, charity is something that can still be accomplished.

There is also the case of a well-known Chinese Emperor of the Ch'ing Dynasty, who acceded to the throne when barely six years old and abdicated at the age of twenty-four to become a Buddhist monk. To occupy the exalted position of Emperor, first in power and wealth throughout the entire realm, dwelling in magnificent palaces, surrounded with luxury beyond imagination, attended by a harem with many thousands of the most beautiful women in the land, his power extending over one and all -- how could such wealth and honor be surpassed? Yet, if we understand the dreamlike, evanescent nature of worldly blessings and pleasures and the true joy of the realm of everlasting True Thusness -- and if we are resolute and determined -- practicing the Dharma in such extraordinary circumstances, however difficult, is a realizable undertaking. Likewise, although cultivation under conditions of extreme poverty and deprivation may be difficult, if we are resolute, it is not something that cannot be done.

An example that comes readily to mind occurred during the lifetime of Buddha Sakyamuni. There was a destitute old woman who had been working as a maid since the age of thirteen, and was still toiling at the age of eighty. She worked without rest all day long, pounding rice until past midnight, waking up again at the crow of the cock to busy herself with mortar and pestle. Cultivating under such trying conditions, with not a single moment of leisure was difficult, to say the least! However, thanks to the teaching of the Elder Mahakatyayana, a senior disciple of the Buddha, each night, when she had finished pounding rice, she would wash up, change her clothing, cultivate well into the night and transfer the merit to all sentient beings before retiring.[98] As a result of her determination and effort, she was reborn as a deity in the Yama Heaven.

***

Dear fellow cultivators! It is difficult to be reborn as a human being, while the Dharma is difficult to encounter. Today you have a human body and the opportunity to read this commentary. Thus, you have already met with a wonderful method to achieve Buddhahood. Even if you should face difficult circumstances, I urge you to recognize the sufferings of this dreamlike, evanescent world and to cultivate resolutely -- so that the precious lotus blossoms of the Pure Land may give birth to many more *beings of the highest virtue!*[99]

Editors' Notes

(1)   *Noumenon/Phenomena*:   a   crucial   distinction   for understanding this text.

(2) As Buddhist practice is basically a question of skillful means or expedients, "fingers pointing to the moon," the level of cultivation (noumenal or phenomenal) of an Elder Master is not necessarily known to his followers.   Witness the following passage, describing the last moments of the Patriarch Honen, founder of the Pure Land school in Japan:

> At the hour of the serpent (10 a.m.), on the same day, his disciples brought him an image of Amida, three feet high, and as they put it on the right side of his bed, asked him if he could see it. With his finger pointing to the sky he said, "There is another Buddha here besides this one. Do you not see him?" Then he went on to say, "As a result of the merit of repeating the sacred name, I have, for over ten years past, continually been gazing on the glory of the Pure Land, and the very forms of the Buddhas and Bodhisattvas, but I have kept it secret and said nothing about it. Now, however, as I draw near the end, I disclose it to you." The disciples then took a piece of cord made of five-colored strands, fastened it to the hand of the Buddha's image, and told Honen to take hold of it. Declining, he said, "This is the ceremony for most men, but hardly necessary for me." (Rev. Harper Havelock Coates and Rev. Ryugaku Ishizuka, tr. *Honen, the Buddhist saint: his life and teaching,* p. 636.)

(3) Practitioners must exercise utmost caution when choosing a Dharma teacher as in Buddhist teaching, the commitment entered into with that teacher extends through many lifetimes.

(4) Complete faith, or utter sincerity, or singlemindedness, or one-pointedness of mind: in practice, these expressions are used interchangeably, as a cultivator cannot have complete faith without being utterly sincere and singleminded (and vice versa). See also note 37.

(5) See Glossary, "Awakening vs. Enlightenment."

(6) The author went on to suggest that Zen might be revived in Vietnam, as a result of the development of Buddhism in the country as well as the influence of monks and nuns returning from Japan and Theravada countries. However, he felt that most cultivators would only be able to follow the practices of Samatha-Vipasyana or the Four Meditations-Eight Samadhis. Few could hope to succeed in kung-an Zen or in the Zen of the Patriarchs, as in earlier centuries. See also the following passage:

> After the Sung period (960-1279) there were indeed first-rate Zen masters directing their disciples along the proven path to Zen enlightenment ... but decline was also evident. Lacking genuinely creative figures, the movement began to stagnate ... In later popular Buddhist religion, which consisted mainly of the Amida cult, Zen -- by nature somewhat elitist -- was able to carry on only at the cost of denying some of its elements. (Heinrich Dumoulin, *Zen Buddhism*, Vol. I, p. 287.)

(7) Non-retrogression in cultivation is one of the most important advantages of rebirth in the Pure Land (compared with rebirth in celestial realms, for example).

(8) Love is considered an affliction in Buddhism because, like all emotions, it disturbs the peacefulness of the mind.

(9) Buddha Sakyamuni compared human beings chasing after the fleeting pleasures of this world to a child licking honey off a sharp knife. There is no way they can avoid hurting themselves.

(10) See Glossary, "Awakening vs. Enlightenment."

(11) Merit and virtue: these two terms are sometimes used interchangeably. However, there is a crucial difference: merits are the blessings of the human and celestial realms; therefore, they are temporary and subject to Birth and Death. Virtues, on the other hand, transcend Birth and Death and lead to Buddhahood. An identical action can lead either to merits or virtues, depending on the mind of the practitioner, that is, on whether he is seeking mundane rewards (merits) or transcendence (virtues). Thus, the Pure Land cultivator should not seek merits because by doing so, he would remain within samsara. This would be counter to his very wish to escape Birth and Death.

(12) Bodhi Mind: also translated as "Bodhicitta," "Bodhi Resolve" or "aspiration for Supreme Enlightenment." See also Glossary.

This section touches on a cardinal feature of Buddhism, as expressed in numerous Mahayana scriptures, such as the *Lotus Sutra*: the true intention of the Buddhas is not simply to rescue sentient beings, who, once saved, play a secondary, subservient role; rather, it is to help sentient beings attain Enlightenment and Buddhahood, i.e., to become equal to themselves in all respects. This is a unique and revolutionary feature of Buddhism.

(13) See Glossary, "Skillful means." See also the following explanation of the expression "skillful means are the ultimate," by Kukai (774-835), the founder of the Japanese Shingon, or Esoteric, school::

> Kukai interpreted the last phrase in two ways. One stresses the imperative sense that skillful means should lead to ultimate enlightenment. The other emphasizes the declarative sense that skillful means themselves are the ultimate. The former expresses the view of self-benefit in seeking enlightenment, and the latter, the view of enlightenment fulfilled in compassion toward others. (Taiko Yamasaki, *Shingon: Japanese Esoteric Buddhism*, p.105.)

(14) Unfavorable expedients: a severe illness, a sudden death or even loss of a job may sometimes jolt the practitioner out of his usual complacency and remind him of the need to cultivate.

Note: whether an unfavorable event is good or bad for one's cultivation depends, in the final analysis, on one's own outlook, one's mind. It can be either an expedient, to help one attain the Way or a "demon," hindering cultivation See also section 63, point 4.

(15) Buddhist cultivation entails ridding ourselves of all attachments, beginning with attachment to our own body and mind (mark of self). Once this is achieved, we will be able to transcend attachment to family and friends (mark of others), attachment to sentient beings other than family and friends (mark of sentient beings) and finally, attachment to the duration of our life (mark of lifespan). The more successful

our cultivation is, the more detachment we achieve, the calmer our mind becomes and the closer we are to the Way.

(16) Unlike sentient beings, the Buddhas do not discriminate, but see sentient beings as their equals, for all possess the same Buddha Nature.

(17) Perseverance is an especially important quality in Buddhism. For example, if we were to rub two pieces of wood together but before fire is produced, we stop to do something else, only to resume later, we would never obtain fire. Likewise, a person who cultivates sporadically (e.g., on weekends or during retreats) but neglects daily practice, can seldom achieve lasting results.

(18) The truth being one and indivisible in Buddhist teaching, a "discriminating" mind can never grasp the whole truth. Thus, such an approach is bound to result in an imperfect understanding of the world as it really is. This is best expressed by the parable of several blind men trying to describe an elephant, each touching a different part of the animal, with no one having the total picture.

(19) There is no distinction between the savior and the saved because at the transcendental level of the Arhats and above the ego has been transcended. It is just like the two hands. Because they belong to the same person, one would automatically clasp the other if hurt and neither would hold a grudge against the other for accidentally striking it (when missing the head of a nail, for example).

(20) According to Mahayana Buddhist teaching, without developing the Bodhi Mind, we cannot achieve Buddhahood. Therefore, developing the Bodhi Mind surpasses eons of *ordinary* cultivation.

(21) At the noumenon level, all pure lands are equal. However, to give practitioners an achor upon which they can easily focus their minds, the Western Pure Land is singled out. See also note 30 below.

(22) All Buddhist teaching stresses the Truth of Impermanence, to spur the cultivator on in his practice.

According to Elder Zen Master Ta-Hui:

> One must paste the words "life-death" on the forehead, and regard them as seriously as if one owed a debt of a millions taels. (Sung-peng Hsu, *A Buddhist Leader in Ming China*, p. 130.)

(23) The existence or non-existence of the Pure Land is a question the answer to which depends on the practitioner and his level of cultivation. Consider the following exchange between two Zen monks:

> *Disciple*: "Master, does the Pure Land exist?"
> *Master*: "Does this world exist?"
> *Disciple*: "Of course it does, Master."
> *Master*: "If this world exists, then the Pure Land exists all the more."

Buddha Sakyamuni taught that ultimately, we are all living in a big Dream. Within this Birth and Death Dream, everything, ourselves and all dharmas exist. In this sense, the Pure Land also exists.

This is not unlike a child who has no chocolate at all dreaming of receiving, for example, ten boxes of chocolates. If upon "awakening," he finds himself with even one box, it can only mean that he is still dreaming. Otherwise, there should be no box of chocolates at all, as everything was just a dream.

Likewise, when we still grasp at the self and still see this world as existent, we are still dreaming the big Dream and therefore everything, including the Pure Land, exists. Only those sages and saints who have transcended all notion of self and dharmas can proclaim that there is no Pure Land (see also this book section 19, question 1 and section 47).

On this point, see also the words of the eminent Zen Master Chu Hung (16th century):

> Some people say that the Pure Land is nothing but mind, that there is no Pure Land of Ultimate Bliss beyond the trillions of worlds of the cosmos. This talk of mind-only has its source in the words of the sutras, and it is true, not false. But those who quote it in this sense are misunderstanding its meaning.
>
> Mind equals object: there are no objects beyond mind. Objects equal mind: there is no mind beyond objects. Since objects are wholly mind,

why must we cling to mind and dismiss objects? Those who dismiss objects when they talk of mind have not comprehended mind. (J.C. Cleary, *Pure Land, Pure Mind*, unpub. manuscript.)

(24) An externalist is someone who does not believe in or follow Buddhist teaching, which can be defined as any teaching conforming to the Dharma seals. (Sakyamuni Buddha taught three "seals," or criteria, to determine the genuineness of Buddhist teachings, namely, impermanence, suffering, no-self. A fourth criterion, emptiness, is also mentioned in the sutras and encompasses the other three.)

(25) True realization of cause and effect can free us from a most pervasive affliction: anger and resentment. Once, it is said, Buddha Sakyamuni was falsely accused of fathering a certain woman's child. When the deceit was discovered, the Buddha's followers wanted to beat the culprit to death. The Buddha calmly stopped them, saying:

"Oh, Bhikkus, in a previous lifetime when I was a king, I was once in a grove together with my courtiers. At the sight of an ascetic, the ladies of the party surrounded him, turning their backs on me. Jealous and angry, I exclaimed, 'How do you know that this ascetic is not a fake? How do you know that he does not spend his nights revelling with women?' It is because of that slanderous remark that I have now had to endure that woman's deceit. Oh, monks, release her and let her go in peace."

In the Buddhist world view, nothing happens without cause. To escape suffering, we must stop causing further suffering. Acting otherwise is no different from trying to escape one's shadow by running in the blazing sun!

(26) These heterodox practices are known today under a variety of names, such as polarity therapy, Dr. Randolph Stone's method, life energy healing arts, spiritual/energy healing, healing ministry, laying on hands ministry.

The reason many externalists take the appearance of monks and nuns is that Buddhism is widely known and respected in Asia. To be taken for a monk or nun is to gain entry to the heart -- and purse -- of the populace.

(27) Nineteen eminent Zen Masters are enumerated in the original commentary, including Yung Ming, Yuan Chao Pen (Viên Chiếu Bản), Fa Chao (Pháp Chiếu), Tao Chen (Đạo Trần), Tao Ch'o (Đạo Xược) ...

(28) In this regard, note the following:

> This section was of great interest to me. I am one of those who in the ordinary frame of mind understands the Pure Land as a metaphor, a "guided visualisation" for advanced meditators. This may have been the original approach to Pure Land practice. But, once in a state of deep meditation, I became convinced that the Pure Land is an actual state of existence, beyond the manifestation of the physical universe. It is analogous to the electromagnetic spectrum. By changing the frequency, x-rays become visible light or infra-red waves (heat), etc. Just as matter and energy are manifestations of the same reality (Einstein), so, too, the Pure Land and our earthly existence are related. (Private communication from Mr. D. Bakhroushin of New York City.)

(29) See notes 23 and 28, section 48, as well as the related passage below:

> In secular western thought awareness of psychological projection as a source of supernatural being has served to demythologize demons, goblins, angels and saints and rob them of their power. The Bardo Thodol [Tibetan Book of the Dead], however, speaks of the deities as "projections" but never as "mere projections." The deities are present and must be dealt with religiously ... not just by intellectual insight."
> (D.G. Dawe in *The Perennial Dictionary of World Religions*, p. 93.)

(30) According to Buddhist teaching, there is an infinite number of pure realms or pure lands in the cosmos. In this text, the term Pure Land, when capitalized, refers to the Pure Land of Amitabha Buddha, the Western Pure Land. See also note 21.

(31) This quote from the *Sutra of Hui Neng (Platform Sutra)* has also been translated as follows:

> To have no thought is correct mindfulness. If there is thought, mindfulness is incorrect. (J.C. Cleary, private communication.)

Note also the explanation of a modern Chinese scholar:

> To have "no-thought," ... is "not to allow the mind to be contaminated

by various objects," and to be "ever detached from objects." (Fung Yu-Lan, *A History of Chinese Philosophy*. Vol. II, p.395.)

Hui Neng (638-713) is the Sixth Patriarch of the Chinese Zen school. The *Platform Sutra*, which records his sermons and sayings, is a standard Zen text and has been canonized in the *Tripitaka*.

(32) See also Wong Mou Lam, Op. cit., p. 38.

(33) "Marks." Forms, characteristics, physiognomy. Marks are contrasted with essence, in the same way that phenomena are contrasted with noumenon. *Real Mark* stands for True Form, True Nature, always unchanging. The *Real Mark* of all phenomena is like space: always existing but really empty; although empty, really existing. The *Real Mark* of the Triple World is No-Birth/No-Death, not existent/not non-existent, not like this/not like that ... *Real Mark* is also called "Self-Nature," "Dharma Body," the "Unconditioned," "True Thusness," "Nirvana," "Dharma Realm."

(34) Master Fa Ta prostrated himself only halfway before the Sixth Patriarch because of conceit at his feat of having recited the *Lotus Sutra* 3,000 times.

At the highest or transcendental level, all attachments (even to the loftiness of the Buddhas and Bodhisattvas) have to be discarded if the Way is to be attained. Thus, Master Pei Ta wrote the names of Manjusri and Samantabhadra, two of the most revered Bodhisattvas in the Mahayana Canon, on his underpants to demonstrate the need to sever all attachments. Please note that such actions are not to be condoned in the case of ordinary persons such as ourselves.

For a glimpse of why we should not blindly borrow the words of the sages or emulate their extraordinary actions, see the following passage concerning Kumarajiva, the renowned T'ang Dynasty monk (who masterly translated some thirty-five sutras into Chinese):

When Kumarajiva went to China in the fourth century of this era, the Chinese Emperor thought that such a wise person ought to have descendents so that his wisdom would carry on. He gave concubines to Kumarajiva, and since they were a royal gift, Kumarajiva had no choice but to accept them. Afterwards, his disciples asked, "Can we have relations with women too?"

Kumarajiva said, "Sure, but first, let me show you something." He took a handful of needles and ate them as easily as if they were noodles. When he finished, he said, "If you can do that, then you can have relations with women." (Sheng-yen, *The Sword of Wisdom*, p. 229.)

(35) See Glossary, "Dharma-Ending Age."

(36) This passage has also been translated as follows: "Better you should speak of existence on the scale of the polar mountain, than speak of non-existence to the extent of a mustard seed." (J.C. Cleary, *Pure Land, Pure Mind.* Unpub. manuscript.)

(37) For heuristic reasons, Dharma Masters explain Faith, Vows and Practice separately, emphasizing the crucial nature of each one. However, these three preconditions for rebirth in the Pure Land are one and indivisible. True Faith naturally leads to Vows and Practice, while correct Practice cannot exist independent of Faith and Vows. As the Patriarch Yin Kuang once wrote:

> The true Pure Land practitioner always fully combines the three criteria of Faith, Vows and Practice during recitation. He is like an infant longing for his mother. When, lonely and crying, he searches for her, he certainly never lacks Faith or the desire (Vow) to see her. Therefore, why do you ask whether "Vows and Practice come separately or together"?

(38) Ordinary blessings are considered delusive because they are likely to lead to the creation of bad karma in future lifetimes. See also Glossary, "Third Lifetime."

(39) See note 37 above.

(40) 100,000 recitations: this number is often cited in commentaries as an ideal for the very serious Pure Land cultivator.

108 recitations: another commonly cited figure, equivalent to the number of beads in a long rosary.

(41) Real Mark:

> The real mark is apart from marks; it is not attached to any

distinguishing characteristics. It has left all dharmas behind, and swept away all marks. This is the investigation of the dhyana [Zen] Dharma-door. Those who truly practice dhyana truly chant the Buddha's name as well. Those who can really recite the Buddha's name are, in fact, investigating dhyana. Dhyana practice and Buddha Recitation both help you to stop your idle thoughts and sweep away your personal desires and random thoughts, so that your original face can appear. This is called real mark recitation. (Hsuan Hua, *Buddha Root Farm,* p. 41.)

(42) Once we are reborn in the Pure Land, in our pure Mind (Mind-Only Pure Land), we have awakened and therefore, all Dharma methods are perfectly comprehensible.

(43) Shift of level: at the transcendental level, reciting the Buddha's name, too, is a form of attachment.

(44) Three truths in the T'ien-t'ai (Tendai) School:

The threefold truth refers to emptiness, conditional existence and the Middle Way, meaning that things are not ultimately existent or non-existent ... The three contemplations: contemplation of the emptiness of conditional things, the relative existence of conditional things, and the Middle Way which is between or beyond being and nonbeing ... The scheme of three truths and three corresponding contemplations is a format used by the T'ien-t'ai school. (Thomas Cleary, *Entry into the Inconceivable: an Introduction to Hua-Yen Buddhism*, p. 212.)

(45) See also Wong Mou-Lam, Op. cit., p. 56-57.

(46) This passage has also been translated as follows:

The Buddha said: "A shramana who practices the Way should not be like an ox turning a millstone. Such a one practices the Way with his body, but his mind is not on the Way. If the mind is concentrated on the Way, what need is there to practice?" (Hsuan Hua, *A General Explanation of the "Sutra in Forty-two Sections,"* p. 81.)

(47) Wordless Sutra: The *Avatamsaka Sutra* states:

It is as if there is a great scripture
Equal in extent to a universe
Existing inside one atom,
And in all atoms as well;
Someone with intelligence and wisdom
Sees all clearly with pure eyes
And breaks the atoms, releasing the scripture

For the benefit of all beings.
Buddha-knowledge, likewise
Is in all beings' minds. (Thomas Cleary, tr. *The Flower Ornament Scripture [Avantamsaka Sutra]*. Vol. II, p. 317.)

This big sutra is wordless, but it also has boundlessly many words ... The true wordless sutra is just the mind-sutra. What is the mind-sutra? It is the embodiment of the tenet that everything is made from mind alone ... It's when a single thought does not arise. If not one thought arises, what words could there be? ... If you can't manage not to have a single thought arise, then you should create more merit and virtue, nurture your basis for Bodhi and foster your Bodhi way. (Hsuan Hua.)

(48) The basic goal of Buddhist teachings is to keep the mind empty and still so that our innate wisdom can manifest itself. (A Buddha is all wisdom at all times.) Thus, Buddhism fosters practices and habits that subdue passions and simplify life, freeing the cultivator for spiritual pursuits. It is in this context that sexual desire, excessive rest and sleep, etc. are considered afflictions. Note: section 35 as a whole is geared to the advanced practitioner!

(49) According to Buddhist (and Taoist) teachings, it is because we have a body that we suffer. Therefore, the true cultivator, when ill, should always remind himself of the need to escape this body and transcend Birth and Death.

(50) When the practitioner sees the signs of impermanence (e.g., parched skin, gray hair) he should redouble his efforts at cultivation, so as to escape Birth and Death. This is, of course, the opposite of common, everyday behavior, which consists in hiding the truth -- coloring one's hair, for example.

(51) Our bodies, our emotions, our environment all exist but their existence is not permanent or absolute. Therefore, in Buddhism, they are said to be illusory but not non-existent. See also Glossary, "Illusion."

(52) All these delusions are termed "upside down thinking" in Buddhism.

(53) Perhaps a correct response on the monk's part would have been to remain silent, while keeping his mind empty and still. See also Glossary, "Vimalakirti Sutra."

(54) All attachments, even to the Buddhas and the Dharma, should ultimately be discarded.

(55) This passage is a quote from the *Avatamsaka Sutra*:

> If an enlightening being conceives a single feeling of anger toward enlightening beings, that produces a million obstacles... Why? I do not see anything that is as big a mistake as for enlightening beings to become angry at other enlightening beings. Therefore, if great enlightening beings want to quickly fulfill the practices of enlightening beings, they should diligently practice ten principles: in their minds, they should not abandon sentient beings; they should think of enlightening beings as buddhas; they should never slander any teachings of the buddhas, they should know that there is no end to different lands; they should be profoundly devoted to enlightening practices; they should not give up the cosmic, space-like, impartial mind of enlightenment; they should contemplate enlightenment and enter the power of buddhas; they should cultivate unobstructed intellectual and expository powers; they should teach and enlighten beings tirelessly; they should live in all worlds without attachment in their minds. (Thomas Cleary, Op. cit., p. 266.)

(56) The difference between personal and common karma can be seen in the following example: Suppose a country goes to war to gain certain economic advantages and in the process, numerous soldiers and civilians are killed or maimed. If a particular citizen volunteers for military service and actually participates in the carnage, he commits a *personal* karma of killing. Other citizens, however, even if opposed to the war, may benefit directly or indirectly (e.g., through economic gain). They are thus said to share in the *common* karma of killing of their country.

(57) Proclaiming the errors of others, whether true or not, is an offence for two main reasons: i) the mind of the "proclaimer" is no longer empty and still, but tarnished by dislike or scorn; ii) the "transgressor" and those who hear of the errors may grow discouraged, abandon further cultivation and retrogress -- thus, potential Buddhas are lost.

(58) Four propositions: a) existence; b) non-existence; c) both; d) neither. The 100 errors are derived from these propositions.

(59) "All eagerness for study gone": the goal of all Buddhist teaching is to stop the mind from wandering, keeping it empty and still, so that our innate wisdom can surface. In that

context, love, hatred and eagerness to study are all attachments that disturb the mind.

"Eating when hungry, sleeping when tired": this Zen statement, which usually baffles non-Buddhists, actually reflects a deep truth. Most people do not eat when hungry, that is, they do not eat what is available or what is good for them, but rather seek special dishes prepared to their taste. Likewise, they do not sleep when tired, but are likely to do other things, such as tossing and turning in bed recalling past wrongs or mulling over future events.

(60) This is a key Buddhist teaching: every action has its source in a single thought. For example, while studying for his examination, a student may suddenly have the thought that there is a good movie to be seen. Later, if the conditions allow it (a friend calls to suggest going out), he may close his books, abandon his efforts to study and possibly, fail his examination, drop out of school, etc.

(61) According to one definition, Pratyeka Buddhas are "those who live in a world where there is no Buddha and awaken by themselves to the truth of impermanence by observing natural phenomena, such as the scattering of blossoms or the falling of leaves." (*A Dictionary of Buddhist Terms and Concepts*, p. 344.)

62) Mind and Realm:

> Amida Buddha is not far from anyone. His Land of Purity is described as being far away to the west but it is, also, within the minds of those who earnestly wish to be born there... To those who have faith, He offers the opportunity to become one with Him. As this Buddha is the all-inclusive body of equality, whoever thinks of Buddha, Buddha thinks of him and enters his mind freely.

> This means that when a person thinks of Buddha, he has Buddha's mind in all its pure and happy and peaceful perfection. In other words, his mind is a Buddha-mind. (*The Teaching of the Buddha*. Tokyo: Bukkyo Dendo Kyokai.)

> From the *ultimate* standpoint, the Pure Land is not to be taken as an existent place in the way ordinary beings are predisposed to understand it. The admonition against such a view of the Pure Land is found in the following passage: "A foolish person in hearing *birth* in the Pure Land understands it as *birth* and in hearing *non-birth* understands it as *non-*

birth. He thus fails to realize the identity of birth and non-birth and of non-birth and birth" ... Having said that, however, the Pure Land proponents acknowledge that the capacity of ordinary, unenlightened people is such that they have no choice but to regard the Pure Land as ontically existent ... The objective presentation of the Pure Land accords with the emotional and intellectual make-up of ordinary beings whose capacity affords only a literal understanding of the sutra description ... Only through their relationship with the Pure Land of form can the ultimate reality be realized.

But the question remains as to how beings are able to realize enlightenment through *grasping at forms* of Pure Land, which strikes as being antithetical to the fundamental Buddhist practice. T'ao-Ch'o [a Pure Land Patriarch] argues: "Although this is grasping onto form, such grasping does not constitute binding attachment. In addition, the form of the Pure Land being discussed here is identical to form without defilements, form that is true form ... It is like lighting fire on top of ice. As the fire intensifies, the ice melts. When the ice melts, then the fire goes out ..." According to this explanation, an ordinary being is able to engage the ultimate realm without that person fully understanding the ultimate nature. This process skillfully uses the form (rooted in truth) to transcend form in order to enter the formless. When the formless is attained, the previous attachment to form disappears ... (Kenneth K. Tanaka, "Where is the Pure Land?" in *Pacific World*, Fall 1987.)

As we recite "Namo Amitabha Buddha," we each create and adorn our own Land of Ultimate Bliss. We each accomplish our own Land of Ultimate Bliss which is certainly not hundreds of thousands of millions of Buddhalands from here. Although it is far away, it doesn't go beyond one thought. It's not hundreds of thousands of millions of Buddhalands from here; it's right in our hearts. The Land of Ultimate Bliss is the original true heart, the true mind, of every one of us. If you obtain this heart, you will be born in the Land of Ultimate Bliss. If you don't understand your own original true heart, you will not. The Land of Ultimate Bliss is within our hearts, not outside ... Amitabha Buddha and living beings do not discriminate between this and that, for the Land of Ultimate Bliss is not so far away. In one thought, turn the light within. Know that you are the Buddha, and your original Buddhahood is just the Land of Ultimate Bliss. (Hsuan Hua, *A General Explanation of the Buddha Speaks of Amitabha Sutra*, p. 110.)

(63) As everything is mind-made, the practitioner sees the marks of men and women because of his own latent lust.

(64) Take the example of a dream of Ms. P.C. Lee (Chihmann), the first person to translate (in 1935) Ch. 40 of the *Avatamsaka Sutra* ("Vows and Practices of the Bodhisattva Samantabhadra"):

In 1931, on the day of 17th November, I prayed to Buddha Amitabha, saying: "I have recited Thy Holy Name for one year and I have not received any answer from Thee, as to whether I will have a chance of re-birth to be born from the Lotus-flower. Today being the date in Thy honour, may I be favoured [with] a sign from Thee, to encourage me and give me strength." At night of the same day, when I went to bed, [I] had a dream that I saw something floating on the surface of the water of a lake. I could not see clearly what it was. Then I went forward to have a close look, and I clearly beheld them. They were all the sprouts of the lotus ... (P.C. Lee, *The Two Buddhist Books in Mahayana.*) Available in university libraries.

(65) Discussions on such subjects as the rise and fall of countries and empires are not recommended because they tend to disturb the mind, diverting it from the larger issue of how to escape Birth and Death.

(66) Celestial demons stand for lust and power, and can take the form of oppression by those in a position of power. (See *A Dictionary of Buddhist Terms and Concepts*, p. 259.)

67) Cultivators should exercise wisdom in receiving the teachings, carefully distinguishing the true from the false and the deviant. See the following passage, by the late founder of the Buddhist Lodge and Buddhist Society (London), on the true goal of all Buddhist practice:

In the West, the need for some guidance in mind-development was made acute ... by a sudden spate of books which were, whatever the motive of their authors, dangerous in the extreme. No word was said in them of the sole right motive for mind-development, the enlightenment of the meditator for the benefit of all mankind, and the reader was led to believe that it was quite legitimate to study and practice mindfulness, and the higher stages which ensue, for the benefit of business efficiency and the advancement of personal prestige. In these circumstances, *Concentration and Meditation* ... was compiled and published by the [British] Buddhist Society, with constant stress on the importance of right motive, and ample warning of the dangers, from a headache to insanity, which lie in wait for those who trifle with the greatest force on earth, the human mind. (Christmas Humphreys, *The Buddhist Way of Life*, p. 100.)

Most ancient masters, including such towering figures as the Patriarch Dogen, the founder of the Japanese school of Soto Zen, held that only monks and nuns could achieve Enlightenment through Zen. (See, for example, Kenneth Kraft, *Zen: Tradition and Transition*, p. 186.)

(68) This is a reference to the high-level form of Buddha Recitation: to recite the Buddha's name is to recite the Mind, to realize our Self-Nature.

(69) The mind of most humans is never at rest, empty and still, but "runs" continuously, like a horse. It also "jumps" from one branch to another, like a monkey in the forest.

(70) See the following passage:

> This [Pure Land] Dharma-door fights poison with poison. False thinking is like poison, and unless you counter it with poison, you will never cure it. Reciting the Buddha's name is fighting false thinking with false thinking. It is like sending out an army to defeat an army, to fight a battle to end all battles. If you have a good defense, other countries won't attack. Constant recitation drives out false thinking so that you may attain the Buddha- recitation samadhi. (Hsuan Hua, *A General Explanation of the Buddha Speaks of Amitabha Sutra,* p. 42.)

(71) This story of the Patriarchs Asanga and Vasabhandhu is particularly interesting as they were the founders and main exponents of the Yogacara or Mind-Only school (which flourished in the 6th century A.D.). The school teaches that everything is a projection of the mind and stresses the practice of meditation. Yogacara has had a strong influence on Zen.

(72) This is an extreme case of attachment on the part of the deceased monk: a temple should be an aid to cultivation, not an end in itself.

(73) According to Buddhist teachings, if there were another obstruction or force as strong as love-attachment, no cultivator could ever hope to attain Enlightenment and Buddhahood.

(74) Master Arya Simha lived in Central Asia during the sixth century A.D. While he was preaching Buddhism in Kashmir, King Dammira, an enemy of Buddhism, razed temples and murdered a number of monks. When he finally beheaded Master Arya Simha, it was said that pure white milk gushed from Arya Simha's neck.

The Patriarch Hui Ku (Hui K'o) was the Second Chinese Patriarch after Bodhidharma.

(75) Maudgalyayana was one of Shakyamuni Buddha's ten major disciples, known as the foremost in occult power. He died before Shakyamuni, killed by a hostile Brahmin while on his alms round.

The Patriarchs Arya Simha and Hui K'o and the Elder Maudgalyayana are all revered figures in Mahayana Buddhism. Through their symbolic deaths, sentient beings are taught the crucial importance of adhering to the precept against killing -- a cornerstone of Buddhist ethics.

(76) See Glossary, "Illusion."

(77) This is a cardinal teaching of Buddhism.

(78) In Buddhism, right thoughts are crucial at the time of death as they play a major role in our future rebirth. Those who have cultivated throughout life naturally develop right thoughts at the time of death. Most of the advice given in this chapter is directed at non-practitioners or those whose practice is perfunctory, as help of last resort, to maximize their chance of rebirth in a favorable realm.

(79) Love-attachment (to family and possessions), the strongest obstruction faced by human beings, is considered one of the greatest dangers at the time of death (see note 73).

The phrase "rebirth as a dog or snake" can be understood as vivid imagery. Any realm being ultimately Mind, a "dog" is "someone" who, at a certain time, experiences overpowering greed and must constantly watch over his property; a "snake" may represent a person afflicted by extreme anger.

(80) Like birds faced with the hunter's gun (which should all scatter, each for itself, and try to regroup later, after the danger has passed), dying practitioners should think of their salvation first, to the exclusion of everything and everyone else. (Incidentally, this is exactly the advice given to airline passengers in case of emergency.) Once reborn in the Pure Land, the cultivator should, of course, aim to rescue all sentient beings.

(81) This is so because the mind cannot then concentrate

singlemindedly on the Buddha. As stated in the Pure Land classic *Direct Pointing to the Source (Qui-Nguyên Trực-Chỉ/Kuei Yuan Chih Chih)*:

> If your illness becomes serious, and you are facing the end, your relatives should not weep or wail or utter sounds of lamentation and distress. This may throw your mind into confusion and make you lose correct mindfulness. They should just join together and recite the Buddha-name to help you to go to the Pure Land. Only after your breathing has stopped for a long time can they weep and wail.
>
> As soon as there is the least bit of longing for the world, it immediately becomes an obstruction, and you will not achieve liberation. If you find people who clearly understand the Pure Land [i.e. good spiritual advisors], let them come frequently to urge you on and encourage you. This would be a great good fortune. (J.C. Cleary, *Pure Land, Pure Mind*, unpub. manuscript.)

Note: Love-attachment is, along with killing, one of the two major impediments to rebirth in the Pure Land. (See, for example, Hsuan Hua, tr. *The Sutra in Forty-Two Sections*, p. 64.)

(82) As stated in the *Ksitigarbha Sutra*:

> In this instance, this sutra should be recited once in a loud voice before the images of Buddhas and Bodhisattvas, and possessions which the sick one loves, such as clothing ... should be offered, saying in a voice before the sick person, "I, so-and-so, before this sutra and image, give all these items on behalf of this sick person." ... The sick [cultivator] should be told three times of the offerings that are being made so that he may hear and know of them. (*Sutra of the Past Vows of Earth Store Bodhisattva [Ksitigharba Sutra]: the Collected Lectures of Tripitaka Master Hsuan Hua*, p. 158.)

See also the same Sutra under the title *The Sutra of Bodhisattva Ksitigharba's Fundamental Vows*, Sutra Translation Committee of the United States and Canada, p. 54-55.

(83) This situation is akin to that of the traveller who has just spent an entire week driving from New York to San Diego and then, just before reaching his destination, takes a wrong turn and winds up across the border in Mexico!

The reader may wish to contrast these guidelines with certain other practices which tend to foster attachment:

In Philip Roth's book, [*Patrimony -- a True Story*] a prodigious teller gives us his father's experience of this new landscape of death and his own. Here the old intimation of mortality has yielded to the physician's second opinion. The last words, the blessing of the young, the washing of the body, the coins on the eyelids, the deathbed confession, the deathbed reconciliation and the deathbed farewell have been succeeded or crowded by the I.V., the respirator, the feeding tubes in the nostrils, the living will, the hospital roommate, the nurses. (*New York Times Book Review*, January 6, 1991, p. 1.)

(84) King Ajatasatru, after usurping his father's throne, ruled for a number of years before becoming incurably ill at age fifty. He then converted to Buddhism and became a well-known disciple of Sakyamuni Buddha.

Please note that it is not the act of disturbing the dying person that causes him to remain in the Triple Realm, but rather his angry thoughts at being disturbed, his lack of correct mindfulness.

(85) Most major religions teach that at the time of death, "the dying person [however sinful] may, by focusing his mind on God [i.e., a transcendental being] and accepting the Light that seems to embrace him, leap to a higher realm." (*World Scripture*, p. 240.)

(86) As stated in the *Ksitigharba Sutra*:

World Honored One, the habitual evil of living beings extends from the subtle to the overwhelmingly great. Since all beings have such habits, their parents or relatives should create merit for them when they are on the verge of dying in order to assist them on the road ahead. This may be done by ... reciting the holy sutras, or making offerings before the images of Buddhas or sages. It includes recitation of the names of Buddhas, Bodhisattvas, and Pratyeka Buddhas in such a way that the recitation of each name *passes by the ear* of the dying one and is heard in his fundamental consciousness.

The evil deeds done by living beings bear corresponding results, yet even if one ought to fall into the Evil Paths, his offenses may be eradicated if his survivors cultivate holy causes for him. During a period of forty-nine days after the death, they should do many good deeds that can cause the dead one to leave the Evil Paths. (*Sutra of the Past Vows of Earth Store Bodhisattva [Ksitigharba Sutra]: the Collected Lectures of Tripitaka Master Hsuan Hua,* p. 168.)

(87) Buddhism makes a distinction between physical (clinical) death and mental death, with the former preceding the latter

by a period of some three to eight hours. Actual death is defined as that moment when the Alaya consciousness (see Glossary) leaves the body -- not when the heart has stopped or brain waves can no longer be detected. This is the reason for the waiting period of at least three hours after clinical death before the body is disturbed.

(88) The two principal dangers to avoid at the time of death are anger and love-attachment.

(89) Some of the texts in which this practice is mentioned include the *Great Heap Sutra*, the *Tibetan Book of the Dead* and a well-known Chinese commentary, *Transcending Life and Death*. Note: this practice is particularly prevalent in Tantric (Esoteric) Buddhism.

(90) As stated in the *Ksitigharba Sutra*:

> The dead one might be due to receive a good retribution and be born among men and gods in his next life or in the future, but because of offenses committed by his family in his name, his good rebirth will be delayed. Everyone must undergo the Evil Paths in accordance with his own deeds; it is even more unbearable when survivors add to those deeds. (Loc. cit., p. 170.)

(91) Killing sentient beings, including slaughtering animals for food, is among the heaviest transgressions in Buddhism. This is not only because such acts create untold suffering but also because they cut short the lives of future Buddhas (as all sentient beings have a common Buddha Nature).

The injunction against all forms of killing (including suicide), covering all sentient beings, is unique to Buddhism. Jainism, for example, approves of the penance of death by self-starvation, while Hindu ceremonies such as the Srauta rites "center on offering into the altar fires oblations of milk, butter, honey ... domestic animals ..." (K. Crim, *Dictionary of Religions*, p. 369 and 790, respectively.)

(92) The reader is referred to C.T. Shen, *The Essence of Samantabhadra's Vows*, p. 18-19. See also Glossary, "Transference of Merit."

(93) To be truly effective in dedicating merit to others, the

practitioner must be utterly sincere and singleminded in his recitation. Even so, the *Ksitigarbha Sutra* teaches that the deceased can only receive a small part of this merit. Furthermore, since the crucial conditions of sincerity and singlemindedness are seldom achieved in full, most intercessions are, at best, partially effective and can seldom erase a lifetime of bad karma. Thus, it is imperative for the practitioner himself to cultivate during his lifetime and not rely on family members, monks or nuns at the time of death.

(94) See note 2 above.

(95) See note 89 above.

(96) The practice of feeling the body at the time of death is common to many Buddhist traditions, including the Yogacara (Mind-Only), Pure Land and Tantric (Esoteric) schools.

(97) Good spiritual advisor: a friend of virtue, a religious counsellor, a guru, who advises the cultivator on the right path. The term can apply to anyone, from the Buddhas and Bodhisattvas to monks and nuns and laymen. Even the non-virtuous or heretics may fulfill the role, albeit in a negative way. See also Glossary.

(98) Transference of merit: see Glossary.

(99) "Beings of the highest virtue": this a reference to the *Amitabha Sutra*.

> Shariputra: the beings who hear this ought to make a vow -- a vow to be born in that land. Why should they? Having succeeded thus, all are then persons of the highest virtue; all are assembled in the same circumstances. (Hozen Seki, *The Buddha Tells of the Infinite*, p. 48).

Please note that Master Thích Thiên Tâm, in the tradition of classical Pure Land exegesis, deliberately quotes from many sutras and commentaries not commonly associated with the Pure Land school (e.g., the *Avatamsaka, Lotus, Platform, Lankavatara, Surangama and Questions of King Milinda Sutras*, etc.). This is to demonstrate that Pure Land concepts can be found throughout the *Tripitaka* and underlie much of popular Buddhist thinking and practice.

I vow that when my life approaches its end,
All obstructions will be swept away;
I will see Amitabha Buddha,
And be born in his Land of Ultimate Bliss.

When reborn in the Western Land,
I will perfect and completely fulfill
Without exception these Great Vows,
To delight and benefit all beings.

The Vows of Samantabhadra

Glossary

Alaya consciousness. Also called "store consciousness," "eighth consciousness," or "karma repository." See also "Eight consciousnesses."

> All karma created in the present and previous lifetimes is stored here. The alaya consciousness is regarded as that which undergoes the cycle of birth and death ... All the actions and experiences of life that take place through the first seven consciousnesses are accumulated as karma in this alaya consciousness, which at the same time exerts an influence on the workings of the seven consciousnesses. (*A Dictionary of Buddhist Terms and Concepts.*)

Amitabha (Amida, Amita, Amitayus). Amitabha is the most commonly used name for the Buddha of Infinite Light and Infinite Life. A transhistorical Buddha venerated by all Mahayana schools (T'ien T'ai, Esoteric, Zen ...) and, particularly, Pure Land. Presides over the Western Pure Land (Land of Ultimate Bliss), where anyone can be reborn through utterly sincere recitation of His name, particularly at the time of death.

Amitabha Buddha at the highest or noumenon level represents the True Mind, the Self-Nature common to the Buddhas and sentient beings -- all-encompassing and all-inclusive. This deeper understanding provides the rationale for the harmonization of Zen and Pure Land, two of the most popular schools of Mahayana Buddhism. See also "Buddha Recitation," "Mind," Pure Land."

Amitabha Sutra. See "Three Pure land Sutras."

Arhat. Arhatship is the highest rank attained by Sravakas. An Arhat is a Buddhist saint who has attained liberation from the cycle of Birth and Death, generally through living a monastic life in accordance with the Buddhas' teachings. This is the goal of Theravadin practice, as contrasted with Bodhisattvahood in Mahayana practice. (*A Dictionary of*

Buddhism.) See also "Sravakas."

Attachment. In the Four Noble truths, Buddha Sakyamuni taught that attachment to self is the root cause of suffering:

> From craving [attachment] springs grief, from craving springs fear; For him who is wholly free from craving, there is no grief, much less fear. (*Dhammapada Sutra.* In Narada Maha Thera, *The Buddha and His Teachings.*)

> If you don't have attachments, naturally you're liberated ... In ancient times, there was an old cultivator who asked for instructions from a monk, "Great Monk, let me ask you, how can I attain liberation?" The Great monk said, "Who tied you up?" This old cultivator answered, "Nobody tied me up." The monk said, "Then why do you seek liberation?" (Hsuan Hua, tr., *Flower Adornment Sutra*, "Pure Conduct," chap. 11.)

For the seasoned practitioner, even the Dharma must not become an attachment. As an analogy, to clean one's shirt, it is necessary to use soap. However, if the soap is not then rinsed out, the garment will not be truly clean. Similarly, the practitioner's mind will not be fully liberated until he severs attachment to everything, including the Dharma itself.

Avalokitesvara. Also called Kuan Yin, the Bodhisattva of Compassion. Usually recognizable by the small Buddha adorning Her crown.

Avatamsaka (Flower Ornament) Sutra. The basic text of the Avatamsaka School. It is one of the longest sutras in the Buddhist Canon and records the highest teaching of Buddha Sakyamuni, immediately after Enlightenment. It is traditionally believed that the Sutra was taught to the Bodhisattvas and other high spiritual beings while the Buddha was in samadhi. The Sutra has been described as the "epitome of Buddhist thought, Buddhist sentiment and Buddhist experience" and is quoted by all schools of Mahayana Buddhism, in particular, Pure Land and Zen.

Awakening vs. Enlightenment. A clear distinction should be made between *awakening to the Way* (Great Awakening) and *attaining the Way* (attaining Enlightenment). (Note: There are many degrees of Awakening and Enlightenment. Attaining the Enlightenment of the Arhats, Pratyeka Buddhas, Bodhisattvas, etc. is different from attaining *Supreme Enlightenment*, i.e., Buddhahood.)

To experience a Great Awakening is to achieve (through Zen meditation, Buddha Recitation, etc.) a complete and deep realization of what it means to be a Buddha and how to reach Buddhahood. It is to see one's Nature, comprehend the True Nature of things, the Truth. However, only after becoming a Buddha can one be said to have truly attained Supreme Enlightenment (attained the Way).

A metaphor appearing in the sutras is that of a glass of water containing sediments. As long as the glass is undisturbed, the sediments remain at the bottom and the water is clear. However, as soon as the glass is shaken, the water becomes turbid. Likewise, when a practitioner experiences a Great Awakening (awakens to the Way), his afflictions (greed, anger and delusion) are temporarily suppressed but not yet eliminated. To achieve Supreme Enlightenment (i.e., to be rid of all afflictions, to discard all sediments) is the ultimate goal. Only then can he completely trust his mind and actions. Before then, he should adhere to the precepts, keep a close watch on his mind and thoughts, like a cat stalking a mouse, ready to pounce on evil thoughts as soon as they arise. To do otherwise is to court certain failure, as stories upon stories of errant monks, roshis and gurus demonstrate.

Another illustration:

To make sure that his disciple would reach the great ocean and not be misled by smaller bodies of water, a Zen Master explained the difference between rivers, lakes and seas, the characteristics of fresh water, salt water, etc. Finally, he took the disciple to the highest mountain peak in the area and pointed to the ocean in the distance. For the first time, glimpsing the ocean with his own eyes, the disciple experienced a Great Awakening. However, only after he followed the long, arduous path and actually reached the ocean, tasting its waters, did he achieve Enlightenment.

Awakening of the Faith (Treatise). A major commentary

by the Patriarch Asvaghosha (1st/2nd cent.), which presents the fundamental principles of Mahayana Buddhism. Several translations exist in English.

Bardo stage. The intermediate stage between death and rebirth.

Bodhi. Sanskrit for Enlightenment.

Bodhi Mind, (Bodhicitta, Great Mind). The spirit of Enlightenment, the aspiration to achieve it, the Mind set on Enlightenment. It involves two parallel aspects: i) the determination to achieve Buddhahood and ii) the aspiration to rescue all sentient beings.

Bodhisattvas. Those who aspire to Supreme Enlightenment and Buddhahood for themselves and all beings. The word Bodhisattva can therefore stand for a realized being such as Avalokitesvara or Samantabhadra but also for anyone who has developed the Bodhi Mind, the aspiration to save oneself and others.

Bodhisattva Grounds. See "Ten Grounds."

Brahma Net Sutra (Brahmajala Sutra). This is a sutra of major significance in Mahayana Buddhism. In addition to containing the ten major precepts of Mahayana (not to kill, steal, lie, etc.) the Sutra also contains forty-eight less important injunctions. These fifty-eight major and minor precepts constitute the Bodhisattva Precepts, taken by most Mahayana monks and nuns and certain advanced lay practitioners.

Buddha Nature. The following terms refer to the same thing: Self-Nature, True Nature, Original Nature, Dharma Nature, True Mark, True Mind, True Emptiness, True Thusness, Dharma Body, Original Face, Emptiness, Prajna, Nirvana, etc.

> According to the Mahayana view, [buddha-nature] is the true, immutable, and eternal nature of all beings. Since all beings possess buddha-nature, it is possible for them to attain enlightenment and become a buddha, regardless of what level of existence they occupy ...

The answer to the question whether buddha-nature is immanent in beings is an essential determining factor for the association of a given school with Theravada or Mahayana, the two great currents within Buddhism. In Theravada this notion is unknown; here the potential to become a buddha is not ascribed to every being. By contrast the Mahayana sees the attainment of buddhahood as the highest goal; it can be attained through the inherent buddha-nature of every being through appropriate spiritual practice. (*The Shambhala Dictionary of Buddhism and Zen.*)

See also "Dharma Nature," "True Thusness."

Buddha Recitation. General term for a number of practices, such as i) oral recitation of Amitabha Buddha's name and ii) visualization/contemplation of His auspicious marks and those of the Pure Land.

In reciting the buddha-name you use your own mind to be mindful of your own true self: how could this be considered seeking outside yourself? (Cited in J.C. Cleary, *Meditating with koans.*)

Reciting the buddha-name proceeds from the mind. The mind remembers Buddha and does not forget. That's why it is called buddha remembrance, or reciting the buddha-name mindfully. (Cited in J.C. Cleary, *Pure Land, Pure Mind.*)

The most common Pure Land technique is recitation of Amitabha Buddha's name. See also "Amitabha," "Pure Land."

Conditioned (compounded). Describes all the various phenomena in the world -- made up of separate, discrete elements, "with outflows," with no intrinsic nature of their own. Conditioned merits and virtues lead to rebirth within samsara, whereas unconditioned merits and virtues are the causes of liberation from Birth and Death. See also "Outflows," "Unconditioned."

Consciousness. See "Alaya consciousness" and "Eight consciousnesses."

Dedication of Merit. See "Transference of Merit."

Definitive (Ultimate) Meaning. See "Two Truths."

Degenerate Age. See "Dharma-Ending Age."

Delusion (Ignorance). "Delusion refers to belief in something that contradicts reality. In Buddhism, delusion is ... a lack of awareness of the true nature or Buddha nature of things, or of the true meaning of existence.

"According to the Buddhist outlook, we are deluded by our senses -- among which intellect (discriminating, discursive thought) is included as a sixth sense. Consciousness, attached to the senses, leads us into error by causing us to take the world of appearances for the world of reality; whereas in fact it is only a limited and fleeting aspect of reality." (*Shambhala Dictionary of Buddhism and Zen.*)

Delusions of Views and Thought. Delusion of views refers to greed and lust for externals (clothing, food, sleep, etc.) which are viewed as real rather than empty in their true nature.

> The delusion of thought consists in being confused about principles and giving rise to discrimination ... Thought delusions are unclear, muddled thoughts, taking what is wrong as right, and what is right as wrong. (Master Hsuan Hua)

Delusions of views, simply put, are delusions connected with seeing and grasping at the gross level. Delusions of thought are afflictions at the subtle level.

Demons. Evil influences which hinder cultivation. These can take an infinite number of forms, including evil beings or hallucinations. Disease and death, as well as the three poisons of greed, anger and delusion are also equated to demons, as they disturb the mind.

The *Nirvana Sutra* lists four types of demon: i) greed, anger and delusion; ii) the five skandas, or obstructions caused by physical and mental functions; iii) death; iv) the demon of the Sixth Heaven (Realm of Desire).

The Self-Nature has been described in Mahayana sutras as a house full of gold and jewelry. To preserve the riches, i.e., to keep the mind calm, empty and still, we should shut the doors to the three thieves of greed, anger and delusion.

Letting the mind wander opens the house to "demons," that is, hallucinations and harm. Thus, Zen practitioners are taught that, while in meditation, "Encountering demons, kill the demons, encountering Buddhas, kill the Buddhas." Both demons and Buddhas are mind-made, Mind-Only.

For a detailed discussion of demons, see Master Thích Thiền Tâm, *Buddhism of Wisdom and Faith*, sect. 51.

Dharma. a) The teachings of the Buddhas (generally capitalized in English); b) duty, law, doctrine; c) things, events, phenomena, everything.

Dharma Door. School, method, tradition.

Dharma-Ending Age, Degenerate Age. The present spiritually degenerate era, twenty-six centuries after the demise of Sakyamuni Buddha.
The concept of decline, dissension and schism within the Dharma after the passing of the Buddha is a general teaching of Buddhism and a corollary to the Truth of Impermanence. See, for example, the *Diamond Sutra* (sect. 6 in the translation by A.F. Price and Wong Mou-lam).
The time following Buddha Sakyamuni's demise is divided into three periods: i) the Perfect Age of the Dharma, lasting 500 years, when the Buddha's teaching (usually meditation) was correctly practiced and Enlightenment often attained; ii) the Dharma Semblance Age, lasting about 1,000 years, when a form of the teaching was practiced but Enlightenment seldom attained; iii) the Dharma-Ending Age, lasting some ten thousand years, when a diluted form of the teaching exists and Enlightenment is rarely attained.

Dharma Nature. The intrinsic nature of all things. Used interchangeably with "emptiness," "reality." See also "Buddha Nature," "True Thusness."

Dharma Realm (Cosmos, Dharmadhatu, realm of reality, realm of Truth). The term has several meanings in the sutras: i) the infinite universe, consisting of worlds upon worlds *ad infinitum*; ii) the nature or essence of all things; iii) the Mind.

Dharma Seals. Sakyamuni Buddha taught three "Dharma seals," or criteria, to determine the genuineness of Buddhist teachings, namely, impermanence, suffering, no-self. A fourth criterion, emptiness, is also mentioned in the sutras. Thus, the Truth of Impermanence is basic to Buddhism ... After seeing an old man, a sick man and a corpse, the young prince Siddhartha (Sakyamuni Buddha) decided to leave the royal life to become an ascetic.

An interesting corollary of the concept of Dharma seals is that much of the current speculation about whether or not this or that sutra is genuine is, in a sense, moot. A sutra is a sutra because it contains the words of the Buddhas *or* because the ideas expressed in it conform to the Dharma seals. An example of the latter is the *Platform Sutra*, which records the words of the Sixth Patriarch of Zen.

Dharmakara. The Bodhisattva who later became Amitabha Buddha, as related in the *Longer Amitabha Sutra*. The Bodhisattva Dharmakara is famous for forty-eight Vows, particularly the eighteenth, which promises rebirth in the Pure Land to anyone who recites His name with utmost sincerity and faith at the time of death.

Diamond Sutra. "An independent part of the *Prajnaparamita Sutra*, which attained great importance, particularly in East Asia. It shows that all phenomenal appearances are not ultimate reality but rather illusions, projections of one's own mind ... The work is called *Diamond Sutra* because it is 'sharp like a diamond that cuts away all unnecessary conceptualizations and brings one to the further shore of enlightenment.'" (*Shambhala Dictionary of Buddhism and Zen.*) See also "Prajnaparamita Sutras."

Difficult Path of Practice (Path of the Sages, Self-Power Path). According to Pure Land teaching, all conventional Buddhist ways of practice and cultivation (Zen, Theravada, the Vinaya School ...), which emphasize self-power and self-reliance. This is contrasted to the Easy Path of Practice, that is, the Pure Land method, which relies on both self-power and other-power (the power and assistance of the Buddhas and Bodhisattvas).

Dusts (Worldly Dusts). A metaphor for all the mundane things that can cloud our bright Self-Nature. These include form, sound, scent, taste, touch, dharmas (external opinions and views). These dusts correspond to the five senses and the discriminating, everyday mind (the sixth sense, in Buddhism).

Easy Path of Practice. Refers to Pure Land practice. The Easy Path involves reliance on the power of the Buddhas and Bodhisattvas, in particular Buddha Amitabha ("other-power") in addition to one's own cultivation ("self-power"). Usually contrasted with primary reliance on self-power (Difficult Path of Practice), taught in other Buddhist schools.

Equal reliance on self-power and other-power distinguishes the Pure Land School from most other schools of Buddhism. The distinction is, however, a matter of emphasis, as all schools of Buddhism rely, to a greater or lesser extent, on both self-power and other-power.

Eight Adversities. The eight conditions under which it is difficult to meet Buddhas and Bodhisattvas or hear the Dharma: 1. rebirth in the hells; 2. rebirth as a hungry ghost; 3. rebirth as an animal; 4. rebirth in Uttarakuru (a world where life is so pleasant that people have no motivation to practice the Dharma); 5. rebirth in any long-life heaven (where one is also not motivated to seek the Dharma); 6. rebirth with impaired faculties; 7. rebirth as an intelligent, educated person in the mundane sense (as such an individual often looks down on religion and on the Dharma); and 8. rebirth in the intermediate period between a Buddha and his successor (e.g., our current period). Thus, even rebirth under "favorable" circumstances (fourth and seventh conditions, for example) may constitute adversity with respect to the Buddha Dharma. (After G.C.C. Chang.)

Eight consciousnesses. The term "consciousness" refers to the perception or discernment which occurs when our sense organs make contact with their respective objects. They are: 1) sight consciousness; 2) hearing consciousness; 3) scent consciousness; 4) taste consciousness; 5) touch consciousness; 6) mind consciousness (Mano consciousness or ordinary mind); 7) klistamanas consciousness (defiled mind); 8) Alaya consciousness. The first five consciousnesses correspond to the five senses. The sixth consciousness "integrates the perceptions of the five senses into coherent images and makes judgments about the external world ..." (*A Dictionary of Buddhist Terms and Concepts.*) "The seventh consciousness is the active center of reasoning, calculation, and construction or fabrication of individual objects. It is the source of clinging and craving, and thus the origin of the sense of self or ego and the cause of all illusion that arises from assuming the apparent to be real ..." (Sung-peng Hsu.) For the eighth or Alaya consciousness, see "Alaya consciousness."

Eight Sufferings. Birth, old age, disease, death, separation from loved ones, meeting with the uncongenial, unfulfilled wishes and the suffering associated with the five raging skandas. (For a detailed exposition of the eight sufferings, see Thích Thiền Tâm, *Buddhism of Wisdom and Faith*, sect. 5.)

Emptiness (Void, Sunyata). Connotes "first, Void in the sense of antithesis of being; second, the state of being 'devoid' of specific character; third, Void in the highest sense, or Transcendental Void, i.e., all oppositions synthesized ...; and fourth, the Absolute Void or the Unconditioned." (Vergilius Ferm, ed. *An Encyclopedia of Religions.*)

Contrasted with "hollow emptiness," or "stubborn emptiness," which is one-sided and leads to nihilism (the belief that nothing exists after death). Thus, we have the Mahayana expression, "True Emptiness, Wonderful Existence" -- True Emptiness is not empty!

Enlightenment. See "Awakening vs. Enlightenment."

Evil Paths. The paths of hells, hungry ghosts, animality. These paths can be taken as states of mind; i.e., when someone has a vicious thought of maiming or killing another, he is effectively reborn, *for that moment*, in the hells.

Expedient means (Skillful means, Skill-in-means, Upaya). Refers to strategies, methods, devices, targetted to the capacities, circumstances, likes and dislikes of each sentient being, so as to rescue him and lead him to Enlightenment. "Thus, all particular formulations of the Teaching are just provisional expedients to communicate the Truth (Dharma) in specific contexts." (J.C. Cleary.) "The Buddha's words were medicines for a given sickness at a given time," always infinitely adaptable to the conditions of the audience.

Externalists.   Literally, followers of non-Buddhist paths. This term is generally used by Buddhists with reference to followers of other religions.

Five Desires (Five Sensual Pleasures).   Desires connected with the five senses, i.e., form, sound, aroma, taste and touch.

Five Grave Offenses (Five Deadly Sins).   Offenses which cause rebirth in the Uninterrupted Hell.   They are: killing one's father, one's mother, or an Arhat, causing dissension within the Sangha, causing the Buddhas to bleed.

Five Meditations.   Basic meditations usually associated with Theravada Buddhism (meditation on impurities of the body, on compassion, on the twelve links of conditional existence, on the auspicious marks of the Buddhas and as well as counting the breath).

Five Periods and Eight Teachings.   All the teachings of Buddha Sakyamuni during His entire lifetime, as categorized by the T'ien-T'ai school.

Five Precepts.   See "Ten Virtues."

Five Signs of Decay.   Refers to symptoms of imminent death and rebirth in a lower realm, experienced by celestials and deities at the end of their transcendental lives, such as body odor, restlessness, etc.   Please note that celestials and deities are still within the realm of Birth and Death.   The Pure Land, being a Buddha land, is beyond Birth and Death.

Five Skandas. Also translated as "components" or "aggregates." They represent body and mind. The five skandas are form, feeling, conception, impulse and consciousness. For example, form is the physical body, consciousness is the faculty of awareness. The best known reference to the five skandas is found in the *Heart Sutra*. By realizing that they are intrinsically empty, the Bodhisattva Avalokitesvara has escaped all suffering. Note the difference between intellectual understanding of this principle and truly internalizing it (a good driver slams on the brakes when another car cuts in front of him, without stopping to think about it). Only by internalizing the Truth of Emptiness, through assiduous cultivation, can suffering be transcended.

Five Turbidities (Corruptions, Defilements, Depravities, Filths, Impurities). They are: 1. the defilement of views, when incorrect, perverse thoughts and ideas are predominant; 2. the defilement of passions, when all kinds of transgressions are exalted; 3. the defilement of the human condition, when people are usually dissatisfied and unhappy; 4. the defilement of the life-span, when the human life-span as a whole decreases; 5. the defilement of the world-age, when war and natural disasters are rife. Please note that these conditions, viewed from a Buddhist angle, can constitute aids to Enlightenment, as they may spur practitioners to more earnest cultivation. (After G.C.C.Chang.)

Flower Store World. The entire cosmos, consisting of worlds upon worlds *ad infinitum*, as described in the *Avatamsaka Sutra*. It is the realm of Vairocana Buddha, the transcendental aspect of Buddha Sakyamuni and of all Buddhas. The Saha World, the Western Pure Land and, for that matter, all lands and realms are within the Flower Store World.

Four Constituents. Earth, water, wind and fire.

Four Fruits. Refers to four levels of Enlightenment, culminating in Arhatship. Arhats are no longer subject to rebirth in samsara, i.e., in the cycle of Birth and Death.

Four Great Debts. The debt to the Triple Jewel, the debt to our parents and teachers, the debt to our spiritual friends, and finally, the debt we owe to all sentient beings.

Four Propositions. a) existence; b) non-existence; c) both existence and non-existence; d) neither. The 100 errors are derived from these propositions.

Four-fold Assembly. The Assembly of monks, nuns, laymen and laywomen.

Good Spiritual Advisor. Guru, virtuous friend, wise person, Bodhisattva, Buddha -- anyone (even an evil being!) who can help the practitioner progress along the path to Enlightenment. This notwithstanding, *wisdom* should be the primary factor in the selection of such an advisor: the advisor must have wisdom, and both advisor and practitioner must exercise wisdom in selecting one another.

Great Awakening. See "Awakening vs. Enlightenment."

Grounds. See "Ten Grounds."

Hui Neng. See "Sixth Patriarch."

Illusion (Maya). One of the key concepts in Buddhism.

> Things in the phenomenal world are not real or substantial, as ordinary people regard them to be. They are transient, momentary, indefinite, insubstantial, and subject to constant alteration. In reality, they are like phantoms or hallucinations. (G.C.C. Chang).

> Phenomenal "existence," as commonly perceived by the senses, is illusory; it is not real inasmuch as, though it exists, its existence is not permanent or absolute. Nothing belonging to it has an enduring entity or "nature" of its own; everything is dependent upon a combination of fluctuating conditions and factors for its seeming "existence" at any given moment." (Fung Yu-Lan.)

Thus, we have the expression, "illusory but not non-existent."

Insight into Non-arising of the Dharmas. See "Tolerance of Non-Birth."

Karma. Action leading to future retribution or reward, in the current or future lifetimes.

Common karma: the difference between personal and common karma can be seen in the following example: Suppose a country goes to war to gain certain economic advantages and in the process, numerous soldiers and civilians are killed or maimed. If a particular citizen volunteers for military service and actually participates in the carnage, he commits a *personal* karma of killing. Other citizens, however, even if opposed to the war, may benefit directly or indirectly (e.g., through economic gain). They are thus said to share in the *common* karma of killing of their country.

Fixed karma: in principle, all karma is subject to change. Fixed karma, however, is karma which can only be changed in extraordinary circumstances, because it derives from an evil act committed simultaneously with mind, speech and body. An example of fixed karma would be a premeditated crime (versus a crime of passion).

Ksana. "The shortest measure of time; sixty ksana equal one finger-snap, ninety a thought, 4,500 a minute." (Charles Luk.)

Lankavatara Sutra. The only sutra recommended by Bodhidharma, the First Zen Patriarch in China. It is a key Zen text, along with the *Diamond Sutra* (recommended by the Sixth Patriarch), the *Surangama Sutra*, the *Vimalakirti Sutra*, the *Avatamsaka Sutra* ... The last four sutras are referred to frequently in Pure Land commentaries.

Lotus Grades. The nine possible degrees of rebirth in the Western Pure Land. The more merits and virtues the practitioner accumulates, the higher the grade.

Lotus Sutra. A major Buddhist text and one of the most widely read sutras in the present day.

> One of the earliest and most richly descriptive of the Mahayana sutras of Indian origin. It became important for the shaping of the Buddhist tradition in East Asia, in particular because of its teaching of the One Vehicle under which are subsumed the usual Hinayana [Theravada] and Mahayana divisions. It is the main text of the Tendai [T'ien T'ai] school. (Joji Okazaki.)

This School has a historically close relationship with the Pure Land School. Thus, Master T'ai Hsu taught that the *Lotus Sutra* and the *Amitabha Sutras* were closely connected, differing only in length.

Mahasthamaprapta (Shih Chih, Seishi). One of the three sages in Pure Land Buddhism, recognizable by the water jar (jewelled pitcher) adorning Her crown. Usually represented in female form in East Asian iconography. Amitabha Buddha is frequently depicted standing between the Bodhisattvas Avalokitesvara and Mahasthamaprapta.

Marks. Characteristics, forms, physiognomy. Marks are contrasted with essence, in the same way that phenomena are contrasted with noumenon. *True Mark* stands for True Form, True Nature, Buddha Nature, always unchanging. The *True Mark* of all phenomena is like space: always existing but really empty; although empty, really existing. The *True Mark* of the Triple World is No-Birth/No-Death, not existent/not non-existent, not like this/not like that. *True Mark* is also called "Self-Nature," "Dharma Body," the "Unconditioned," "True Thusness," "Nirvana," "Dharma Realm." See also "Noumenon/Phenomena."

Meditation Sutra. One of the three core sutras of the Pure Land school. It teaches sixteen methods of visualizing Amitabha Buddha, the Bodhisattvas and the Pure Land. This sutra stresses the element of meditation in Pure Land. See also "Three Pure Land Sutras," "Vaidehi," "Visualization."

Merit and Virtue. these two terms are sometimes used interchangeably. However, there is a crucial difference: merits are the blessings (wealth, intelligence, etc.) of the human and celestial realms; therefore, they are temporary and subject to Birth and Death. Virtues, on the other hand, transcend Birth and Death and lead to Buddhahood. Four virtues are mentioned in Pure Land Buddhism: eternity; happiness; True Self; purity.

An identical action (e.g., charity) can lead either to merit or virtue, depending on the mind of the practitioner, that is, on whether he is seeking mundane rewards (merit) or transcendence (virtue). Thus, the Pure Land cultivator should not seek merits for by doing so, he would, in effect, be choosing to remain within samsara. This would be counter to his very wish to escape Birth and Death.

Middle Way (Madhyamika). The way between and above all extremes, such as hedonism or ascetism, existence or emptiness, eternalism or nihilism, samsara or Nirvana, etc. The Middle Way is a basic tenet of Buddhism. See also "Nagarjuna."

Mind. Key concept in all Buddhist teaching.

> Frequent term in Zen, used in two senses: (1) the mind-ground, the One Mind ... the buddha-mind, the mind of thusness ... (2) false mind, the ordinary mind dominated by conditioning, desire, aversion, ignorance, and false sense of self, the mind of delusion ... (J.C. Cleary, *A Buddha from Korea.*)

The ordinary, deluded mind (thought) includes feelings, impressions, conceptions, consciousness, etc. The Self-Nature True Mind is the fundamental nature, the Original Face, reality, etc. As an analogy, the Self-Nature True Mind is to mind what water is to waves -- the two cannot be dissociated. They are the same but they are also different.

To approach the sutras "making discriminations and nurturing attachments" is no different from the Zen allegory of a person attempting to lift a chair while seated on it. If he would only get off the chair, he could raise it easily.

Similarly, the practitioner truly understands the Dharma only to the extent that he "suspends the operation of the discriminating intellect, the faculty of the internal dialogue through which people from moment to moment define and perpetuate their customary world of perception." (J.C. Cleary, *Pure Land, Pure Mind*, Introduction.)

See also the following passage:

> The mind ... "creates" the world in the sense that it invests the phenomenal world with value. The remedy to this situation, according to Buddhism, is to still the mind, to stop it from making discriminations and nurturing attachments toward certain phenomena and feelings of aversion toward others. When this state of calmness of mind is achieved, the darkness of ignorance and passion will be dispelled and the mind can perceive the underlying unity of the absolute. The individual will then

have achieved the state of enlightenment and will be freed from the cycle of birth and death, because such a person is now totally indifferent to them both. (Burton Watson, *The Zen Teachings of Master Lin-Chi.*)

Mind-Only School. See "Yogacara School."

Mindfulness of the Buddha. Synonymous with Buddha Recitation. See "Buddha Recitation."

Nagarjuna. (2nd/3rd cent.) "One of the most important philosophers of Buddhism and the founder of the Madhyamika school. Nagarjuna's major accomplishment was his systematization ... of the teaching presented in the *Prajnaparamita Sutras.* Nagarjuna's methodological approach of rejecting all opposites is the basis of the Middle Way ..." (*Shambhala Dictionary of Buddhism and Zen.*) See also "Middle Way."

Nature and Marks. See "Marks."

Nine Realms. All realms in the cosmos, with the exception of the Buddha realms.

Non-Birth (No-Birth). "A term used to describe the nature of Nirvana. In Mahayana Buddhism generally, No-Birth signifies the 'extinction' of the discursive thinking by which we conceive of things as arising and perishing, forming attachments to them." (Ryukoku University.) See also "Tolerance of Non-Birth."

Non-Dual. Key Buddhist truth. Can be understood as not two and not one -- transcending two and one. Equivalent to Reality, Truth, Emptiness.

Noumenon/Phenomena. *Noumenon:* principle, essence of things, always one and indivisible. *Phenomena:* All things and events. Used in plural form to contrast with noumenon.

"Noumenon" (principle) is reason, the realm of enlightenment, and belongs to the sphere of "nature." "Phenomena" are expedients, practices, deeds, "form," and fall under the heading of "marks." However, in the end, phenomena are noumenon, nature is mark, and both belong to the same truth-like Nature, all-illuminating, all-pervading. In cultivation, noumenon and phenomena are the two sides of a coin, interacting with one another and helping one another. (Thích Thiền Tâm.)

Thus, for example, the word "Buddha" can mean the Buddha with His thirty-two auspicious marks (phenomena) or, at a higher level, the True Nature inherent in all sentient beings (noumenon). See also "Marks."

Ocean Seal Samadhi. A state of concentration of the highest level, mentioned, *inter alia*, in the *Avatamsaka Sutra*. The mind is likened to the ocean, which, when calm and without a single wave, can reflect everything throughout the cosmos, past, present and future.

Ocean-Wide Lotus Assembly. The Lotus Assembly represents the gathering of Buddha Amitabha, the Bodhisattvas, the sages and saints and all other superior beings in the Land of Ultimate Bliss. This Assembly is "Ocean-Wide" as the participants are infinite in number -- spreading as far and wide as the ocean. The term Ocean-Wide Assembly is generally associated with the *Avatamsaka Sutra*, a text particularly prized by the Pure Land and Zen schools alike.

One-Life Bodhisattva. A Bodhisattva who is one lifetime away from Buddhahood. The best known example is the Bodhisattva Maitreya.

One-pointedness of mind. Singlemindedness or singleminded concentration.

Original Nature. See "Buddha Nature."

Other-Power. See "Easy Path of Practice."

Other shore. A metaphor for Enlightenment and Buddhahood.

Outflows. "With outflows" = leaking, i.e., mundane or conditioned. "Without outflows" = without leakage, transcendental or unconditioned. See also "Conditioned,"

"Unconditioned."

Paramita. Means "the perfection of" or "reaching the other shore" (Enlightenment) as contrasted with this shore of suffering and mortality. The paramitas are usually six in number (charity, discipline, forbearance, diligent practice, concentration, wisdom) or expanded to ten (adding expedients, vows, power and knowledge). Mahayana emphasizes the paramita of expedients, or skill-in-means.

Path of Sages. See "Difficult Path of Practice."

Perfect Teaching (Round Teaching). Supreme teaching of the Buddhas, as expressed in the *Avatamsaka* and *Lotus Sutras*.

Platform Sutra. See "Sixth Patriarch."

Prajnaparamita Sutras. "Term for a series of about forty Mahayana sutras gathered together under this name because they all deal with the realization of prajna [intuitive wisdom] ... Best known in the West are the *Diamond Sutra* and the *Heart Sutra*. Their most important interpreter was Nagarjuna." (*Shambhala Dictionary.*) The Truth of sunyata, or emptiness, is central to these sutras, which teach non-attachment to self or dharmas. See also "Diamond Sutra."

Pratyeka Buddhas. "These buddhas become fully enlightened ... by meditating on the principle of causality. Unlike the Perfect Buddhas, however, they do not exert themselves to teach others" (A. Buzo and T. Prince).

Pure Land. Generic term for the realms of the Buddhas. In this text it denotes the Land of Ultimate Bliss or Western Land of Amitabha Buddha. It is not a realm of enjoyment, but rather an *ideal place of cultivation*, beyond the Triple Realm and samsara, where those who are reborn are no longer subject to retrogression. This is the key distinction between the Western Pure Land and such realms as the Tusita Heaven. There are two conceptions of the Pure Land: as different and apart from the Saha World *and* as one with and the same as the Saha World. When the mind is pure and undefiled, any land or environment becomes a pure land (*Vimalakirti,*

Avatamsaka Sutras ...). See also "Triple Realm."

Pure Land School. When Mahayana Buddhism spread to China, Pure Land ideas found fertile ground for development. In the fourth century, the movement crystallized with the formation of the Lotus Society, founded by Master Hui Yuan (334-416), the first Pure Land Patriarch. The school was formalized under the Patriarchs T'an Luan (Donran) and Shan Tao (Zendo). Master Shan Tao's teachings, in particular, greatly influenced the development of Japanese Pure Land, associated with Honen Shonin (Jodo school) and his disciple, Shinran Shonin (Jodo Shinshu school) in the 12th and 13th centuries. Jodo Shinshu, or Shin Buddhism, places overwhelming emphasis on the element of faith.

[Pure Land comprises the schools] of East Asia which emphasize aspects of Mahayana Buddhism stressing faith in Amida, meditation on and recitation of his name, and the religious goal of being reborn in his "Pure Land" or "Western Paradise." (Keith Crim.)

Note: An early form of Buddha Recitation can be found in the *Nikayas* of the Pali Canon:

In the *Nikayas*, the Buddha ... advised his disciples to think of him and his virtues as if they saw his body before their eyes, whereby they would be enabled to accumulate merit and attain Nirvana or be saved from transmigrating in the evil paths ... (D.T. Suzuki, *The Eastern Buddhist*, Vol. 3, No. 4, p. 317.)

Pure Land Sutras. See "Three Pure Land Sutras."

Saha World. World of Endurance. Refers to this world of ours, filled with suffering and afflictions, yet gladly endured by its inhabitants.

Samadhi. Meditative absorption. "Usually denotes the particular final stage of pure concentration." There are many degrees and types of samadhi (Buddha Recitation, Ocean Seal, Pratyutpanna ...)

Samantabhadra. Also called Universal Worthy or, in Japanese, Fugen. A major Bodhisattva, who personifies the transcendental practices and vows of the Buddhas (as compared to the Bodhisattva Manjusri, who represents transcendental wisdom). Usually depicted seated on an elephant with six tusks (six paramitas). Best known for his "Ten Great Vows."

Samatha-Vipasyana. "Tranquility and contemplation; stopping evil thoughts and meditating on the truth." (Hisao Inagaki.)

Samsara. Cycle of rebirths; realms of Birth and Death.

Sariputra. Major disciple of Sakyamuni Buddha, foremost in wisdom among His Arhat disciples.

Self-Power. See "Difficult Path of Practice."

Seven Treasures. Gold, silver, lapis lazuli, crystal, agate, red pearl and carnelian. They represent the seven powers of faith, perseverance, sense of shame, avoidance of wrongdoing, mindfulness, concentration and wisdom.

Singlemindedness. See "One-pointedness of mind."

Six Directions. North, South, East, West, above and below, i.e., all directions. In the *Avatamsaka Sutra*, they are expanded to include points of the compass in between and are referred to as the Ten Directions.

Six Dusts. See "Dusts."

Six Paths. The paths within the realm of Birth and Death. Includes the three Evil Paths (hells, hungry ghosts, animality) and the paths of humans, asuras and celestials. These paths can be understood as states of mind. See also "Evil Paths."

Sixth Patriarch. Refers to Master Hui Neng (638-713), the Sixth Patriarch of the Chinese Zen school and author of the *Platform Sutra*.

Skillful Means. See "Expedient Means."

Spiritual power. Also called miraculous power. Includes, *inter alia,* the ability to see all forms (deva eye), to hear all sounds (deva ear), to know the thoughts of others, to be anywhere and do anything at will.

Sravakas. "Lit., 'voice-hearers': those who follow [Theravada] and eventually become arhats as a result of listening to the buddhas and following their teachings" (A. Buzo and T. Prince.) See also "Arhat."

Subhuti. One of Buddha Sakyamuni's major disciples. Foremost among Arhats in understanding the doctrine of the Void (Emptiness). However, the Buddha predicted in the *Lotus Sutra,* chapter 6, that he would achieve Buddhahood with the title Name-and-Form Buddha, thus demonstrating that Emptiness is Form and Form is Emptiness -- the two are not different (*Heart Sutra.*)

Sudden (Abrupt) Teaching. A teaching which enables one to attain Enlightenment immediately. It is usually associated with the *Avatamsaka Sutra.*

Sudhana (Good Wealth). The main protagonist in the next-to-last and longest chapter of the *Avatamsaka Sutra.* Seeking Enlightenment, he visited and studied with fifty-three spiritual advisors and became the equal of the Buddhas in one lifetime. Both his first advisor and his last advisor (Samantabhadra) taught him the Pure Land path.

Suffering. See "Eight Sufferings."

Surangama Sutra. Also called *Heroic Gate Sutra.*

The "Sutra of the Heroic One" exercised a great influence on the development of Mahayana Buddhism in China [and neighboring countries]. It emphasizes the power of samadhi, through which enlightenment can be attained, and explains the various methods of emptiness meditation through the practice of which everyone ... can realize ... enlightenment ... The Sutra is particularly popular in Zen. (*Shambhala Dictionary of Buddhism and Zen.*)

Tathagata. Usually translated as "Thus Come One."

He who came as did all Buddhas, who took the absolute way of cause and effect, and attained to perfect wisdom; one of the highest titles of a Buddha (Charles Luk).

Ten Evil Acts (Ten Evil Deeds, Ten Sins). 1. Killing; 2. stealing; 3. sexual misconduct; 4. lying; 5. slander; 6. coarse language; 7. empty chatter; 8. covetousness; 9. angry speech; 10. wrong views. (Note: taking intoxicants is not included in this formulation.) See also "Ten Virtues."

Ten Great Vows. The famous vows of the Bodhisattva Samantabhadra in the *Avatamsaka Sutra*. These vows represent the quintessence of this Sutra and are the basis of all Mahayana practice. Studying the vows and putting them into practice is tantamount to studying the *Avatamsaka Sutra* and practicing its teachings. See also "Samantabhadra."

Ten Grounds (Bodhisattva Grounds, Ten Stages). According to the Mahayana sutras, there are a total of 52 (or 53) levels of attainment before a cultivator achieves Buddhahood. The 41st to 50th levels constitute the Ten Grounds. Above these are the levels of Equal Enlightenment, Wonderful Enlightenment (and Buddhahood).

Ten Mysterious Gates (Ten Esoteric Doors, Ten Mysteries, Ten Profound Propositions). Ten aspects of the interrelationship of all phenomena, as seen from the enlightened point of view. To explain such relationship and harmony,

> The [Avatamsaka] School advances the Ten Profound Propositions: 1) All things are co-existent, corresponding to one another. 2) The intension and extension of one thing involve those of others without any obstacle. 3) The One and the Many are mutually inclusive. 4) All things are identical with one another. 5) The hidden and the manifested mutually perfect each other. 6) All minute and abstruse things mutually penetrate one another. 7) All things reflect one another. 8) Truth is manifested in facts and facts are the source of Enlightenment. 9) The past, present and future are inter-penetrating. 10) All things are manifestations and transformations of the mind." (Vergilius Ferm.)

Ten Precepts. See "Ten Virtues."

Ten Recitations. "Ten recitations" refers to the Ten

Recitations method, based on the lowest grade of rebirth described in the *Meditation Sutra*. It is taught to persons busy with mundane activities, so that they, too, can practice Buddha Recitation and achieve rebirth in the Pure Land. The method consists of uttering Amitabha Buddha's name approximately ten times each time one inhales or exhales. The real intent behind this practice is to use the breath to concentrate the mind. Depending on the cultivator's breath span, he may recite more than ten utterances or fewer. After ten inhalations/exhalations (or some fifty to one hundred utterances in total) the cultivator should proceed to transfer the merits accrued toward rebirth in the Pure Land.

Ten Stages. See "Ten Grounds."

Ten Thousand Conducts. All the countless activities and cultivation practices of the Bodhisattvas.

Ten Virtues (Ten Good Deeds, Ten Precepts). Abstaining from the Ten Evil Acts. The Ten Virtues include an expanded version of the Five Precepts of body and mouth (not to kill, steal, engage in illicit sex, lie, engage in slander, coarse language or chatter) with the addition of the virtues of the mind (elimination of greed, anger and delusion). See also "Ten Evil Acts."

Third Lifetime. In the first lifetime, the practitioner engages in mundane good deeds which bring ephemeral worldly blessings (wealth, power, authority, etc.) in the second lifetime. Since power tends to corrupt, he is likely to create evil karma, resulting in retribution in the third lifetime. Thus, good deeds in the first lifetime are potential "enemies" of the third lifetime.

To ensure that mundane good deeds do not become "enemies," the practitioner should dedicate all merits to a transcendental goal, i.e., to become Bodhisattvas or Buddhas or, in Pure Land teaching, to achieve rebirth in the Pure Land -- a Buddha land beyond Birth and Death.

In a mundane context, these three lifetimes can be conceived of as three generations. Thus, the patriarch of a prominent family, through hard work and luck, amasses great power, fortune and influence (first lifetime). His children are then able to enjoy a leisurely, and, too often, dissipated life (second lifetime). By the generation of the grandchildren, the family's fortune and good reputation have all but disappeared (third lifetime).

Three Doors to Liberation. "Liberation is possible only through these three realizations: 1) All things are devoid of a self (emptiness). 2) There are no objects to be perceived by sense-organs (signlessness). 3) No wish of any kind whatsover remains in the ... [practitioner's] mind, for he no longer needs to strive for anything (wishlessness)." (G.C.C. Chang.)

Three Evil Paths. See "Evil Paths."

Three Pure Land Sutras. Pure Land Buddhism is based on three basic sutras:

a) *Amitabha Sutra* (or *Shorter Amitabha Sutra*, or *Smaller Sukhavati-Vyuha*, or the *Sutra of Amida*);

b) *Longer Amitabha Sutra* (or *Larger Sukhavati-Vyuha*, or the *Teaching of Infinite Life*);

c) *Meditation Sutra* (or the *Meditation on the Buddha of Infinite Life*, or the *Amitayus Dhyana Sutra*).

Sometimes the last chapter of the *Avatamsaka Sutra* ("The Practices and Vows of the Bodhisattva Samantabhadra") is considered the fourth basic sutra of the Pure Land tradition. Note: in Pure Land, the *Longer Amitabha Sutra* is considered a shorter form of the *Lotus Sutra*.

Three Treasures (Triple Jewel) The Buddha, the Dharma and the Sangha (community of monks).

T'ien T'ai (Tendai) School. A major school that takes the *Lotus Sutra* as its principal text. Historically, it has had a close relationship with Pure Land. See also "Lotus Sutra."

Tolerance of Non-Birth. "Tolerance" (insight) that comes from the knowledge that all phenomena are unborn. Sometimes translated as "insight into the non-origination of all existence/non-origination of the dharmas."

A Mahayana Buddhist term for the insight into emptiness, the non-origination or birthlessness of things or beings realized by Bodhisattvas who have attained the eighth Stage [Ground] of the path to Buddhahood. When a Bodhisattva realizes this insight he has attained the stage of non-retrogression. (Ryukoku University.)

The Pure Land School teaches that anyone reborn in the Pure Land attains the Tolerance of Non-Birth and reaches the stage of non-retrogression, never to fall back into samsara. See also "Non-Birth."

Three Realms. See "Triple Realm."

Transference of Merit. The concept of merit transference, or sharing one's own merits and virtues with others, is reflected in the following passage:

Some of us may ask whether the effect of [evil] karma can be ... [changed] by repeating the name of Kuan-Yin. This question is tied up with that of rebirth in Sukhavati [the Pure Land] and it may be answered by saying that invocation of Kuan-Yin's name forms another cause which will right away offset the previous karma. We know, for example, that if there is a dark, heavy cloud above, the chances are that it will rain. But we also know that if a strong wind should blow, the cloud will be carried away somewhere else and we will not feel the rain. Similarly, the addition of one big factor can alter the whole course of karma ...

It is only by accepting the idea of life as one whole that both Theravadins and Mahayanists can advocate the practice of transference of merit to others. With the case of Kuan-Yin then, by calling on Her name we identify ourselves with Her and as a result of this identification Her merits flow over to us. These merits which are now ours then counterbalance our bad karma and save us from calamity. The law of cause and effect still stands good. All that has happened is that a powerful and immensely good karma has overshadowed the weaker one. (Lecture on Kuan-Yin by Tech Eng Soon - Penang Buddhist Association, c. 1960. Pamphlet.)

Triple Jewel. See "Three Treasures."

Triple Realm (Three Realms, Three Worlds). The realms of *desire* (our world), *form* (realms of the lesser deities) and *formlessness* (realms of the higher deities). The Western Pure Land is outside the Triple Realm, beyond samsara and retrogression. See also "Pure Land."

True Thusness (True Suchness). Equivalent to Buddha Nature, Dharma Body, etc. See also "Buddha Nature," Dharma Nature."

Two Truths. 1) *Relative* or conventional, everyday truth of the mundane world subject to delusion and dichotomies and 2) the *Ultimate* Truth, transcending dichotomies, as taught by the Buddhas.

> According to Buddhism, there are two kinds of Truth, the Absolute and the Relative. The Absolute Truth (of the Void) manifests "illumination but is always still," and this is absolutely inexplicable. On the other hand, the Relative Truth (of the Unreal) manifests "stillness but is always illuminating," which means that it is immanent in everything. (Hsu Heng Chi/P.H. Wei.)

Pure Land thinkers such as the Patriarch Tao Ch'o accepted "the legitimacy of Conventional Truth as an expression of Ultimate Truth and as a vehicle to reach Ultimate Truth. Even though all form is nonform, it is acceptable and necessary to use form within the limits of causality, because its use is an expedient means of saving others out of one's compassion for them and because, even for the unenlightened, the use of form can lead to the revelation of form as nonform" (David Chappell). Thus to reach Buddhahood, which is formless, the cultivator can practice the Pure Land method based on form.

Unconditioned (Transcendental). Anything "without outflows," i.e., free of the three marks of greed, anger and delusion. See also "Conditioned," "Outflows."

Vaidehi. The Queen of King Bimbisara of Magadha, India. It was in response to her entreaties that Buddha Sakyamuni preached the *Meditation Sutra*, which teaches a series of sixteen visualizations (of Amitabha Buddha, the Pure Land ...) leading to rebirth in the Land of Ultimate Bliss.

Vairocana. The main Buddha in the *Avatamsaka Sutra*. Represents the Dharma Body of Buddha Sakyamuni and all Buddhas. His Pure Land is the Flower Store World, i.e., the entire cosmos.

Vimalakirti Sutra. Also called *Vimalakirti Nirdesa Sutra*. A key Mahayana sutra particularly popular with Zen and to a lesser extent Pure Land followers. The main protagonist is a layman named Vimalakirti who is the equal of many Bodhisattvas in wisdom, eloquence, etc. He explained the teaching of Emptiness in terms of non-duality ... "The true nature of things is beyond the limiting concepts imposed by words." Thus, when asked by Manjusri to define the non-dual Truth, Vimalakirti simply remained silent.

Virtue. See "Merit and Virtue."

Visualization. See *Meditation Sutra* for explanation.

The visualizations [in the *Meditation Sutra*] are distinguished into sixteen kinds [shifting from earthly scenes to Pure Land scenes at Visualization 3]: (1) visualization of the sun, (2) visualization of water, (3) visualization of the ground [in the Pure Land], (4) visualization of the trees, (5) visualization of the lake[s], (6) unified visualization of the [50 billion] storied-pavilions, trees, lakes, and so forth, (7) visualization of the [lotus throne of Amitabha Buddha], (8) visualization of the images of the Buddha [Amitabha] and Bodhisattvas [Avalokitesvara and Mahasthamaprapta], (9) visualization of the [Reward body of Amitabha Buddha, i.e., the form in which He appears in the Pure Land], (10) visualization of Avalokitesvara, (11) visualization of Mahasthamaprapta, (12) visualization of one's own rebirth, (13) [see below], (14) visualization of the rebirth of the highest grades, (15) visualization of the rebirth of the middle grades and (16) visualization of the rebirth of the lowest grades. (K.K. Tanaka, *The Dawn of Chinese Pure Land Doctrine.*)

The 13th Visualization has been summarized as follows:

If one cannot visualize the [Reward body of Amitabha Buddha], focus on the small body, which is sixteen cubits high (the traditional height of Sakyamuni while he dwelt on earth); contemplate an intermingling of the [Reward] and small bodies. (Joji Okazaki, p. 52.)

Visualizations 14-16 refer to the nine lotus grades (of rebirth), divided into three sets of three grades each.

Way. The path leading to Supreme Enlightenment, to Buddhahood.

Wisdom-life. The life of a Buddha or Bodhisattva, which is sustained by wisdom, just as the life of an ordinary being is sustained by food.

Worldly Dusts. See "Dusts."

Yogacara School. Another name for the Mind-Only school, founded in the fourth century by the brothers Asanga and Vasubandhu.

Zen. A major school of Mahayana Buddhism, with several branches. One of its most popular techniques is meditation on koans, which leads to the generation of the Great Doubt. According to this method:

> The master gives the student a koan to think about, resolve, and then report back on to the master. Concentration intensifies as the student first tries to solve the koan intellectually. This initial effort proves impossible, however, for a koan cannot be solved rationally. Indeed, it is a kind of spoof on the human intellect. Concentration and irrationality -- these two elements constitute the characteristic psychic situation that engulfs the student wrestling with a koan. As this persistent effort to concentrate intellectually becomes unbearable, anxiety sets in. The entirety of one's consciousness and psychic life is now filled with one thought. The exertion of the search is like wrestling with a deadly enemy or trying to make one's way through a ring of flames. Such assaults on the fortress of human reason inevitably give rise to a distrust of all rational perception. This gnawing doubt [Great Doubt], combined with a futile search for a way out, creates a state of extreme and intense yearning for deliverance. The state may persist for days, weeks or even years; eventually the tension has to break. (Dumoulin, *Zen Buddhism*, Vol. I, p. 253.)

Realms of worlds in empty space might reach an end,
And living beings, karma and afflictions be extinguished;
But they will never be exhausted,
And neither will my vows.

The Vows of Samantabhadra

Bibliography

Andrews, Allen A., "Nembutsu in Chinese Pure Land Tradition." In *The Eastern Buddhist,* Vol. 3, No. 2, October 1970, p. 20ff.

Asvaghosha, *The Awakening of the Faith.* S. Yoshito Hakeda, tr. New York: Columbia University Press, 1967.

Birnbaum, Raoul, *The Healing Buddha.* Boston, Ma: Shambhala, 1989.

Buzo, Adrian and Tony Prince, tr., *Kyunyo-jon: The Life, Times and Songs of a Tenth Century Korean Monk.* Sydney, Australia: Wild Peony, 1993.

Ch'en, Kenneth K.S., *Buddhism in China: A Historical Survey.* Princeton, NJ: Princeton University Press, 1964.

Chih I (Patriarch), "Ten Doubts about Pure Land." In *Pure Land Buddhism: Dialogues with Ancient Masters.* Master Thích Thiên Tâm, tr. New York: Sutra Translation Committee of the United States and Canada, 1992.

Chihmann (P.C. Lee), tr., *The Two Buddhist Books in Mahayana.* Taipei: Corporate Body of the Buddha Educational Foundation [no date]. Originally published in early 1930's.

Cleary, J.C. *Pure Land, Pure Mind.* (Unpublished manuscript.)

Cleary, Thomas, tr., *The Flower Ornament Scripture: A Translation of the Avatamsaka Sutra.* (Three vols.) Boston, Ma and London: Shambhala, 1984-1987.

------- *No Barrier [Wu-men kuan]: Unlocking the Zen Koan.*New York: Bantam, 1993.

Cook, Francis, *Hua-Yen Buddhism: The Jewel Net of Indra*. University Park, Pa and London: Pennsylvania State University Press, 1977.

Crim, Keith, et al., ed., *The Perennial Dictionary of World Religions*. San Francisco, Ca.: Harper & Row, 1989.

A Dictionary of Buddhism: Chinese-Sanskrit-English-Thai. Bangkok: The Chinese Budddhist Order of Sangha in Thailand, 1976.

A Dictionary of Buddhist Terms and Concepts. Tokyo: Nichiren Shoshu International Center, 1983.

Dumoulin, Heinrich, *Zen Buddhism: A History*. James W. Heisig and Paul Knitter, tr. New York and London: Macmillan, 1988.

Eliade, Mircea, ed., *The Encyclopedia of Religion*. New York: Macmillan.

Fung Yu-Lan, *A History of Chinese Philosophy*. Derk Bodde, tr. Princeton, NJ: Princeton University Press.

Goddard, D., ed., *A Buddhist Bible*. Boston, Ma: Beacon Press, 1970.

Han-Shan Te-Ch'ing, *Pure Land of the Patriarchs: Zen Master Han-Shan on Pure Land Buddhism*. Master Lok To, tr. New York: Sutra Translation Committee of the United States and Canada, 1993.

Hsu, Heng Chi, *What's Buddhism? Theory and Practice*. P.H. Wei, tr. Hong Kong: Hong Kong Buddhist Books Distributor, 1989.

Hsu, Sung-peng, *A Buddhist Leader in Ming China*. University Park, Pa and London: State University of Pennsylvania Press, 1979.

Hsuan Hua (Master), *A General Explanation of the Buddha Speaks of Amitabha Sutra*. San Francisco: Buddhist Text Translation Society, 1974.

Hui Seng, *The Buddha Speaks the Brahma Net Sutra*. Talmadge, Ca: Buddhist Text Translation Society, 1982.

Humphreys, Christmas, *The Buddhist Way of Life*. London: Unwin Paperbacks, 1980. (Originally pub. 1969.)

Hurvitz, Leon, tr., *Scripture of the Lotus Blossom of the Fine Dharma (The Lotus Sutra)*. New York: Columbia University Press, 1976.

Inagaki, Hisao, *A Dictionary of Japanese Buddhist Terms*. Union City, Ca: Heian, 1988.

Kraft, Kenneth, *Zen: Tradition and Transition.* New York: Grove Press, 1988.

Layman, Emma, *Buddhism in America.* Chicago, Il: Nelson-Hall, 1976.

Luk, Charles, tr., *The Vimalakirti Nirdesa Sutra.* Boston, Ma: Shambhala, 1972.

Murcott, Susan, *The First Buddhist Women: Translations and Commentary on the Therigatha.* Berkeley, Ca: Parallax Press, 1991.

Narada Maha Thera, *The Buddha and His Teachings.* Singapore: Singapore Buddhist Meditation Centre. (Originally pub. c. 1973.)

Okazaki, Joji, *Pure Land Buddhist Painting.* Elizabeth ten Grotenhuis, tr. Tokyo: Kodansha, 1977.

Price, A.F. and Wong Mou-Lam, tr., *The Diamond Sutra & The Sutra of Hui Neng.* Boston, Ma: Shambhala, 1969.

Prince, A.J. (Tony), "The World of Hua Yen Buddhism." Reprinted in *Phật Học (Sepulveda, Ca)*, No. 6, 1986, p. 135-136.

Red Pine, tr., *The Zen Teaching of Bodhidharma.* Berkeley Ca: North Point Press, 1989.

Sangharakshita, *The Eternal Legacy: An Introduction to the Canonical Literature of Buddhism.* London: Tharpa Publications, 1985.

Saso, Michael and David W. Chappell, ed., *Buddhist and Taoist Studies I.* Honolulu: University of Hawaii Press, 1987.

Seki, Hozen, *Buddha Tells of the Infinite: the "Amida Kyo" [Shorter Amitabha Sutra]* New York: American Buddhist Academy, 1973.

The Shambhala Dictionary of Buddhism and Zen. Boston, Ma: 1991.

Sheng-Yen (Master), *Faith in Mind: A Guide to Ch'an Practice.* Taipei: Tungchu Pub., 1989.

Shih Shing-yun (Master), ed., *Bilingual Buddhist Series.* Taipei: Buddhist Cultural Service, 1962.

Snelling, John, *The Buddhist Handbook: A Complete Guide to Buddhist Schools, Teaching, Practice and History.* Rochester, Vt: Inner

Traditions, 1991.

------- *The Elements of Buddhism.* Longmead, England: Element Books, 1990.

Sutra Translation Committee of the United States and Canada, tr., *The Buddhist Liturgy.* 2nd ed. New York, San Francisco, Toronto: 1993.

Suzuki, D. T., "The Development of the Pure Land Doctrine in Buddhism." In *The Eastern Buddhist*, Vol. III, No. 5, Jan.-Mar. 1925, p. 285-326.

------- *An Introduction to Zen Buddhism.* New York: Grove Weidenfeld, 1964.

------- "Zen and Jodo, Two Types of Buddhist Experience." In *The Eastern Buddhist*, Vol. IV, No. 2, Jul.-Sept. 1927, p. 89-121.

------- tr., *The Lankavatara Sutra: A Mahayana Text.* Boulder Co: Prajna Press, 1978.

Tay, C.N., "Kuan-Yin: The Cult of Half Asia." In *History of Religions*, Vol. 16, No. 2, Nov. 1975, p. 147-175.

Thích Thiên Tâm (Master), *Pure Land Buddhism: Dialogues with Ancient Masters.* New York: Sutra Translation Committee of the United States and Canada, 1992. (Reprinted by The Corporate Body of the Buddha Educational Foundation, Taipei.)

------- tr., *Pure-Land Zen, Zen Pure-Land: Letters from Patriarch Yin Kuang.* New York: Sutra Translation Committee of the United States and Canada, 1993. (Reprinted by The Corporate Body of the Buddha Educational Foundation, Taipei.)

Thurman, Robert, tr., *The Holy Teaching of Vimalakirti: A Mahayana Scripture.* University Park, Pa and London: Pennsylvania State University Press, 1981.

Watson, Burton, tr., *The Zen Teachings of Master Lin-chi: A Translation of the Lin-chi Lu.* Boston, Ma and London: Shambhala, 1993.

Wilson, Andrew, ed., *World Scripture: A Comparative Anthology of Sacred Texts.* New York: Paragon, 1991.

Yamazaki, Taiko, *Shingon: Japanese Esoteric Buddhism.* Richard and Cynthia Peterson, tr. Boston, Ma and London: Shambhala, 1988.

Selective Index
(Entries in boldface refer to Glossary)